MW01503393

Radical Islamic Fundamentalism:

Radical Islamic Fundamentalism:

The Ideological and Political Discourse of Sayyid Quṭb

Ahmad S. Moussalli

American University of Beirut

Published by the American University of Beirut

Printed in Beirut, Lebanon
Second Printing, 1995
Cover Design By: Anis-El-Koury

CONTENTS:

ACKNOWLEDGEMENT

I am greatly indebted to Dr. Lawrance I. Conrad, of the Wellcome Institute for the History of Medicine, and Dr. George N. Atyieh, of the Library of Congress, who read and evaluated the manuscript and made substantive suggestions.

Also, I want to express deep gratitude to Professor Charles E. Butterworth, of the University of Maryland, for his unstinting encouragement and guidance and for directing my interests towards Islamic thought and history in general and modern Islamic ideologies in particular.

My thanks go to A.U.B. University Research Board whose financial aid in the summer of 1990 allowed me to travel and pursue my research at the Library of Congress. My appreciation goes also to A.U.B. Publications Committee for approving the publication of the manuscript and to the University Publication Office for undertaking its publication.

INTRODUCTION

The intended goal of this book is to set forth a more accurate explanation of Islamic fundamentalism on the basis of Sayyid Quṭb (1906-66) as an example. Sayyid Quṭb's œuvre is massive, his works are not easy to work with, and they represent a process of dramatic changes in thinking.

Of course, the entire topic of fundamentalism is difficult, for it is charged with so many value-laden connotations which obscure our view and which differ from one commentator to the next. Thus, to work through all the relevant material in order to provide the theoretical and political underpinnings of Islamic fundamentalism requires tremendous caution and objectivity.

The subject of this study is neither Islamic political history and movements nor contemporary politics, but rather fundamentalist Islamic political discourse as elaborated primarily by Sayyid Quṭb. I intend to show, *first*, that fundamentalism is not only a political movement but is equally an intellectual one which provides philosophical principles that have evolved into a system of thought worthy of serious study. *Secondly*, although fundamentalism appears conservative, it is actually a progressive program, more progressive than Islamic modernism - but unwittingly, it has contributed to historicism and positivism. *Thirdly*, fundamentalism, when compared to modernism, exhibits a better understanding of science as well as its impact on the structure of society and its values, but is less aware of the benefits of philosophy. To show this, I follow two levels of discourse, the first of which is the immediate task of explaining Quṭb's thought. The second is to compare the opinions and arguments of other fundamentalists with Quṭb's and to contrast fundamentalism with modernism. This comparative analysis is found in the conclusions of *Chapters II* and *III*. Also, at the end of *Chapter II*, I have attempted to relate Quṭb's basic notions of knowledge to Western principles in order to show that in fact Quṭb owes many of his principles to modern Western thought, notwithstanding his rejection of the West.

Therefore, no attempt is made here to treat individual thinkers, and I opted to include their arguments in *Chapters II* and *III*. This method avoids repetition and shows what Quṭb has borrowed, accepted or rejected, and what he has sharpened, radicalized, and invented. Because my concern is the justification as well as the logic and adequacy of ideas, the method employed here is topical, analytical and philosophical, not historical. Consequently, ideas are to be discussed under such headings as religion, social justice, political theory, philosophy, and science. Throughout the study, Quṭb's arguments are developed first, then my analysis follows. Furthermore, since the fundamentalists and the modernists have dwelt on Western thought and its advantages and disadvantages, one cannot escape doing the same. Hence, there are sections in *Chapter II* that deal with philosophy and science, and in *Chapter III*, with political principles. And because both groups used Western thought selectively, I have limited my comments to a number of specific topics. For example, Marxism is not treated in depth by Muslim thinkers, but some principles like class struggle are dealt with. Hence, my discussion of Marxism is also limited to the issue of class struggle.

Chapter I is a biography of Quṭb's life and a bibliography of his work. *Chapter II* focuses on the theoretical foundations of fundamentalism and its conceptions of religion, of Islam, of philosophy, and of science. *Chapter III* dwells on fundamentalism as an ideology and compares it with Islamic and Western notions of government and politics. *The Conclusion* is a critical summary of Quṭb's thought, showing its benefits and disadvantages.

But here, a word on fundamentalism, the general subject of this work, is in place. Fundamentalist Islamic political thought has been treated in general as a passing political phenomenon dependent on unfavorable specific social and political circumstances. The movement has been studied by political scientists as a movement that lacks any deep-rooted and meaningful principles and is often dismissed as religious fanaticism.

Thus, the rise of fundamentalism is, in most cases, attributed to social, psychological and/or economic causes, and there have been few attempts to understand fundamentalism on its own terms. The important question that needs to be addressed is not whether a specific group will react; of course, every action provokes some reaction. The most important question is how and why. Why do fundamentalists, for instance, want to change governments? Is it only because of economic reasons or is there something deeper than that? Why do they espouse Islam as an ideology instead of, for instance, socialism? These and similar questions should be addressed by scholars on the Middle East. In political science, the Middle East is approached in the same manner, i.e. socio-economics- as other areas of the Third World, which accounts for the failure of political scientists to predict, for instance, the Iranian Revolution. To study the Middle East correctly and intelligibly, religion should be viewed as one of the major causes of change. Some examples may illustrate my point. Manfred Halpern, in his ***The Politics of Change in the Middle East and North Africa,*** tries to explain changes in terms of economics and middle class orientation. For him, religion is nothing but a negative attitude toward life and progress, and Islamic movements are fascist movements. He states:

> *The neo-Islamic totalitarian movements are essentially fascist movements. They concentrate on mobilizing passion and violence to enlarge the power of their charismatic leader and the solidarity of the movement. They view material progress primarily as a means for accumulating strength for political*

expansion, and entirely deny individual and social freedom. They champion the values and emotions of a heroic past, but repress all free critical analysis of their past roots or present problems.[1]

This description actually reveals a misunderstanding of Islamic movements since these movements do not in principle attempt to build societies on state regulation or absolute authority or deny or repress freedom. Another example of not focusing on substantive issues in Islamic activism is Hisham Sharabi's "Islam and Modernism in the Arab World" and Majid Khadduri's "From Religious to National Law," in ***Modernization and the Arab World.***[2] The two authors' analyses do not address the question of why Muslims in this century are reacting in the manner they do. Instead of treating causes and events, they focus on the latter. Similar views and analysis can be found in ***Islamic Resurgence in the Arab World,*** (ed. Ali H. Dessouki), where most authors try to interpret Islamic movements in terms of socio-economics and events without reference to the thought of the leaders and the thinkers (an exception is the article by Charles E. Butterworth where the focus is theoretical). A similar book is ***Religion and Politics in the Middle East***.[3]

Another discourse on, for instance, the Muslim Brethren, the most distinguished and powerful fundamentalist organization, runs as follows:

The Muslim Brotherhood was a militant group which believed in the sufficiency and supremacy of Islam and in **literal interpretation of the Koran** *and the Sunna. It worked for the revival of the principle of jihad, holy war. Unlike the Wahhabis, however, it believed in reform and in the utilization of certain Western methods. Unlike Abduh, the Brotherhood* ***did not think that a restatement of Islamic doctrines was necessary.*** [4] (Emphasis added)

The above statement- especially the in bold phrases- does not capture accurately and does not account for a variety of interpretations put forward by the Muslim Brethren's leaders such as Sayyid Quṭb, the subject of this study, let alone other fundamentalist thinkers like Abū al-Aʿlā al-Mawdūdī (1903-80), the founder of the Islamic movement in Pakistan. None of these authors, not even Ḥasan al-Bannā (1906-49), the founder of the Muslim Brethren, advocates a literal interpretation of the Holy Qur'an or thinks that Islamic doctrines are in no need of restatement.[5]

More recent books and articles such as "The Blood of Brothers" in ***Holy Terror*** and "The Sunni Revolution" in ***Radical Islam, Medieval Theology and Modern Politics*** as well as ***The Rise of Islamic Fundamentalism, Faith and Power*** and ***Political Perspectives on the Muslim World***,[6] and Shepard's "Islam as a system in the later writings of Sayyid Qutb" are more substantive in dealing with Islamic fundamentalism and pay more attention to fundamentalist ideology and its general framework. However, more objective and substantive studies on ideological and political discourses are needed in order to obtain a better understanding of the fundamentalist phenomenon.

In fact Islamic fundamentalism has contributed to the intellectual discourse which has been going on for hundreds of years in the East and the West. At the least, fundamentalism constitutes a critique of philosophy, of political ideology, and of the sciences. Philosophically, it rejects the claim made by man to be the possessor of truth and the claim that all knowledge is relative. More essentially, it offers a way of life and thought, a way that is regulated by God's laws and by nature. Politically, it rejects the notion that authority belongs to the people and that societies are no more than market-places or places where desires are satisfied. Also, it strives to erect societies whose basic components are justice, virtues, and equality. It is a movement that aims at making the two fundamentals, the *Qur'ān* and the *sharīʿah,* the bases of Muslim life and society and of the Islamic state.

But the contribution of the fundamentalists, in their thought as well as in their action, as a result of the negative image applied to them by Arab and foreign media, scholars, and governments, has been viewed superficially. Consequently, this association has precluded any serious in depth study of their assumptions and doctrines. Whereas the student of contemporary Islam finds a substantial output by Westerners on modernist reformers such as Jamāl al-Dīn al-Afghānī, Muḥammad ᶜAbduh, and Muḥammad Iqbāl, there is less theoretical discussion concerning fundamentalist thinkers such as Ḥasan al-Bannā and Abū al-Aᶜlā al-Mawdūdī. But the least discussed and understood thinker is Sayyid Quṭb, whose output cannot be matched by any other contemporary Muslim writer, not even by al-Mawdūdī. Of his 41 published books and 30 unpublished works and hundreds of articles in newspapers and journals, only two books had been translated into English by Westerners and two others by Muslim organizations. Moreover, until recently, nothing major had been written on him. Articles by Yvonne Haddad, focusing on Quṭb's concept of revolution and the ideology of the fundamentalists, have now appeared, as well as one by Sylvia Haim describing his attitude toward women and a discussion by Charles E. Butterworth outlining Quṭb's basic notions within the context of fundamentalism. Also, articles dealing with some aspects of Sayyid Quṭb's ideology such as "The Sunni Revolution" in ***Radical Islam, Medieval Theology and Modern Politics*** and Shepard's "Islam as a 'system' in the late writing of Sayyid Quṭb," have appeared. They are very inconclusive and short and are not meant to cover all of the ideological and political aspects of fundamentalism. Passing references can be found here and there, such as in Rodinson's ***Islam and Capitalism,*** Mitchell's ***The Society of Muslim Brothers,*** Mortimer's ***Faith and Politics,*** Taheri's ***The Inside Story of Islamic Terrorism,*** and Hiro's ***The Rise of Islamic Fundamentalism.*** To complicate matters, the secondary sources in Arabic are poorly written and suffer from partisanship and lack of critical analysis.[7]

Nonetheless, Quṭb's importance and influence on fundamentalist movements and contemporary Islamic revival are acknowledged by Westerners and Easterners; he has been long considered one of the most distinguished contemporary fundamentalist thinkers, and numerous labels have been bestowed on him- by Asaf Hussain as "the ideologue of the Ikhwan," by Haddad as "the most noted advocate of the interpretation of Islam as revolution," by President Sādāt of

Egypt as "an eminent leader of the Brethren," by Abū al-Ḥasan al-Nadawī as "one of Islam's new crusaders, a great author and scholar," by S. Badrul Ḥasan as "a matchless writer," by Muḥammad Barakāt as "the only thinker who enjoys purity in intellectual methodology and straightforwardness in action." He is also characterized by ᶜAbbās Muḥammad ᶜAbd Allah as "one of greatest thinkers of contemporary Islamic thought," by Mahdī Faḍl Allah as "the most famous personality in the Muslim world in the second half of the twentieth century," by Muḥammad Quṭb (not a relative of his) as "the revolution of contemporary Islamic thought," and by Olivier Carré as "le grand inspirateur de ce nouveau souffle".[8] He is also described by Dilip Hiro as "the leading ideologue of the Muslim Brotherhood" and by Edward Mortimer as "The leading writer and theorist of the Egyptian Brothers after Banna's death." Interest in him reached the point that some individuals, like Jacques Berque, attempted to save Quṭb's life by contacting Jamāl ᶜAbd al-Nāṣīr, then President of Egypt, both personally and through others.[9] Even Quṭb's death played a symbolic role in perpetuating the Islamic revival,[10] and as recently as February and March of 1985, the Journal ***Al-Muslimūn*** (The Muslims), a weekly concerned with Islamic thought and movements, serialized and published in five of its issues the last document that Quṭb wrote before his execution.[11]

Footnotes:

1 Manfred Halpern, *The Politics of Change in the Middle East and North Africa,* 4th ed. (Princeton: Princeton University Press, 1970), pp. 60-135; also see Part III, Chapter 8.

2 J.H. Thompson and R.J. Reischauer (Princeton: D. Van Nostrana Co., 1966).

3 Michael Curtis, ed., (Boulder/Colorado: Westview Press 1981).

4 Yahaya Armajani, *Middle East: Past and Present* (New Jersey: Prentice-Hall, Inc., 1970), pp. 287-88.

5 See the comparative section in Chapter II.

6 Amir Taheri: *The Inside Story of Islamic Terrorism* (Johannesburg: Hutchinson Ltd., 1987).
Emmanuel Sivan, *Radical Islam, Medieval Theology and Modern Politics* (New Haven and London: Yale University Press, 1985). Dilip Hiro, *The Rise of Islamic Fundamentalism* (New York: Routledge, 1989).
Edward Mortimer, *Faith and Power: The Politics of Islam* (London: Faber and Faber, 1982).
Asaf Hussain, *Political Perspectives on the Muslim World* (New York: St. Martin's Press, 1984).

7 For bibliographical details on Arabic and English sources, see below, footnotes 8-10, and *Chapter II,* footnotes 2-3.

8 Hussain's remark, see *Islamic Movements in Egypt, Pakistan, and Iran* (Great Britain: Mansell Publishing Limited, 1983), p. 9. This book is a good annotated bibliography. It brings together Arabic and Western sources on these movements. In her "The Qur'anic Justification for an Islamic Revolution: The View of Sayyid Quṭb," *Middle East Journal,* Winter, 1983, vol. 37, p. 17, Yvonne Haddad speaks of Quṭb in these terms and provides an adequate but sparse exposition of his thought. Sādāt's remark can be found in *In Search of Identity* (New York: Harper, 1978), p. 66. For S. Badrul Hasan's remark, see *Syed Quṭb Shaheed* (Sayyid Quṭb, A Martyr) (Lahore: International Pakistani Publishers, 1980), p. 17; (hereafter cited as *Shaheed*). This book is an informative biography and a summary of some of Quṭb's books. However, it lacks in scholarship, for his references are not precise and the reader would not benefit much in terms of sources and secondary books on Quṭb. Muḥammad Tawfīq Barakāt's quote can be found in *Sayyid Quṭb: Khulāṣat Ḥayātuh, Minhājuhu fī al-Harakah wa-al-Naqd al-Mūwajah ilāyh* (Sayyid Quṭb: A Summary of his Life, His Method in Activism, and the Criticism Directed at Him) (Bayrūt: Dār al-Da'wah, 197?), p. 3; (hereafter cited as Barakat, *Khulāṣah*). ʿAbbās Muḥammad ʿAbd Allah's remark is quoted from his *Miftāḥ fī Kunūz fī Ẓilāl al-Qur'ān* (The Key to the Treasures in 'In the Shades of the Qur'an') (ʿAmmān:

Maktabat al-Aqṣā), 1972, pp. 3-4. This is an index of the names and topics in Quṭb's *Fī Ẓilāl al-Qur'ān* (In the Shades of the Qur'an), discussed in *Writings*. Mahdī Faḍl Allah's *Ma^ca Sayyid Quṭb fī Fikrihī al-Siyāsī wa-al-Dīnī,* (Bayrūt: 2nd. ed. 1979) is the author's dissertaton at the Sorbonne in France. Because it is out of print, the quotation in the text is taken from Sylvia Haim's "Sayyid Qutb," *Asian and African Studies,* 16, (1982), p. 147. The author delineates Quṭb's perception and arguments concerning women and their role in Muslim society. Muhammad Quṭb's remark is taken from *Sayyid Quṭb, Al-Shahīd al-A^czal* (Sayyid Quṭb, the Unarmed Martyr) (Al-Qāhirah: al-Mukhtār al-Islāmī, 2nd ed., 1972), p. 23; also see p. 29 (hereafter cited as Quṭb, *Al-Shahīd al-A^czal*). This is a basic biography, but does not cite references.

Also, see Hiro, *The Rise of Islamic Fundamentalism,* p. 67 and Mortimer, *Faith and Power,* p. 271.

Olivier Carré's note can be found in *"Le combat-pour-Dieu et l'Etat islamique chez Sayyid Quṭb, l'inspirateur du radicalisme actuel,"* (The Struggle-For-God and the Islamic State in Sayyid Quṭb, the Inspirer of Contemporary Islamic Radicalism), *Revue francaise de science politique,* No. 4, August 1983, vol. 33, p. 681. It is a short article on Quṭb's life and radicalism.

9 Jacques Berque, "Islam and Innovation," in *Islam, Philosophy and Science* (Paris: UNESCO, International Seminar on Islam, 1981), p. 90.

10 Maxime Rodinson, *Islam and Capitalism,* 1st. 1966, trans. Brian Pearce (Austin: University of Texas Press, 1978), pp. 237-38.

11 The title of the article is "Why Did They Execute Me?" (*Li-Mādhā 'A^cdamūnī?)*. It had been published in *Al-Muslimūn* (The Muslims). This journal is published in London, and 1985 was the first year of publication).

These articles have been published as a book under the same title by the Saudi Corporation for Research and Marketing in London. It includes photographs of Quṭb and some of his contemporaries as well as photocopies of some pages of the original document.

CHAPTER I

THE LIFE AND WRITINGS OF SAYYID QUṬB

Sayyid Quṭb lived through a very critical phase of Egyptian history and witnessed and worked against Egypt's royal regime till its collapse. He fervently supported the Revolution of 1952 and believed that it would make his dreams come true. Instead, he entered into a vicious circle of nightmares and conspiracies. He was made by the great events in Egypt and the world and, in turn, he made a great impact on Egypt and the world by means of his ideological and political discourse and activism. To the extent that his philosophy of life was mainly a consequence of his social and political involvement in the affairs of Egypt, his political discourse is abstracted from reality and reified into an absolute system of ideas. In order to throw some light on his actions and interactions, this *Chapter* treats the life and works of Quṭb in the context of Egyptian life.

It is divided into two sections: the first, the biographical, describes Quṭb's life and how he came to adhere to Islamic fundamentalism; the second, the bibliographical, discusses the style, the structure and range of his publications as well as his sources of information.

1 - Life

In ***Maʿālim fī al-Ṭarīq*** (Signposts on the Road), Quṭb described himself as someone who lived in the *jāhilīyyah.* (period of ignorance) for many years devoting himself to the quest for knowledge and studying whatever sciences came to his hand.[1] However, he entertained no regrets; for this period of about forty years in the *jāhilīyyah* acquainted him with and made him study many and diverse fields of human knowledge. Among other things, this experience resulted in profound changes in his intellectual and political outlook that led to his convicton of the irreconcilability of the *jāhilīyyah* with Islam and to his belief in the infutility of human knowledge as a source of truth and happiness.[2] The *jāhilīyyah* is a conceptual framework used by Quṭb not to indicate only the historical epoch before the Prophet Muhammad's time, but as an indication of condemnation for those whose life styles do not conform to divine guidance. *Jāhilīyyah* (ignorance) is found when the individual lives according to his whims and wishes. More specifically, it was conceived by Quṭb as a moment of turning away from the Islamic method. It covers all societies, including the Western and Eastern societies as well as the Islamic ones. Thus, *jāhilīyyah* is an epistemological device that allowed him to reject Western, Eastern and Islamic philosophies and thought. Also, it is a social and political device that allowed him to reject Eastern, Western and Islamic political orders and international organizations.

Quṭb did not make al-Mawdūdī's distinction between pure *jāhilīyyah,* and partial and mixed *jāhilīyyahs.* Pure *jāhilīyyah*, to al-Mawdūdī, is the one that rejects God completely; mixed *jāhilīyyahs* associate religion with infidelity and do not rule by God's order. For Quṭb, the whole world lives one pure *jāhilīyyah.*

In his forties, Quṭb considered Islam the true and only foundation of truth in all aspects of life; therefore, any study of Quṭb needs to account for this transformation that moved him from social liberalism and political socialism to Islamic fundamentalism. This metamorphosis resulted in a tremendous output of Islamic literature which gained him a great reputation.

Sayyid Quṭb was the eldest of five children. Quṭb's family was famous; besides Sayyid Quṭb, it produced Muḥammad, a thinker well-known for his writings on Islamic topics and activism. Also, his sister Amīnah was renowned for her involvement in the propagation of Islam *(daʿwah),* and her writings could be found in numerous periodicals; and Ḥamīdah was also involved with the Muslim Brethren and was imprisoned for seven years. The third sister's name is not known.

Quṭb was born in 1906 in a village called Mūshā in the district of Asyūṭ. Although a generation or two ago Quṭb's family was well-off, during his childhood it was not. Nonetheless his family was very respected in the village because his father was known as an educated man. Quṭb had an ordinary life, but his childhood was distinguished by his curiosity about knowledge and love of reading. He was sent to the usual school in the village, the *kuttāb,* where the Holy Qur'ān and other traditional disciplines were taught. At the age of ten he memorized the Holy Qur'ān because his mother, a devout Muslim, wanted him to be educated at the University of *al-Azhar,* the prestigious Sunnite center for Islamic learning, in order to become a religious scholar.[3] In the 1919 revolution, his school was closed and the principal addressed the students on the duty to revolt. Meanwhile his father started selling parts of his land in order to meet the necessities of life since his salary was insufficient. In a dialogue with his mother, she made him promise her to get the land back.

At the age of thirteen, his family moved close to Cairo (to Ḥalwān), and he entered a preparatory and secondary school called *Tajhīzīyyat Dār al-ᶜUlūm.* In 1929 he joined *Dār al-ᶜUlūm's* Teachers' College.[4] Four years later, in 1933, Quṭb obtained a B. A. in Arts of Education. Upon graduation, he was appointed instructor at the same institution because he had distinguished himself.[5] For one thing, his book ***Mahammat al-Shāᶜir fī al-Hayāh*** (The Poet's Responsibility in Life) was published in 1933. Quṭb was also employed by the Ministry of Education as a teacher from 1933 till 1939.

His attachment to literature and poetry was traceable from the beginning of his career, and his earlier life. His literary works dominated the years from the 1930's to the late 1940's. His writings were of a nonreligious nature such as poems, composition, education, two autobiographies, literary criticism and commentaries, and love stories dealing with political and psychological topics.[6]

For example, ***Ashwāk*** (Thorns) is a love story and is dedicated to his beloved. It is the story of a man who, on the night of his engagement, is shocked to discover that his would-be fiancée is in love with her neighbor, an army officer. He is saddened by his discovery. Knowing of her fiancée's love for her, the girl is tortured beyond any human capacity. For one thing, her family has refused to let her marry the man she loves because of social conditions (he being from a poorer and less prestigious family). Her fiancée, accepting her feelings, withdraws from the engagement and tries to help her. After many intricate events and meetings, he and the woman come to the same conclusion: that her family will never accept the young officer who has given up loving her, let alone marrying her. During that time, the woman falls in love with her former fiancee but it is too late. Now, she cannot marry him because she stands emotionally naked before him; she cannot tolerate him staring at her psychological nudity.[7] ***Ashwāk*** refers to the pains experienced during the relationship and the scars left after its ending.

It is a very moving love story of frustration, pain and pleasure, criticizing the social and traditional customs of marriage and relationships. It is abundant with psychological and emotional insights into human interactions and nature. Physical attraction and attributes of his beloved are unusually well described.

The strongest influence on Quṭb's intellectual and political development during this period was that of ᶜAbbās Maḥmūd al-ᶜAqqād,[8] a famous Egyptian thinker; actually, Quṭb became his ardent student and defender. Quṭb followed similar lines of argumentation and discourse as those of al-ᶜAqqād and other Egyptian thinkers like Ṭahā Ḥusayn who were staunch proponents of Westernization. But his views were closer to al-ᶜAqqād. Both were self-made, joined the *Wafd* party then turned against it after the death of Saᶜd Zaghlūl, did not marry, and turned sharply against Western concepts and towards Islam. Al-ᶜAqqād introduced Quṭb to most journals and newspapers. After a long friendship of 25 years, Quṭb broke with him because al-ᶜAqqād refused to write an introduction to one of his works. Through them, he became acquainted with the West and its civilization. The reader of his earlier works does not fail to see the numerous references to and analyses of Western literary figures such as the English poet Thomas Hardy (1840-1928). Furthermore, liberalism, individualism, and modernism were principal features in his and, his mentor, al-ᶜAqqād's writings. To the Egyptian liberal thinkers at that time (and still now), the West was the model to be followed and imitated, and its political and social values were accepted. Quṭb was no exception; he showed, for instance, in his novel ***Ashwāk,*** profound existentialism, skepticism and liberalism, and even advocated, in an article, complete nudity; an idea that is totally unacceptable to Muslims in general.[10]

Quṭb's fame started with the publication of numerous articles in the literary, social, and political spheres. His articles were published along with well-known and respected figures such as al-ᶜAqqād, Ṭahā Ḥusayn, and Aḥmad al-Zayyāt.[11] He contributed to the debates in political and literary circles on literary criticism, methods, and styles. In the 1940's he was especially vocal in criticizing the royal government and was called the first critic in Egypt.[12] Once, while delivering a lecture at the Faculty of Arts at Cairo University which was modeled on a Western-like structure, he described the professors as ignorant, notwithstanding their doctorates. Quṭb's activism and criticism of prevailing social and political conditions put him at odds with the Egyptian government. Tired of working for the government, he wanted to resign his post as Inspector in the Ministry of Education which he held since 1939, but Dr. Ṭahā Ḥusayn, who was the Ministry's Adviser, would not allow that to happen. Instead, Quṭb was sent to the countryside to conduct research on the teaching of Arabic in public schools. Quṭb preferred the countryside because he was touched by an incident that had happened while he was graduating from *Dār al-ᶜUlūm.*

The Egyptian Parliament was in the process of studying the law on elementary education. One very prevalent opinion in the Parliament was that the education of the children of poor families was a danger to society because it would lead to an increase in the numbers of the unemployed who would revolt against the system and would direct the efforts of the peasants away from the fields. Quṭb also discredited the government for its "half-solutions" with the British and censured the corruption of Egyptian parties and advocated nothing less than their complete abolition.[13]

Apparently, the situation between him and the government did not improve; and, in 1947, Quṭb attempted to quit his job in the government by becoming the editor-in-chief of two journals: ***Al-ᶜAlam al-ᶜArabī*** (the Arab World) and ***Al-Fikr al-Jadīd*** (New Thought). But he did not last long in the former, and King Fārūq closed down the latter.[14] ***Al-Fikr*** directed its attention to developing a method of resisting tyranny and aggression and calling for the setting-up of a Muslim society as opposed to the corrupt, capitalist, and feudalist society of that time. Only six issues were produced before Quṭb was out of work. In fact, three of these issues were sequestrated. He continued, however, writing in other journals and newspapers such as ***Ṣaḥīfat al-Ḥizb al-Waṭanī*** (National Party newspaper) ***Al-Liwa'*** (the Banner) the ***Ṣaḥīfat Ḥizb Miṣr al-Fatāt*** (Young Egypt party newspaper), ***Al-Ishtirākīyyah*** (Socialism). Furthermore, his dissatisfaction led to his resignation from the Sa'adist Party which he joined in 1942 after breaking away from the Wafd party.[15] In fact, Quṭb was raised in a family that was very concerned with the political affairs of the time. His father was a member of *Al-Ḥizb al-Waṭanī* (National Party). Quṭb defended the *Wafd* and became one of its members at an early age.

In 1948, Quṭb left for the United States of America by ship. Officially, the Ministry of Education had sent Quṭb there to study modern systems of education and training. He studied at Wilson's Teachers' College (now, University of the District of Columbia), Washington, D.C.; the Teacher's College, an institute in the University of Northern Colorado, in Greeley, Colorado; and Stanford University, California. From the Teacher's College he obtained a Master's degree in Education. He visited New York, San Francisco, Los Angeles, and other cities; and on his way back to Egypt in 1951 he stayed for some time in England, Switzerland, and Italy.[16]

While Quṭb was in the United States, his ***Al-ᶜAdālah al-Ijtimāᶜīyyah fī al-Islām*** (Social Justice in Islam) was published, which showed for the first time fundamentalist tendencies in his political views on social justice and government and contained harsh attacks on feudalism and exploitation in the forties.[17] The real intention of the Ministry of Education was to positively impress Quṭb with American culture. Indeed Quṭb was impressed but not in the manner that the Ministry hoped for. His visit and observation of a materialistic culture had a profound influence in shaping and directing the future of his life. His visit turned out to be a focal point in his intellectual and political development. At least, it led him to repudiate the Western way of life more than he did in ***Social Justice***.[18] In fact, it should be noted that 1948-1949 were tragic years for the Arabs: Israel was established as a state whose existence was guaranteed by the USA. The USA competed with Britain over control of oil fields and succeeded in breaking the monopoly of Britain. Also, they were the beginning of the cold war between the USA and the Soviet Union which affected the Middle East. These years witnessed also the dissolution of the Muslim Brotherhood and the death of Ḥasan al-Bannā, the supreme guide of the Muslim Brotherhood.

From his book, ***Amrikā allatī Ra'aytu*** (America that I Saw) one can discern three features, among others, that shocked Quṭb and propelled his mind towards further rejection of the West as the model to be emulated. The three features were materialism, racism, and sexual permissiveness. "Americans," he proclaimed "are not a people without virtues. But their virtues were those of production, organization, reason, and work. Their virtues were neither of social and human leadership nor of manners and emotions".[19] In other words, Quṭb contended that the American leadership was that of production and materialistic attainment but not of moral leadership. His contention was motivated by many reasons. Believing that the Americans produced for the sake of production itself, he felt that production was not directed at moral and spiritual well-being and was devoid of compassion. As their machines did, the Americans functioned day and night and lived in a circle. But, he asked, where was man? And, how could he be distinguished from his machine? Furthermore, he added, the Americans were neither at rest nor at peace with themselves, let alone with others. Of course, reason was capable of keeping pace with change and science, Quṭb argued. But, more importantly, the conscience was in need of fixity and tranquility; for the human conscience was tired of the changeable.

On the other hand, Quṭb did not or could not deny the place of the West in the advancement of science; the West had done wonders in the material and industrial fields. But in terms of brotherhood and morality, Quṭb withheld his appreciation; for he believed that the West was bankrupt in its principles. According to Quṭb, the principles of the French Revolution- liberty, fraternity, and equality- had lost their role in history and were incapable anymore of generating tranquility and happiness. Having exhausted these principles, Western civilization was impoverished and was unable to provide fresh and new moral and political principles. For individual freedom was transformed into the freedom to pursue lusts and desires, and equality became unattainable because of the economic structure of the world. Furthermore, Westerners did not know what real fraternity meant; for real fraternity required, at least, the abandonment of narrow-minded nationalism. The solution to humanity's problems was in its return to God. God offered freedom which science could not.[20]

While Quṭb was in Washington, D.C., Colorado, and California, he joined some churches' clubs. His purpose was to study the church in American society. Two things amazed him, the number of churches and the manner in which the churches attracted the youth. Here I find it informative to quote Quṭb's ***Amrikā allatī Ra'aytu*** at some length in order to show the manner and content of his observations in the United States as well as his temperament.

No one builds as many churches as the Americans do. In a

town of no more than ten thousand people, I counted more than twenty churches. No other people go [as much] to churches on Sundays, day and night; on holidays; for the celebrations of local saints...

Notwithstanding all this, there is no one as removed from feeling the spirituality, respect, and sacredness of religion than the Americans.

While the church is a place of worship in Christendom... it is in America for everything except worship. It would be very hard for you to distinguish it from places of fun and amusement... At best they [the Americans] consider it a necessary social tradition and a place for meeting, friendliness, and having a good time. This is the feeling not only of the public but also of the church and its clergy.

Most churches have clubs composed of both sexes: [especially] young men and women. The priest of the church tries his utmost to bring to the church as many people as possible, especially since there is a great competition among the different doctrines and sects. For this reason, the churches compete by advertising themselves in published pamphlets and by [projecting] colored lights on doors and walls [of the church] in order to attract attention. And [also, they] offer attractive and pleasant programs, in the same fashion employed by stores and movies and play theaters, in order to attract crowds. There is no problem in employing the town's best looking and attractive girls skilled in singing, dancing, and relaxation...

This is, for instance, the content of an announcement of a party for the church, which was attached to a hall at one college in order to attract students to a specific church in the small university town.

'Sunday, October 1, 1950; 6.00 pm.
Light Dinner. Magic Tricks. Quizzes.
Competitions. Amusement. Dance.'

Nothing in this (announcement) is strange because the priest does not feel that his job is different from that of a stage manager or store manager. Success is first and prior to anything else. Means are unimportant; for success brings him good consequences: money and prestige. The greater the number of church-goers, the greater his income, prestige, and influence in the town. The American is, by nature, taken by great sizes and numbers. They are the first yardstick for feeling and respect.

One night I was at one of the churches in Greeley, Colorado... Concluding the sermon after young men and women joined in the hymn and others played [the music], we entered from a side door to a dance hall adjacent to the prayer hall... The 'father' went to his office, and each man held the hand of a woman...

The dance hall was lit with red and blue flashes and a few white lamps. While [people] listening to tones of a gramophone, dancing intensified, the dance floor started swarming with legs [i.e. dancers], hands embraced [others'] waists, and lips touched. The whole atmosphere was of romance. Then the father came down from his office, gave a searching look at the place and the people present, and encouraged those who were sitting and not taking part in the dance to participate. Suddenly he noticed that the white lamps were getting brighter, which might spoil the romantic atmosphere,... [and] turned off the lights one by one while avoiding obstructing the movement of the dance. Actually the place appeared more romantic. Then he went to pick out another dance record suitable to the atmosphere, and encouraged those who were sitting to take part in the dance. He picked out a famous song called 'But baby it's cold outside.'[21]

The other feature in the United States that disturbed Quṭb was sexual behavior. Without paying attention to debates going on in American society on morality, love, and sex and their relationship, and putting aside the sexual revolution and its causes, Quṭb showed, citing a few examples from his experience, his strong astonishment at the perception of sex as an issue separate from morality. One of the instances he gave was a dialogue with a young American woman at the institute in Greeley, Colorado. The woman told him:

The issue of sexual relations is purely a biological matter. You... complicate this matter by imposing the ethical element on it. The horse and mare, the bull and the cow... do not think about this ethical matter... and, therefore, live a comfortable, simple, and easy life.

Another incident involved a teacher who gave a lecture on the traditions of American society at the Wilson's Teachers' College. In a response to a foreigner's observation that young girls and boys enjoyed full sexual relations, she answered, "Life on earth is very short, and there is no time to waste from the age of fourteen."[22]

Not only was Quṭb disturbed by sexual permissiveness but also by racism. Quṭb probably felt personal discrimination in the late forties and early fifties due to his dark skin. Furthermore, he predicted- wrongly, of course- the end of domination by the white man because his civilization had been exhausted in terms of goals. "The White Man's Mission," after a very productive period that resulted in the Magna Carta, the French Revolution, and the American Revolution was sterile. Its sterility stemmed from destroying the meaning of Christianity and erecting a false religion, abuse of reason, and the manipulation of science for selfish ends and wants. These dominating characteristics were about to destroy the white man's civilization because of its antagonism to nature.[23]

One more feature that antagonized Quṭb was what he called the international crusade (imperialism and colonialism) and Zionism. For instance, imperialism and colonialism had been attempting to impose their domination over the Muslim world by trying to restrict Islam to the domain of personal belief. As a consequence of their endeavors, Mustafa Kemal Ataturk, for instance, had won a battle for them by terminating the Caliphate and by separating politics from religion.[24] Moreover, the creation of Israel did not have any positive outcomes or encourage good relations between the Arabs and the Americans. On the contrary, the creation of Israel led to disenchantment with the West; Quṭb perceived that the West had betrayed the Arabs. The British, for instance, defaulted on their promises of independence for the Arabs and had been attempting to stifle the spirit of the Egyptian people as well as the movement of the Muslim Brethren's fighting forces in Palestine. Also, the United States had betrayed the Arabs by siding in the United Nations with the Zionists on the question of Palestine and by sponsoring and approving the creation of the Jewish state. Furthermore, Quṭb added, the Arabs who lived in the United States knew first hand the discrimination against the Arabs and the anti-Arab and pro-Jewish propaganda in the media, newspapers, broadcasts, movies, and other sources of information that distorted the Arab image by fostering contempt for their dignity and reputation.[25]

For this and the above mentioned reasons, Quṭb terminated his trip to the United States in the Summer of 1950. Quṭb, if he wished, could have stayed in the United States and studied for a Ph. D. because his fellowship was open.[26] On the other hand, this trip affirmed his belief that Islam was a superior creed and ideology; that an Islamic revival was necessary; that the West entertained deep hatred for Islam; that Western civilization could not be used as the basis of a moral and political regeneration of Islam; that the fate of materialism was the destruction of those people who espoused it; that the Muslims had to depend on themselves for success in this life and the life to come; and that Islam was the correct and true path for a political and moral regeneration and strength.

Two events in particular from his sojourn in the United States made him entertain joining the Muslim Brethren. The first was "the happy and joyous American reception" in 1949 of the assassination of Ḥasan al-Bannā, the founder of the Muslim Brethren.[27] The second was his meeting with a "British agent," identified by Quṭb as James Heyworth-Dunne, who told him that the Muslim Brethren was the only movement that stood as a barrier to Western civilization in the East. Dunne also showed Quṭb "intelligence reports" on al-Bannā and his organization.[28] These two incidents, among many other things, motivated Quṭb to study in depth more of al-Bannā's books and to increase his interest in the Muslim Brethren.

Hence, the most tangible effect of his trip to the States was his sympathy toward and readiness to co-operate with the Muslim Brethren. Upon his return to Egypt, Quṭb wrote in the Brethren's journal ***Al-Daᶜwah*** (The Call) as well as in other journals such as ***Al-Risālah*** (The Message) and ***Al-Liwā' al-Jadīd*** (New Banner).[29] Moreover, Quṭb resigned his new post in 1951 as Adviser to the Ministry of Education, a very prestigious position held previously by no less a personality than Dr. Ṭaha Ḥusayn. All this was crowned in 1953 by his joining the Muslim Brethren.[30]

Quṭb and the Muslim Brethren met intellectually when the former published ***Naqd Kitāb Mustaqbal al-Thaqāfah fī Miṣr*** (A Critique of [Ṭahā Ḥusayn's] Book 'The Future of Education in Egypt') which the Brethren adopted in their publications. Ṭahā Ḥusayn divided the world into East and West and argued that Egypt belonged to the West. But Quṭb pointed out that there was a third power, the Islamic World, to which Egypt belonged. Yet a more important event was Quṭb's publication of ***Al-ᶜAdālah al-Ijtimāᶜīyyah fī al-Islām*** (Social Justice in Islam). This book was confiscated by the government because it was dedicated to a Muslim vanguard movement that dedicates its life to Islam, which the government understood as the Muslim Brethren. The book was released and published again when the dedication was deleted.[31] But, more importantly, the content of the book argued for an ideology very similar to that of the Muslim Brethren (like the adherence to Islam and opposition to Western thought and domination).

In 1953 Quṭb was appointed editor-in-chief of the weekly ***Al-Ikhwān al-Muslimīn*** (The Muslim Brethren). But this journal was banned in 1954, and the Muslim Brethren was dissolved, and many of its members, including Quṭb, were jailed. But when the court could not find sufficient evidence of conspiracy, the Brethren was allowed to continue its activities and the ban on the journal was lifted. Then Quṭb was appointed member of the Working Committee and of the Guidance Council, the highest branch in the organization, as well as head of the propaganda section.[32] This section was in charge of endorsing and sanctioning the writing of books in the name of the organization. Under Quṭb, increasingly numerous books dealing with diverse topics of Muslim civilization and Brethren literature were sanctioned and published; and Richard Mitchell attributed this increase to Quṭb- "In fact, Sayyed Quṭb was the center as well as the main ideologist of the Muslim Brotherhood."[33] Moreover, added Mitchell, under Quṭb, a more "scientific approach" was followed.

> *This section for the propagation of the message now began to make use of talent available to it among its professional members in the fields of law, economics, society, education, chemistry, engineering, and zoology.*[34]

The Muslim Brethren was the civil organ of the 1952 revolution. It was in charge of protecting foreign institutions and minorities. Moreover, it was to provide support for revolution among the civilian population.[35] Among the Brethren, Quṭb played a special role in this revolution and was, according to one of the Free Officers (the leaders of the revolution), very instrumental in preparing for the revolution. He is described by the officer as "our leader and teacher Sayyid Quṭb who tended the revolution from the beginning till its occurrence and who ordered us to be ready." He added that he went to Quṭb's house on July 19th (a week before the revolution) and some of the revolution's leaders were there, including Jamāl ᶜAbd al-Nāṣir. Moreover, Quṭb was the only civilian who attended the Revolutionary Council.

In August 1952, Quṭb delivered his lecture "Intellectual and Spiritual Liberation in Islam" to the Officers' Club, which was attended by well-known intellectuals- in fact, Dr. Ṭahā Ḥusayn introduced him- and politicians like Jamāl ᶜAbd al-Nāṣir.[36] Also, Quṭb was appointed adviser to the Revolutionary Council on matters of culture. Other posts were offered such as director of Liberation Rally and minister of Education which Quṭb declined to accept. The only post which Quṭb accepted after persuasion was director of *Hay'at al-Taḥrīr* (Liberation Rally), a pro-government organization.[36]

But after a few months, Quṭb resigned because of differences about the political line to be followed and Nāṣir himself occupied the post; Quṭb also refused Nāṣir's invitation to establish "les statuts et programmes du futur Rally de la Liberation".[37] Quṭb's main difference with Nāṣir was the former's exhortation to the latter to apply Islamic principles. For instance, whereas the Brethren wanted to prohibit the selling of alcohol and to shut down bars and liquor stores, the government, instead, restricted the hours of service. The Brethren refused the invitation of the Revolutionary Council to participate in the government by refraining from nominating any of their members to the cabinet. For although they aimed at strengthening the government and at guiding it as long as the principles of Islam were followed, they envisioned the Revolutionary Council as an adequate transitional tool which would either apply the principles of Islam or surrender the government to civilians.[38]

More importantly, the Revolutionary Council rejected the Brethren's request for civilian constitutional rule; and ***Al-Daʿwah,*** the Brethren's journal, asked repeatedly for a constitution based on Islam and for a free press. Confident that the country would opt for an Islamic constitution, they requested a public referendum in order to determine the kind of constitution the people wanted.[39] This was the beginning of the falling-out, but the straw that broke the camel's back was the Brethren's harsh denunciation of the July, 1954 Anglo-Egyptian Agreement. Their objections centered around the provision that the British enjoyed the right to re-enter Egypt and the Middle East whenever the area was threatened and around the provision that the British could keep some troops at the Suez Canal. The Brethren and Muḥammad Najīb, the leader of the Revolution and Prime Minister, were particularly critical of the Agreement and condemned Nāṣir; and Ḥasan al-Huḍaybī, the Muslim Brethren's guide, asked the government to submit the Agreement to public referendum.[40] Meanwhile, Muḥammad Najīb and the Brethren agreed on a return to civilian rule, the creation of a popularly elected parliament, the re-establishment of all freedoms, and the release of the arrested.[41] The situation escalated to a point where the Brethren and the police clashed repeatedly. Then a charge surfaced that the Brethren were dealing with the communists; a charge dismissed by Mitchell as impossible. Mitchell limited the cooperation to the distribution of each other's pamphlets, and Quṭb's name was, as the head of the propaganda section, linked with the liaison.[42]

Then, under charges of conspiracy to overthrow the government and terrorism, the movement of the Brethren was declared illegal, its journals banned, and its leaders and thousands of its followers arrested and jailed. Quṭb was arrested and held from January until March of 1954, again he was arrested in October after the *al-Manshīyyah* (Park) incident and was accused of being a member of the Secret Section in the Muslim Brethren and in charge of their secret publications. This incident, according to Quṭb, was set up in order to sever the relations between the Free Officers and the Brethren. The real reason, it has been argued, was the junta's fear of losing power.[43] (General Najīb also was removed as the head of the Revolutionary Council and as Premier and was put under house arrest). In July 1955, the "People's Court" sentenced Quṭb, in absentia, to fifteen years in prison. Quṭb and others were tortured ferociously. The Syrian Weekly, ***Al-Shihāb*** (The Meteor), indicating the magnitude of torture inflicted on Quṭb, described the manner of his arrest and jail. It reported that when military officers entered Quṭb's house to arrest him, he was running a high fever. He was handcuffed and taken to jail on foot. Due to extreme agony he was fainting and falling on the ground. Whenever he regained consciousness the words *Allah* ***Akbar*** (God is Most Great) and *Lillah al-Ḥamd* (Praise be to God), the slogans of the Muslim Brethren, would pass his lips. When he was sent to the military jail he came across Ḥamzah Bisūnī, commander of the jail, at the gate and officers of the Intelligence Police. No sooner had he stepped into the jail, than the jail staff beat and abused him for two hours. A trained military dog was let loose at him, which, holding his thigh with its jaws, dragged him back and forth. After this initial chastisement he was taken to a cell where he was continuously interrogated for seven hours. On May 3rd, 1955 he was admitted to a military hospital, suffering from chest ailments, cardiac weakness, and arthritis and various other diseases.[44]

In fact, from his early life, Quṭb was plagued with poor he that dictated many limitations on his work. He lived in Ḥal... because of lung troubles and needed dry, sunny weather. He looked pale with sleepy eyes. His illness was one of the reasons for his introvertedness, isolation, depression and concern.[45]

While in prison, one of Quṭb's most important works, ***Fī Ẓilāl al-Qur'ān*** (In the Shades of the Qur'an) was completed and published.[46] Quṭb was allowed to write because the Press, *Dār Iḥyā' al-Kitāb al-ᶜArabī* (Arabic Books Revival), sued the Government for obstructing Quṭb's fulfillment of the terms of his contract.

In prison, Quṭb abstracted himself from all except the Qurānic text, which became his only intellectual framework and reference to life. Being absorbed in the text made him far removed from the realities of life and allowed him to structure a utopian political existence, as opposed to wicked universal institutions webbed together under the umbrella of colonialism and Zionism, and permitted him to imagine the existence of an angelic Muslim vanguard opposed to the reality of a devilish hypocritical society. This period produced a tremendous output of books which constituted a systematic, ideological and political discourse for political activism that was to be picked up later by many radical movements in the Islamic world. Also, after the dissolution of the Muslim Brethren and while behind bars, he managed to establish an effective, secret organization for the Brethren and became its chief spokesman.[47] Quṭb came to the conclusion that the movement had to set up a shield, i.e., an armed organization, against external attacks, destruction, torture and dislocation of families as happened to the Muslim Brethren in Egypt in 1948, 1954 and 1957 and to the Islamic movement (*al-Jamāᶜah al-Islāmīyyah*) in Pakistan.

The protection of the Islamic movement required in his mind training a group of Muslims in ideology and military actions. Military actions were not to be directed at the overthrowing of the regime in Egypt but considered as the last resort in preventing attacks on and torturing of the Brethren. But the virtual beginning of his armed band dates from 1959.

Specifically, the events of 1954 and the harshness of the regime as well as its violence were the catalyst for Quṭb's belief in the legitimate use of force against governmental violence. Also, he perceived that the destruction of the Muslim Brotherhood was a Zionist goal as well as a colonialist objective.

The massacre that took place in the prison of *Liman Ṭara* in 1957 had a terrifying effect on Sayyid Quṭb. In that massacre 23 Brethren were shot dead and 46 were injured, out of 180 Brethren. Quṭb was at the hospital where the injured were treated. It seems that this event had made him convinced that the Egyptian regime was definitely un-Islamic and *jāhilī* and consequently could be overthrown legitimately. This period constituted the beginning of his radical contemplation that resulted in the belief of *al-ḥākimīyyah* of God and *al-jāhilīyyah* of societies that were to be taken up later by quite important radical organizations such as *al-Takfīr wa al-Hijrah* and *al-Jihād*.

Sayyid Quṭb, while in prison, was very much influenced by Abū al-A^{c}lā al-Mawdūdī who founded the Islamic movement (*al-Jamā^{c}ah al-Islamīyyah*) in India and attempted to and succeeded in establishing an Islamic state in 1947. But he did not consider the political rule in Pakistan as Islamic and asked his followers to migrate to a small village so that men would receive a proper Islamic education. Al-Mawdūdī called on the government to implement and follow the *sharī^{c}ah* and to cancel any contrary law. He was under arrest for a year and a half, then was pardoned upon the intercessions of many Islamic governments. He was the first Muslim thinker to use *al-jāhilīyyah* and *al-ḥākimīyyah* as political doctrines directed against fellow Muslims. One difference should be noted: al-Mawdūdī modified his views later in his life; Quṭb did not.

Quṭb stayed in prison till 1964. And upon the intercession of ^{c}Abd al-Salām ^{c}Arif, then President of Iraq, Quṭb was released but kept under police surveillance. The Iraqi President invited Quṭb to live in Iraq but the latter declined the offer, preferring to stay in Egypt. Eight months after his release, Quṭb along with his brother Muḥammad and his sisters Ḥamīdah and Amīnah and over twenty thousand people were jailed. The charge, this time, was preparation of an armed revolt and terrorism.[47]

In fact, once out of prison, the concepts he formed while in prison came to fruition in a small group of one hundred individuals. Its framework was based on a set of ideological rules:

1 - All human societies were far removed from Islamic ethics, system and *sharīᶜah*. Hence, there was a need to re-educate people in the true essence of Islam whether in terms of metaphysics or politics.
2 - Those who responded to this education were to undertake a study of the Islamic movements throughout history in order to set a course of action related to Zionism and "Colonialist Crusades."
3 - No organization was to be set up except after this highly ideological training had been applied.
4 - The organization was not to demand the implementation of an Islamic order at the outset of its action but was to concern itself with educating the rulers and the ruled about the true Islam.
5 - Setting up an Islamic order was not to be achieved by a coup but by a willed change by the people.
6 - Military action was only warranted when the movement was under virtual attack.

The military plan of action included the assassination of the President of the Republic, the prime minister, head of the intelligence section, head of the military police and others, as well as the destruction of some essential establishments such as lines of communication and transportation. But later on, and in a discussion with the leaders of this organization it was agreed that the essential establishments and parts of the infrastructure such as bridges were excluded from the plan.[48]

But, according to Barakāt, the trial was a mockery of justice, and a charade of a trial was conducted. Quṭb and other leaders of the Brethren were sentenced to death.[49] The charge was divided into two categories: the first was destructive and terrorist activities, the second, encouraging sedition. But, according to

Ḥasan in ***Milestones***[50] and the late President Sādāt in ***In Search of Identity***,[51] the government could not furnish a single piece of evidence to support its first charge. As to the second category, encouraging sedition, it was based on Quṭb's ***Maᶜālim.*** It was true that this book exhorted Muslims to activism but the line of activism proposed was the dissemination of Islamic message and thought in a free and peaceful manner to build a Muslim character and to create a vanguard of Muslims who, by consent of the people and through education and election, would take final charge of the affairs of the government.[52] Quṭb was not advocating the immediate overthrow of the government but a gradual transformation of the whole society and its government. Moreover, it is worth mentioning that Ḥasan believed that on the basis of certain indications, it could be asserted that one of the factors in crushing the movement and sentencing Quṭb and other leaders to death was to please a certain power, i.e., the Soviets. This was because the writings of Quṭb and other Brethren thinkers stood against communist propaganda and countered its influence. The main reason for this suggestion is that President Nāṣir, while on a visit to the USSR, announced his intention of taking punitive action against the Brethren. Following his return, mass arrests took place which culminated in Quṭb's execution.[53]

Ignoring world reactions and entreaties, on August 29th, 1966, Quṭb and two other leaders of the Brethren, Muḥammad Yūsuf ᶜAwash and ᶜAbd al-Fattaḥ Ismāᶜīl, were hanged by the Egyptian government. The death sentences of four other leaders, among them al-Huḍaybī, were commuted to life imprisonment.[54] The execution of Quṭb was a tragic blow to many Muslims, especially to the Muslim Brethren, but Quṭb's spirit manifested in his books is still very alive. And many of those books have been published numerous times and some have been translated into many languages. Now, I turn to discuss Quṭb's writings in order to throw some light on the diversity of the topics he treated and the volume of his writings.

2 - Writings:

Sayyid Quṭb is a literary figure, a poet, a novelist, a lecturer, a political reformer, a political thinker, and an intellectual. Moreover, Quṭb was very prolific and produced a number of published and unpublished works. His publications consist of hundreds of articles in journals and newspapers such as ***Al-Risālah*** (The Message), ***Al-ᶜAlam al-ᶜArabī*** (The Arab World), and ***Al-Ahrām*** (The Pyramids).[55] Also, he was editor-in-chief of many journals (such as the ones mentioned earlier). His articles are usually two to seven pages long, easy to read, and are directed at social, political, and literary issues.[56]

Long before joining the religious camp, Quṭb attracted attention and controversy.[57] For Quṭb enjoyed a very persuasive style that led to republishing many of his books quite a few times (some books now are in their tenth edition).

In ***Naẓarīyyat al-Taṣwīr al-Fannī*** (The Theory of Artistic Imagery), Khālidi, a student of literature, considered Qutb's ***Al-Taṣwīr al-Fannī fī al-Qur'ān*** (The Theory of Artistic Imagery in the *Qur'an*) as a unique and original book. He commended Quṭb for his exposition of the Qur'anic artistic way of expression and imagery. Quṭb argued that the power of the Holy *Qur'ān* did not lay in a single sentence or expression, but resulted from the style and method of conveying its message. Moreover, Khālidī credited Quṭb with outlining the general characteristics of the *Qur'an's* charm. Quṭb argued that Qur'anic charm was its harmonious and integral thesis. What linked the Holy *Qur'ān* together was neither the historical narrations nor the sequence of chapters. It was the sensitivity of the Qur'anic discourse as represented in the usage of images and tones and its employment of psychological and spiritual shades in order to imprint its message and views.[58] Quṭb, more than any writer, emphasized the need for understanding the discourse of the Holy *Qur'ān* by paying due attention to the psychological, intuitive, and spiritual message represented by imagery and dialogues and by toning down the traditional concern with grammatical and linguistic structures. His literary structure is based on using rhetorical language in order to convey lively cases of action and interaction.

His emphasis on the unity of the message, as the primary

important factor in the Holy *Qur'ān,* provided Quṭb with a key to his own writings, his treatises on Islam enjoyed an organic and psychological unity. Neither structure nor grammar is explained in his writings; he always tries to fathom the depth of the treated issues and disregards explaining structural and grammatical differences. His belief in the unity of the Islamic message prevented him from accepting what he viewed as diluted messages such as "Islamic socialism".[59] His textualism resulted from his belief that the Qur'anic text is the only reference to what is absolutely true. Tension is always present in his mockeries of writers who claim to picture realities of life. At times, he confused realities with ideals, in that his ideals are based on realities but reified in ideals that seem to be disconnected with life (like his concept of *jāhilīyyah*).

Also, in emphasizing the unity of the message he was led to reject with shallow arguments a whole culture or system of thought. For Quṭb did not view it as necessary to involve himself in the particulars of, for instance, Greek culture in order to reject it. Quṭb had general notions of Greek culture, its gods, and governments. But all the particulars of this culture became irrelevant to him when measured against its paganism. Also, his rejection of modern Western culture was motivated by his dismissal of materialism. Quṭb felt no obligation to account for the particulars of this doctrine nor its secondary sources; his primary argument was that materialism negated the existence of God and attributed the creation to matter. Many of his arguments were in fact ad hominem such as in rejecting Western society as a result of his one-sided experience.

Scholars might not be satisfied with Quṭb's style and want to see more details and arguments. But it should be noted that Quṭb was not writing for a profession or a class of scholars but his message was directed at the public in general; thus, it is important to keep the nature of his audience in mind. His audience, the average man, did not need detailed scholarship or philosophy. His writings were political essays that were written to stir reform and to attract the Muslims back to Islam. For Quṭb was writing at a time when Egypt was an arena of intellectual conflicts; there were the liberals, the socialists, the communists, and the Muslim activists. As mentioned earlier, Quṭb moved from liberalism to Islamic reform and then to fundamentalism, and the educated public was familiar with Western thought through writers such as al-ᶜAqqād and Ṭāha Ḥusayn. Quṭb's message was that Islam was the purest form of monotheism; that Islam contained the correct doctrine of justice, social and political; that Islam was a dynamic force; and that real victory was tied to the application of Islamic principles. His discourse on Western thought was polemical, but served to highlight the advantages of Islam over other ideologies and philosophies. Consequently, when he dwelt on the doctrine of Trinity, for example, his purpose was not to lecture on or elaborate the details of Trinity but to argue that Christianity had lost its pure monotheism.

Of course Quṭb showed emotionalism in his writing; for his work as a political reformer could not lead to its final destination without emotions. In a sense he had a belief that he had a mission to fulfill, i.e., the reform of the'*ummah*. For the public is not usually persuaded by reasoning but emotions, thus, his ordinary reader was taken away from place and time. But involving emotions, for Quṭb, was not wrong per se since he was not addressing the mind only but also the heart. As said before, he broke with al-ᶜAqqād, whose writings he considered dry because of their "pure intellectualism," and considered that the proper discourse between man and man had to involve emotions and intellect.

Another reason that accounts for his emotionalism was a feeling that Muslim culture and territories were threatened by local and foreign forces. His outrage was motivated by the vulgaritics and superficiality of human existence as a result of the dominance of human systems and philosophies. Disturbed by the materialism of Marxist and Western countries and by the tyranny of the former and the liberalism of the latter, he launched continous attacks on their ideologies. Thus, criticism of ideology became a dominant feature of his writing. Also, Arab and Muslim regimes were not spared criticism; for he considered them tyrannical, unjust, and unproductive.

His fiery style was capable of provoking great emotions of dignity, solidarity, unity, universality, and similar feelings and could, for instance, uplift the reader to the greatness of Islam. On the other hand, his style was capable as well of stimulating, through his criticism, profound anger and revulsion; a fact proved by Quṭb's experience at the Ministry of Education which led to his resignation. His books, and ***Maᶜālim*** in particular, were the basis of the government's charges against the Brethren, namely, harboring terrorism and encourging sedition. They were considered as, for instance, a stumbling block against, communism. In fact, the Egyptian communists denounced him during the 1950's as a Western agent.

A main source of irritation for his adversaries was his unwillingness to compromise. In practice, he refused to compromise with the Ministry of Education and with Jamāl ᶜAbd al-Nāṣir and finally resigned. In theory, he attributed polytheism *(shirk)* to those Muslim societies that accepted un-Islamic ideologies and laws.[60] He refused to fuse Islam with other concepts, be it democracy, socialism or others. Part of the refusal to compromise was his uncompromising belief in the ability of Islam to accommodate itself to modernity without reference to or adoption of anti-Islamic or even un-Islamic values, ideologies, and practices.

Such understanding of Islam, coupled with Qutb's belief in its divinity, oriented him towards purification of Islam from what he considered contrary or detrimental to Islam. On the one hand, traditionalism and imitation of the West and the East were thrown out of his vocabulary as acceptable means of regenerating Islam. On the other hand, purity of thought and values became the centerpiece of his concerns and manifested in the concept of *tawḥīd* and its impact on theology, jurisprudence, and politics.[61]

Hence, the repetition of certain notions and arguments became a characteristic of his books. A concept like social justice is treated in the discussion of peace, equality or rights and duties. Therefore, the reader of more than one book- or even one book- will detect this kind of repetition that serves, in most cases, to impress an idea on the mind of the reader.

A final note should be directed to the sources Quṭb uses in his arguments. The Holy *Qur'ān* functioned as the permanent and fundamental source of reference and authority, employed in order to support his arguments; for each argument he made he provided several verses. The *ḥadīth* (the Prophet's sayings and actions) was used much less. Other references can be divided into two categories, Arabic and English. Some of the modern Muslim authors referred to were Jamāl al-Dīn al-Afghānī (1837-96), Muḥammad ᶜAbduh (1849-1905), Abū al-Aᶜlā al-Mawdūdī (1903-1980), and Muḥammad Iqbāl (1876-1938).[62] Some earlier Muslim authors were referred to but less frequently such as Imām Mālik, Imām Muslim, al-Bukhārī, and al-Māwardī.[63]

Western references were to translations and not to original texts. Although Quṭb studied in English-speaking institutions, he did not quote any source in its English text. Two things can be suggested: First, his English was inadequate, but this seems a very weak suggestion because he had lived and studied at English-speaking institutions. Secondly, his interest was in referring his readers to sources that they could read and use. On the other hand, Quṭb made much use of and referred the reader to the books and conclusions of Iqbal, al-Mawdūdī, al-ᶜAqqād, Asad, and al-Nadawī in treating Western civilization- some of which are discussed in *Chapter II.*

Following is a list of some Western authors he referred to regularly: Plato, Aristotle, Descartes, Charles Darwin, Alexis Carrel, Bertrand Russell, John Foster Dulles, T.W. Arnold, Henri Bergson, Robert Briffault.[64] However, Quṭb did not have deep knowledge of philosophy, science, history or even traditional sciences, and though his knowledge was very comprehensive and touched on so many fields, he was not a scholar in the strict sense of the word- as will be shown in *Chapters II and III.*

Quṭb's published works, leaving out those in journals, can be divided into two intellectual stages which coincided also with two historical phases. The first phase stretches from 1933 till 1948; the second, from 1949 to his execution in 1966. This division is based on his shift from liberalism to the analysis of general social and political issues from an Islamic perspective and, then, to radical fundamentalism, which affected the nature of his writings. Whereas in the first phase Quṭb deals with poetry, fiction, literary studies, in the second he focuses completely on religious and political aspects of Islam.[65]

I will start first by citing the books written before 1949. The titles themselves are revealing of the subject matter, and, therefore, no attempt is made to explain the books unless there is something that is not readily obvious. Their value is historical and literary, revealing the way Quṭb dealt with literature. Because my interest is Quṭb the fundamentalist, I have given synopses of his books written in the second phase; most of which are used to expose and analyze Quṭb's thought in this work, and by which Quṭb has become known as a Muslim reformer and thinker.

First Phase

1 . ***Muhimmat al-Shāʿir fī al-Hayat wa-Shiʿr al-Jīl al-Muʿāṣir*** (The Poet's Responsibility in Life and the Poetry of the Contemporary Generation), 1933. This book was later denounced as un-Islamic by Quṭb. The books that Quṭb denounced were those that viewed life in non-Islamic or irreligious terms.

2 . ***Al-Shāṭī' al-Majhūl*** (The Unknown Beach), 1934. It is a collection of poetry on different social themes.

3 . ***Naqd Kitāb Mustaqbal al-Thaqāfah fī Miṣr*** (A Critique of 'The Future of Culture in Egypt'), 1935. It is a critique of Ṭahā Ḥusayn's *Mustaqbal al-Thaqāfah fī Miṣr*. The basic contention that Quṭb takes up is Ḥusayn's notion that Egypt is part of Western civilization and not part of the Muslim's.

4 . ***Al-Taṣwīr al-Fannī fī al-Qur'ān*** (Artistic Imagery in the Qur'ān), 1945. This book is the first to deal with the Holy Qur'ān, but its subject is the literary, not the political or social aspect of Islam.

5 . ***Al-Aṭyāf al-Arbaʿah*** (The Four Spirits), 1945. It is co-

authored with his brother and two sisters. It is composed of some experiences of the two brothers and the two sisters (the four spirits). Later Quṭb denounced this book as un-Islamic.

6 . ***Ṭifl fī al-Qaryah*** (A Child in the Village), 1946. It is an autobiography of Quṭb's childhood. Also, this book was denounced as un-Islamic. It was dedicated to Ṭahā Ḥusayn who wrote his autobiography *al-Ayyām* (The Days). Quṭb followed the same method as Ḥusayn's in describing his upbringing in the village and commenting on its customs and ignorance and his life in the city. In short, it is a critique of life in the Egyptian village and city.

7 . ***Al-Madīnah al-Mas'ḥurah*** (The Entranced City), 1946. Here it is argued that reality is elusive and man cannot comprehend reality. This book was not denounced because Quṭb persisted in holding the notion that man could not comprehend reality.

8 . ***Kutub wa-Shakhṣīyyāt*** (Books and Personalities), 1946. It is a critique and an appreciation of the writings of some famous literary figures like Thomas Hardy and ᶜAbbās M. al-ᶜAqqād.

9 . ***Ashwāk*** (Thorns), 1947. This is a love story which he later denounced as un-Islamic.

10 . ***Mashāhid al-Qiyāmah fī al-Qur'ān*** (Scenes of the Day of Resurrection in the *Qur'ān*), 1947. It describes and explains the characteristics of the Qur'anic imagery and discourse concerning the Day of Resurrection. It is also a literary work and has been translated into Perisan.

11 . ***Rawḍat al-Ṭifl*** (The Garden of the Child), n.d. It is a textbook for the Ministry of Education and is co-authored with Amīnah al-Saᶜid and Yusūf Murād.

12 . ***Al-Qaṣaṣ al-Dīnī*** (Religious Story-telling), n.d. It is another textbook for the Ministry and is co-authored with ᶜAbd al-Majīd al-Sahar.

13 . ***Al-Jadīd fī al-Lughah*** (What is New in Language), n.d. Again, it is a textbook written for the Ministry.

14 . ***Al-Jadīd fī al-Maḥfūẓāt*** (What is New in Memorized

Poetry), n.d. This book is written for the Ministry as well.

15 . ***Al-Naqd al-Adabī: Uṣūluhu wa-Manāhijuhu*** (Literary Critique: Its Principles and Methods), 1948.

Second Phase

This phase of Qutb's life and writing, which is my interest, starts around 1948. All the books below are concerned with explaining Islam, activism, *tawḥīd* (oneness of God), social justice, and economics.

16 . ***Al-ᶜAdālah al-Ijtimāᶜīyyah fī al-Islām*** (Social Justice in Islam), 1st. ed. 1949. It has been translated into English,[66] Hebrew, and Persian. It is the first of Quṭb's books on Islamic political thought and is dedicated to those individuals who struggle for and dedicate their lives to God. It deals with religion and society in both Christianity and Islam. Quṭb traces the history of the separation between religion and politics and considers this separation as un-Islamic because it originated with Christianity. The thesis of the book is that Islam is revealed for all ages, though the Holy *Qur'ān* was delivered at a specific historical time and provides fixed guidelines, general principles, and comprehensive rules that are continuously valid. It lays down the true spirit and foundation of justice.

The book is composed of eight chapters ranging from social justice, its nature, foundations, instruments, to the function of money and to Islam, its historical reality and the future.

The book devotes a chapter to the relation between God, the universe, life and man. God is the center and is the originator of everything else. This idea should be consulted whenever man wants to understand the ultimate truths. Another chapter deals with "Financial Policies in Islam" and a third focuses on "Political Rule in Islam". The two chapters constitute a set of rules for an Islamic political and economic order. In this book, the author indicates the possibility of co-existence between Marxism and capitalism.

17 . ***Maᶜrakat al-Islām wa-al-Ra'simālīyyah*** (Islam's Battle with Capitalism), 1950. It has been translated into Persian. The

book starts with a warning to the Muslims about the dangers that are surrounding the Muslim world. Because of the spread of corruption and injustice, Egypt's conditions are unnatural and are not going to last (in fact a revolution took over the country in 1952). It is considered as a call for revolt against the authorities of Egypt at that time and a condemnation of corruption and luxury. The author directs all kind of accusations against "Those who participated in corrupting Egypt and the Arab world" including the media, men of religion, arts and politicians. He shows his dissatisfaction with the prevailing social conditions that humiliate mankind. Also, he attempts to clarify "the myth" that the people are the source of authority.

Moreover, the book deals with issues such as the distribution of wealth, unequal opportunity, corruption of labor, and weakness of production. The message of the book is that Islam is necessary in the political arena and is the road to victory and dignified life. Furthermore, the book is full of criticism of tyranny, of shaykhs (religious scholars), the treatment of women, chauvinism, colonialism and other related topics.

18 . ***Al-Islām wa al-Salām al-ᶜĀlamī*** (Islam and Universal Peace), 1951. It has been translated into Persian and English.[67] The book describes the process of building a peaceful structure. Peace can be true only when it starts with the individual and extends to the individual family, society, and the world. Islam attempts to ingrain peace in the conscience of the individual first. If peace does not spring forth from the innermost feeling of the individual, it is not peace but a shaky truce. It can neither be imposed by the world on a society nor by a society on an individual. Hence, peace has to be understood first as a spiritual act that manifests itself in politics, psychology, morality and other disciplines. True peace cannot be attained without reference to God which is embodied in the *Qur'ān,* the *sunnah,* and their teachings such as *shūrah* (consultation), divine law, and social guarantees.

Also, the book shows the essential way for setting up a Muslim society; it is based on the divine *sharīᶜah* and completed by an ethical education and legal guarantees. However, peace is not surrender, humiliation or oppression. It is an honorable victory of man over the material and political impediments in life.

After the Revolution of 1952, a complete chapter "Al-Ān" (Now), which deals with the "hypocrisy of the United States policies in the Middle East" was deleted by the government.

19 . ***Fī Ẓilāl al-Qur'ān*** (In the Shades of the Qur'ān); vol. 1 1952. It was completed, published, and revised in prison. It represents one of Quṭb's highest achievements. It is an eight-volume work; ten editions are in circulation, and it is also published in Persian. Ayatollah Khāmin'ī, the current Guide of the Islamic Republic of Iran, translated some volumes of the book.[68] In English, Part 30 has been published as ***In the Shades of the Qur'ān*** and is introduced by Quṭb's brother, Muḥammad. Most of the book has been translated and serialized in ***The Muslim,*** the organ of the Federation of the Students of Islamic Societies in U.K. and Eire.[69]

Fi Zilāl al-Qur'ān is Quṭb's interpretation of the *Qur'an* as experienced by him. His method is unusual in that he interprets the Qur'an in terms of his own understanding and experience. In the third edition, the ***Ẓilāl*** is made into a method of political activism; i.e., the activism of ***Al-Maᶜālim.***

The language of the interpretation is simple and modern. Every *sūrah* (chapter) has an introduction and a conclusion that draw the themes of the *surāh* into one picture. His method is comprehensive in the sense that he turns the *sūrah* or *āyah* (verse) every way in order to find all of the possible meanings relating to nature, politics, reality and so forth. This was done instead of the traditional method of indulging in legal disputes, linguistic differences and niceties. Moreover, he is very much interested in showing the psychological prototypes of faith, belief, the good, the evil, infidelity, and tries to relate these to human nature *(fiṭrah)* and the harmony between man, the universe, and God.

20 . ***Dirāsāt Islāmīyyah*** (Islamic studies), 1953. It is a collection of articles from other books on different Islamic topics.

21 . ***Hādhā al-Dīn*** (This Religion), 1962. This book has been translated into English and Persian.[70] Written after imprisonment, it focuses on activism of Islam as the proper method for the well-being of the world. The attainment of this unique method is obligatory on the Muslims. ***Hādhā al-Dīn*** is one of the books of the later period, i.e., of the prison period which also includes ***Fi Ẓilal al-Qur'ān; Al-Mustaqbal li-Hādhā al-Dīn*** (The Future Belongs to this Religion), and ***Maᶜālīm fī al-Ṭarīq*** (Signposts on the Road).

It is directed at the young Muslims of the Islamic movement in order to stress the point that the success of religion needs to be embodied in a movement that works in a hard manner. The Muslims should tolerate all kinds of hardships in order to spread the divine method. Islam should become the all-embracing system of life because it alone can free man from submission to another man. By doing this, man returns to his true nature and *fiṭrah* and resolves all of his problems and difficulties.

The author stresses the importance of creed as the only method for resolving conflicts between different countries, nations and peoples and for uniting human beings into one entity by removing mankind from *al-jāhilīyyah.*

In dealing with reason, Quṭb expounds the notion of its inability to fathom ultimate questions on being. But mankind, due to its arrogance, sees itself as the holder of truth. Also, material advances have not softened man's agony and isolation, but have created new gods: the god of money, the god of fame, and the god of desire.

22 . ***Al-Mustaqbal li-Hādhā al-Dīn*** (The Future Belongs to this Religion), 196?, was translated into English.[71] The focus of this book is the notion of Islam's comprehensiveness as a system of thought and life and theory and practice. Other systems of life such as liberalism and Marxism have proved their poverty. Religion is defined as the manner in which a person or a nation conducts his or its life, and its importance is highlighted. ***Al-Mustaqbal li-Hādhā al-Dīn*** is an attempt to discuss in detail Western civilization and its future. This civilization is slipping towards destruction and collapse. Its replacement is nothing but

Islam because it is a comprehensive method that deals with the multiple facets of life.

Human methods, according to Quṭb, are under the impacts of their founders and are flawed by whims and desires. They have produced dislocations in man's mind and body and in the material and the spiritual energies of humanity. This was done by separating life into the religious and the secular and by waging a relentless war against religion. But the future is for Islam if Muslim vanguards struggle to overcome the obstacles erected by human authorities and if they acquire the necessary knowledge and technology.

23 . ***Khaṣā'iṣ al-Taṣawwur al-Islāmī wa-Muqawwamātuhu*** (The Characteristics and Components of the Islamic Concept, 1962). Originally, this book was to be published under ***Fikrat al-Islām ᶜan al-Kawn wa-al-Ḥayāt wa-al-Insān*** (The Idea of Islam on the Universe, Life, and Man), which Professor Mitchell could not find. The book was made into two volumes, the second of which was published in 1986. Volume One is, in my opinion, the most profound book that Quṭb has ever written because it deals with the philosophical bases of Islam. Without reading this book- a common feature in current scholarship on Quṭb- the understanding of Quṭb's thought is partial.

This book is divided into six chapters, each dealing with some characteristics of the Islamic universal concept that underlines all other aspect of Islamic intellectual and practical life. They are *ṭawḥīd* (oneness), *ulūhīyyah* (divinity), *thabāt* (permanence), *shumūlīyyah* (comprehensiveness), *tawāzun* (equilibrium), *'ījābīyyah* (positiveness), and *wāqiᶜīyyah* (realism). The consequences of those characteristics are discussed and compared with Western concepts (elaborated in *Chapter II)*.

Without such a concept, no guarantee can be given of the correctness of an action. Proper actions should be grounded in proper concepts.

The author finds inspiration for these characteristics in the Qur'an itself without referring to past philosophies, ideologies or literature. For he believes that the ultimate infidelity occurs when man legislates and rules instead of God. This constitutes a breach in *tawḥīd,* which is the basis and center of justice.

Volume Two, ***Muqawwamāt al-Taṣawwur al-Islāmī*** (The Components of the Islamic Concept), saw the light after many years of waiting. Quṭb's brother wrote the introduction and edited the text. Two chapters were lost from the manuscript.

Al-ḥākimīyyah is one of the concepts that is treated in depth. Those rulers who claim a right to *al-ḥākimīyyah* in fact claim the right to divinity. Those individuals who concur with this share in the rulers' polytheism *(shirk).*

Another concept is the *jāhilīyyah* of reality. It is found when man's conceptual distortions dominate materially over the world and over God's divine concepts. Knowledge is useless if it is not embodied in an active movement that destroys *al-jāhilīyyah* and uproots its doctrines. The Muslims should not accept *al-jāhilīyyah* on any grounds. Its partial acceptance legitimizes its existence, but its totality is illegitimate and has no right to exist. It has infringed on God's divinity and consequently should be abolished.

Quṭb elaborates the following doctrines:

1 - Human nature has an instinctive part that does not change in time. The spiritual part in man is constant and permanent.

2 - The Islamic concept is divine, complete, comprehensive, timeless, revealed in accordance with man's nature.

3 - The Islamic concept aims at setting up a non-*jāhilī* life capable of development. Its pivot is permanent and extends to the development of mankind. It rejects the legitimacy of *al-jāhilīyyah.*

24 . ***Al-Islām wa-Mushkilāt al-Ḥaḍārah*** (Islam and the Problems of Civilization), 1962. This is a book inspired by Quṭb's two-year visit to the United States of America. There, Quṭb conceived of a set of problems and evils of a materialistic civilization. The book deals with contemporary human life and its styles which Quṭb perceived as unfit for man's dignity and value. Marxism, on one hand, cannot save man from the

materialism of capitalism because Marxism is grounded as well in materialistic interpretations. All in all, Western civilization is on the way to the abyss.

The book discusses three important issues in both Western civilization and Islamic civilization. They are, first, man's essence, secondly, relations between men and women, and thirdly, social and economic orders. He elaborates on God's method and its difference from other methods: God's method is directed at man qua man while other methods deal with man as an object. Thus, mankind will be saved only when it returns to God's religion. Man is a unique being, not because of his biological existence but due to his intellectual and spiritual capacities. Those individuals who forfeit their spirituality are unfit to be called human.

25 . ***Maᶜālim fī al-Ṭarīq*** (Signposts on the Road), 1964. It has been translated into English.[72] It was used against Quṭb in the trial that ended in his being sentenced to death. Because of its exhortation of people to action, anyone who owned a copy of this book was liable to be put on trial on the charge of sedition. *Maᶜālim* provides the activists with signposts that should be followed in order to arrive at the objective of establishing an Islamic order. It describes the fundamental rules for activism such as organization and ideology. It focuses on the concept of *al-jāhilīyyah* as a point of departure between the Muslim activists and other individuals, societies and states. Thus, the Qur'anic generation *(al-jīl al-Qur'ānī)* is born and lives in isolation from corrupt societies. This isolation, however, should lead ultimately to setting up an Islamic state, which is to shoulder a world-wide responsibility in spreading Islam.

Also, *al-ḥākimīyyah* is a characteristic of the Muslim society because the Muslims are united by creed. Any legitimate constitution or political rule, therefore, sould be based on al-ḥākimīyyah. All this requires tremendous and costly sacrifices, without which the divine method ends in futile argumentation.

The book consists of thirteen chapters ranging from the characteristics of Qur'anic generations and of Muslim society to Islam as the right path to good society.

26 . ***Afrāḥ al-Rūḥ*** (Joys of the Soul). It was published posthumously in 1971. It is composed of Quṭb's letters to his family and friends during his stay in the United States. They were published first in ***Majallat al-Fikr*** (The Journal of Thought).

27 . ***Naḥwa Mujtamaᶜ Islāmī*** (Towards an Islamic Society), 1969. This book was published posthumously in *Al-Aqṣā* library in Amman. It is a collection of articles from ***Majallat al-Ikhwān*** (The Journal of the Brethren) in 1951.

The book centers around the idea that Islam's mission is serious, dangerous and fruitful since it is not related only to the Muslim Nation but also to all of mankind. Its mission is to save humanity from errors in concepts and means. The Islamic method cannot die and is everlasting.

The writer makes a distinction between *al-sharīᶜah* (law) and *al-fiqh* (jurisprudence). *Al-sharīᶜah* is what was revealed to and transmitted by the Prophet Muḥammad; *al-fiqh* is the human attempt to understand *al-sharīᶜah*. This leads him to discuss the characteristics of the ideal Muslim society such as divinity which should become a universal ideal.

The thesis of this book is that the Islamic *daᶜwah* is a human necessity because humanity is now plagued with materialism. There is a paramount need for the Islamic divine message, and Islam is a universal system that can offer human brotherhood and love as well as equality.

Communism will one day dominate the West when the economic resources are depleted and when very few individuals control the lives and destinies of millions of people. Neither democracy nor liberalism will be able to fight communism. The only ideology that will stand up to and, ultimately, defeat communism is Islam. The reason is that Islam is in accordance with human nature while communism is not.

28 . ***Fī al-Tarīkh: Fikrah wa-Minhāj*** (On History: An Idea and A Method). This book also was published posthumously. It is composed of two articles published in ***Al-Ikhwān al-Muslimūn*** in

its 1st. and 2nd. editions in 1951 and two other articles extracted from other works.

It is a very essential work for the understanding not only of Quṭb's conception of history and historiography but also of the possibility of achieving an ideal society. The first chapter deals with his theory of the arts and their value in the individual life and in society. Islam is treated as a comprehensive and uncompromising positive revolution. Furthermore, individuals and their rights are discussed in Chapter Four.

29 . ***Maʿrakatunā Maʿa al-Yahūd*** (Our Battle with the Jews), 1970. This work was also published posthumously but appeared first in the weekly ***al-Daʿwah.*** It is a collection of articles on the conflicts with Jews and the colonialists.

30 . ***Tafsīr Sūrat al-Shūrah*** (Interpretation of the Chapter on Shūrah), 196 . This a reproduction of the chapter dealing with *shūrah* in the *Ẓilāl.*

31 . ***Tafsīr Āyāt al-Ribā*** (The Interpretation of the Verses on Usury), n.d. Also, this a reproduction of the verses on ***ribā*** (usury) in ***Ẓilāl.***

32 . ***Fiqh al-Daʿwah*** (Understanding of the Call), 1970. This is a collection of articles that deal with activism and propagation of the Islamic message collected from ***Ẓilāl.*** (In the title, *Fiqh* means understanding and not jurisprudence).

33, 34 & 35 . ***Islām aw lā Islām*** (Islam or no Islam), ***Ilā al-Mutathāqilīn ʿan al-Jihād*** (To those who are slow to respond to *jihād*), and ***Risālat al-Ṣalāh*** (Treatise on Prayer) are collections of numerous articles obtained from diverse sources. No date is given.

36 . ***Amrikā allatī Ra'aytu*** (America that I Saw), n.d. There are different views on the publication of this book. Khālidī states that it is unpublished. Although I have not seen the book, it seems to me that it has been published because Sayyid Quṭb quotes and refers to it in numerous places such as ***Al-Islām wa-Mushkilāt al-Ḥaḍārah*** (Islam and the Problems of Civilization). Also, parts of this book can be found in three articles published

in ***Al-Risālah*** in 1951 (Part 19, vol. 2, no. 957, pp. 1245-47; no. 959, pp. 1302-6; and, no. 961, pp. 1357-60).

This book deals with Quṭb's observations in the United States. The content of the book can be derived from previous quotations. In short, it is a critique of the Western way of life.

37 . ***Sīnā' bayna Aṭmā^{c} al-Isti^{c}mārīyyin wa al-Ṣihyūnīyyīn*** (Sinai between the Ambitions of the Colonialists and the Zionists), 1967. It was published posthumously and is a collection of three articles; two of the articles were written by Ḥasan al-Bannā, the founder of the Muslim Brethren, and Kemāl Sharīf, another leader of the Brethren.

38 . ***Al-Jihād fī Sabīl Allah*** (Struggle in God's Way), 1970. This work is a collection of articles written by Quṭb, al-Bannā, and Abū al-A^{c}lā al-Mawdūdī, the leader of *al-Jamā^{c}a al-Islāmīyyah* in Pakistan.

39 . ***Laḥn al-Kifāḥ*** (The Melody of Struggle), 1972. It is composed of poems written by Quṭb and Hāshim al-Rifā^{c}ī.[73]

Quṭb's books, especially of the late period, have constituted the gospel of action for numerous known and unknown Islamic groups and movements. His philosophy of action is based on a philosophy of the divine and the human elements and their proper place in an all-embracing order, which is our next topic.

Footnotes:

1 Sayyid Quṭb, *Ma^c alim fī al-Ṭarīq* (Signoposts on the Road), (Bayrūt: Dār al-Shurūq, 7th ed. 1980), pp. 134-44; (hereafter cited as *Ma^c ālim*).

2 The *jāhilīyyah* means literally the time of ignorance. Historically it denotes pre-Islamic poetry and culture. According to Philip Hitti in *History of the Arabs,* 1st. ed. 1937 (New York: St. Martin's Press, 1981), pp. 87-88 & 91, it extends from the creation of Adam down to Muḥammad's mission. Some of its features are paganism, poetry, raids. Eloquence with archery and horsemanship are the three basic attributes of the "perfect man." With Quṭb, the *jāhilīyyah* is transformed from a historical concept denoting pre-Islamic culture to a set of permanent political doctrines that functions as a basis for rejecting foreign, un-Islamic, and anti-Islamic ideas and systems.

Ma^c ālim or *Signposts* are the guidelines to those who are actively involved or want to be involved in the creation of an Islamic state. See also *Writings* below. Al-Mawdūdī's view can be found in his *Al-Ḥukūmah al-Islāmīyyah* (Islamic Government), (Al-Qāhirah: Dār al-Mukhtār al-Islāmī, 1980) pp. 15-20.

3 These facts are based on his autobiography, *Ṭifl fī al-Qaryah* (A Child in the Village), discussed below. For more details, see, S. Badrul Hasan, *Syed Qutb Shaheed* (Lahore: International Pakistani Publishers, 1980) pp. 4-7 (hereafter cited as Hasan *Shaheed;* S. Badrul Hasan, tr., *Milestones* (Karachi: International Islamic Publishers, 1981), pp. 1-2, (hereafter cited as Hasan, *Milestones*). *Milestones* is a translation of Quṭb's *Ma^c ālim.* And see Ṣalaḥ ^c Abd al-Fattāḥ Khālidī, *Sayyid Quṭb al-Shahīd al-Ḥayy* (Sayyid Quṭb, the Living Martyr), (^c Ammān: Makatabat al-Aqsā, 1981),. p. 46; (hereafter cited as Khālidī, *Quṭb*). For instance, Quṭb co-authored with his brother and two sisters *Al-Aṭyāf al-Arba^c ah* (The Four Spirits). Khālidī's book is one of the latest and best biographies on Quṭb. The information is well-documented and its sources are known.

See also, ^c Ādil Ḥamūdah, *Sayyid Quṭb: Min al-Qaryah ilā al-Mishnaqah* (Al-Qāhirah: Dār Sīnā, 1987), pp. 39-41; hereafter cited as *Sayyid Quṭb.*

See also, Muḥammad Tawfīq Barakāt, *Sayyid Quṭb: Khulāṣat Ḥayatuhu, Minhājuhu fī al-Ḥarakah,* pp. 9-10, and, Khālidī, *Maẓarīyyat al-Taṣwīr al-Fannī ^c inda Sayyid Quṭb* (Quṭb's Theory of Artistic Imagery), (^c Amman: Dār al-Furqān, 1983), p. 10 and *passim;* (hereafter cited as Khālidī, *Naẓarīyyat*. This book deals with literary originality in one of Quṭb's writings- discussed below. It sheds light on Quṭb's understanding of the literary aspect of the Holy Qur'an which later affected his own style.

Al-Azhar University was founded in 970-72 but modernized and expanded in 1961 in order include modern sciences.

4 *Dār al-^c Ulūm* was founded in Cairo in 1872 by Muḥammad Alī, the builder

of modern Egypt. Originally, it was opened to train students as Arabic teachers for the state primary and secondary schools and became the first secular institute for higher learning. Its first students were from al-Azhar University, the Sunnite Center for learning. Now, it gives advanced and modern training and preparation in Arabic, among other subjects.

5 Hasan, *Milestones,* p. 4. But Ibrāhīm Ibn ^{c}Abd al-Raḥmān al-Balīhī states that Quṭb obtained a B. A. in literature and a diploma in education. See *Sayyid Quṭb wa-Turāthuhu al-Adabī wa-al-Fikrī* (Sayyid Quṭb, His Literary and Intellectual Heritage), (Riyadh, 1972), p. 42; (hereafter referred to as al-Balīhī, *Turāth*). This book is a summary of some of Quṭb's books.

6 See *Writings* above.

7 Quṭb, *Ashwāk* (Al-Qāhirah: Dār Sa^{c}d, n. d.), p. 7; hereafter cited as *Ashwāk.* Later references are to this edition. This book was denounced by Quṭb as un-Islamic. For details on books denounced, see *Writings* above; Barakāt, *Khulāṣah*, pp. 3-4; and, Hasan, *Milestones,* p. 32. It is worthwhile to note that Quṭb did not marry.

8 ^{c}Abbas M. al-^{c}Aqqād (1889-1964) is a well-known literary figure and a journalist. Some of his famous books are *Allāh* and *^{c}Abqarīyyat Muḥammad* (Muḥammad's Genius). He held very high positions like the Chairmanship of the Committee on Poetry in the Higher Council of Arts. See also footnote 12.

9 Ṭahā Ḥusayn (1889-1973) was a famous writer. Some of his books are *The Future of Culture in Egypt* and *On pre-Islamic Poetry.* He occupied many high ministerial offices and became Minister of Education. Also, see footnote 12.

10 On Quṭb and al-^{c}Aqqād and other writers dealing with Western civilization see, Barakāt, *Khulāṣah,* pp. 10-11 & 13; al-Balīhī, *Turāth, pp. 32-36; Muhammd Quṭb, Sayyid Quṭb al-Shahīd al-A^{c}zal*, p. 25. Yvonne Haddad, *Contemporary Islam* (p. 17) and, Maḥmud ^{c}Abd al-Ḥamīd, *Al-Ikhwān al-Muslimūn* (The Muslim Brethren), Vol. 1, (Al-Qāhirah: Dār al-Da^{c}wah, 1978), p. 190 and *passim;* (hereafter cited as *al-Ikhwān*). Also, see Abu al-Ḥasan al-Nadawī, *Mudhakkarāt Sā'iḥ,* p. 25. And see also, Khālidī, *Quṭb,* pp. 105-8 & 165 and footnote 12. See also Ḥamūdah, *Sayyid Quṭb,* pp. 51-52.

On Quṭb's advocacy of nudity, see, Ḥamid, *Al-Ikhwān,* (p. 191-9) where Ḥamid mentions that he intended to write an article to respond to Quṭb's advocacy of nudity in *Al-Risālah.* (I could not find the article or its title). But Ḥasan al-Bannā prevented him from doing so in order not to attract public attention. Also, see, for instance, Quṭb's description of the fiancée in *Ashwāk* (p. 45). She appears average looking but one of her features is "seductive, outstanding breasts that overwhelm the looker so much that he becomes incapable of further judgement." see also Ḥamūdah, *Sayyid Quṭb,* pp. 51-52.

11 Aḥmad Ḥasan al-Zayyāt (1885-1968) issued and edited *Al-Risālah* in 1933. He also was professor of literature at the American University in Cairo.

12 Khālidī, *Naẓarīyyat,* pp. 64-66. Also, see Olivier Carré, *"Le combat-pour-Dieu et l'Etat islamique chez Sayyid Qutb, l'inspirateur du radicalisme actuel," Revue francaise de science politique,* No. 4, August 1983, p. 681. See also, Ḥamūdah, *Sayyid Quṭb,* p. 48.

Al-^{c}Aqqād, Aḥmad Luṭfī al-Sayyid (1872-1963) and others were moderate in their criticism of the government, but were very harsh in their attacks on Islam. (Luṭfī al-Sayyid wrote numerous books like *Al-Muntakhabāt* (Selections) and *Mabādi' fī al-Sīyāsah wa-al-Adab wa-al-Mujtama^{c}* (Principles in Politics, Literature, and Society) and also translated Aristotle's *Politics* and *Poetics* into Arabic. He also was editor-in-chief of *Lisān al-Ḥal,* the Ummah Party's newspaper, and was a well-known advocate of women's rights.) They did not see much use for Islam; Ṭahā Ḥusayn's *On Pre-Islamic Poetry* and ^{c}Ali ^{c}Abd Al-Rāziq's *al-Islām wa-Uṣūl al-Ḥukm* (Islam and the Principles of Government) were perceived by the traditional *'ulamā* as directed against Islam as a religious and political order. ^{c}Abd al-Rāziq's book, for instance, argued that Islam did not require the existence of the caliphate or, in other words, its existence was not a religious matter. Throughout the 1920's and the 1930's al-^{c}Aqqād, Ṭahā Ḥusayn, and Tawfīq al-Ḥakīm saw Europe as the ideal and, even, disliked being associated with the Arabs; for instance Ṭahā Ḥusayn's *The Future of Culture in Egypt* maintained that Egypt was not an Arab country but Pharaonic; a claim that was not acceptable to the traditional centers of power. But in the late thirties, al-^{c}Aqqād and the other modernists shifted alliance and joined with the religious camp. This event resulted in the writing of many books on the validity of Islam like Ṭaha Ḥusayn's *^{c}Alā Hāmish al-Sīrah,* and al-^{c}Aqqād's *^{c}Abqarīyyat Muḥammad.* Quṭb was one of those who "converted" to advocating Islam. Many reasons can be given for this conversion: the rise of nationalism, corrupt political parties and so forth. On intellectual life in Egypt in the first half of this century, see, for instance, P. J. Vatikiotis, *The Modern History of Egypt* (New York: Praeger Publishers, 1969), "From the Old Order to the New, 1930-62".

13 See *Al-Risālah,* vol. 19, part 2, no. 681, July 1946, pp. 796-97. See also Muḥammad Ḥāfiz Dīyāb, *Sayyid Quṭb, al-Khiṭāb wa al-Aydiolojīyyah* (Sayyid Quṭb: The Discourse and Ideology), (Bayrūt: Dar al-Ṭali^{c}ah, 2nd ed. 1988), pp. 65-66. hereafter cited as *Al-Khiṭāb.* Also, see, Quṭb, *Ma^{c}rakatunā ma'a al-Yahūd* (Our Battle with the Jews), (Riyadh, 1970), pp. 21-24 & 30; hereafter cited as *Ma^{c}rakatūnā.*

14 *Al-^{c}Ālam al-^{c}Arabī* was published in 1947 as a scientific, literary, and social monthly journal. *Al-Fikhr al-Jadīd* was published in 1948 as a general weekly that treated different aspects of society. See also, Yusuf al-^{c}Aẓm, *Rā'id al-Fikr al-Islāmī, al-Shahīd Sayyid Quṭb* (The Pioneer of Contemporary Islamic Thought, the Martyr Sayyid Quṭb), (Bayrūt: Dār al-

Qalam, 1980), pp. 227-228; hereafter cited as *Rā'id al-Fikr.*

15 See Khālidī, *Quṭb,* pp. 94 & 134; Hasan, *Milestones,* p. 4 and *passim;* and Balīhī, *Turāth,* pp. 43-49. For more information on Quṭb's party life, see Khālidī, *Quṭb,* pp. 100-134. *Sa^cd Zaghlūl* established the *Wafd* in 1918. Its basic demand was the independence of Egypt by peaceful means and limiting the power of the king. Its leaders came mainly from the bourgeoisie. The *Sa^cdist* was established in 1938. It was a breakaway from the *Wafd* which, in the *Sa^cdists'* opinion, was very timid with the British and was corrupted. But the *Sa^cdists* themselves participated in the government and allied themselves with the British. They wanted to enter the Second World War with the British, whereas most other parties did not. See for instance ^cAli al-Dīn Hilāl, *Al-Sīyāsah wa-al-Ḥukm fī Miṣr: 1923-52* (Politics and Government in Egypt: 1923-1952), (Al-Qāhirah: Maktabat Nahḍat al-Sharq, 1977), pp. 200-8. See also, ^cAẓm, *Rā'id al-Fikr,* pp. 205-207.

16 See Ḥasan, *Milestones,* pp. 4-5; Balīhī, *Heritage,* p. 43; and Khālidī, *Quṭb,* p. 125 and *passim.* Khālidī argues that the mission was actually not to obtain a master's degree but to acquire knowledge of techniques and disciplines in education. It has been suggested that Quṭb's mission to the United States was politically motivated due to his anti-government publications and disagreement with his superiors in the Ministry of Education. (Barakāt, *Khulāṣah,* pp. 14-15; and Khālidī, *Quṭb,* pp. 98-125). It is not clear how long Quṭb stayed in each location.

17 Khālidī, *Quṭb,* p. 125. On the theme of *Social Justice in Islam,* see *Writings* above.

18 Khālidī, *Quṭb,* p. 125; and Asaf Hussain, *Islamic Movements,* p. 9. One cannot fail to see the critical attitude that Quṭb espoused in his articles and his book *Social Justice.* See *Writings* above and the article mentioned earlier on his disagreement with the Government and the parties. See also, Ḥamūdah, *Sayyid Quṭb,* pp. 83-86.

19 Sayyid Quṭb, "Amrikā allatī Ra'aytu" in *Al-Risalah,* Vol. 19, Part 2, no. 961, p. 1360. This article is a part of his book *Amrikā.* I could not find the book; and *Dār al-Shurūq,* the Press that publishes Quṭb's books said that it was out of print. See also *Writings* above.

20 See, Quṭb, *Naḥwa Mujtama^c Islāmī* (Towards a Muslim Society), (Bayrūt: Dār al-Shuruq, 5th ed., 1982), pp. 11-12; (hereafter cited as *Naḥwa Mujtama^c.* Nationalism and equality are elaborated in *Chapter III.* Also see, Sayyid Quṭb, *Al-Mustaqbal li-Hādhā al-Dīn* (The Future Belongs to This Religion), (Al-Qāhirah: Maktabat Wahbah, 1965), pp. 71-90; (hereafter cited as *Al-Mustaqbal.*

To substantiate his argument, Quṭb quotes at length two well-known individuals, Alexis Carrel, the author of *Man, the Unknown* (New York: Harper and Brothers Publishers, 1935), and John Foster Dulles, President Eisenhower's Secretary of State and the author of *War or Peace* (New York:

The Macmillan Company, 1950). Both men, Dulles and Carrel, believe that humanity is threatened, and the focus of their writings is on the dangers facing humanity. Carrel's thesis is that man is a stranger in this world and that man's environment is unbeneficial. Curing humanity's problems requires new blood. This should manifest in a new method that reaches the depth of human consciousness. "We must liberate ourselves from blind technology and grasp the complexity of wealth of our own nature... We know how we have transgressed natural laws. We know why we are punished, why we are lost in darkness. Nevertheless, we faintly perceive through the mist of dawn a path which may lead to our salvation." (p. 321)

Similarly, Dulles deprecates materialism and the lack of social justice in the world and believes that the new material and scientific knowledge is dangerous if not accompanied by a spiritual leadership. "The trouble is not material. We are establishing an all-time world record in the production of material things. What we lack is a righteous and dynamic faith. Without it, all else avails us little." (p. 253) Also, "The difficulty is that we, ourselves, are unclear as to our faith and the relationship of that faith to our practices. We can talk eloquently about liberty and freedom, and about human rights and fundamental freedoms, and about the dignity and worth of the human personality; but most of our vocabulary derives from a period when our own society was individualistic. Consequently, it has little meaning for those who live under conditions where individualism means premature death. Also, we can talk eloquently about the material successes we have achieved, about the marvel of mass production, and about the number of automobiles, radios, and telephones owned by our people. That materialistic emphasis makes some feel that we are spiritually bankrupt. It makes others envious and more disposed to accept communist glorification of 'mass' efforts to "develop the material life of society." (pp. 257-58).

21 Sayyid Quṭb, *Amrikā allatī Ra'aytu* as quoted in his *Al-Islām wa-Mushkilāt al-Ḥaḍarah* (Islam and the Problems of Civilization), (Bayrūt: Dār al-Shurūq, 8th ed., 1983), pp. 843-87; (hereafter cited as *Mushkilāt*).

22 Quṭb, *Amrikā* as quoted in *Mushkilat,* pp. 77-78.

23 Quṭb, *Al-Mustaqbal,* pp. 14-65. This topic is to be discussed in *Chapter III.*

24 *Ibid.,* pp. 5-6, Quṭb frequently attacks Wilfred C. Smith. Smith, in *Islam and the Modern World* (London: Oxford University Press, 1957; p. 163) argues that "Already the Turkish interpretation of religion, implicit if not overt, is an emergence of real Islam." In other words, true Islam is (Ataturk's) secularism which relegated Islam to the domain of personal life and not the public.

25 On this topic, see Sayyid Quṭb, *Maᶜrakat al-Islām wa-al-Ra'simālīyyah* (Islam's Battle with Capitalism), (Bayrūt: Dār al-Shurūq, 4th ed., 1980), pp. 32-33 & *passim;* (hereafter cited as *al-Ra'simālīyyah*). Also, see Quṭb, *Maᶜrakatunā,* pp. 23-33.

26 Khālidī, *Quṭb,* p. 125; and al-Balīhī, *Turāth,* p. 43.

[27] See Khālidī, *Quṭb,* p. 136. This contention that Quṭb joined the *Ikhwan* beause "he witnessed the ecstasy of the American general public at the assassination of Ḥasan al-Bannā" cannot be proven. It is only a conjecture and unlikely. Also, see Hussain, *Islamic Movement.* p. 17. However the *New York Times* (Feb. 13th, 1949) reported the assassination of the al-Bannā in the following manner: "In Cairo the leader of the outlawed terrorist Moslem Brotherhood Hassan el Banna, was killed by an assassin." The *New York Times* went on to say: "Sheikh Hassan el Banna, 39-year-old head of the outlawed Moslem Brothrhood extremist Egyptian nationalist movement that was banned after authorities had declared it responsible for a series of bombing outrages and killings last year, was shot five times by a group of young men in a car and died tonight in a hospital." Furthermore, the Brethren were fanatical, and the Brotherhood enjoyed "mystical and fascist overtones." What is apparent here is that although there was no ecstasy, the newspaper was not unhappy with the event because it equated the Brotherhood with "terrorism."

[28] Khālidī, *Quṭb,* pp. 130 & 136. James Heyworth-Dunne published *Religious and Political Trends in Modern Egypt* (Washington, 1950); the date of publication coincided with Quṭb's stay in the U.S.A. Also, see Sayyid Quṭb, "Li-Mādha 'A^{c}damūnī?", *Al-Muslimūn,* 1st. year 1985, Feb. No. 2, p. 3. The article is the one mentioned in the *Introduction.* It sheds light on some ambiguous issues in Quṭb's life, like his involvement in the politics of the Brethren and his perception of the United States as the indirect cause behind the liquidation of the Brethren. Quṭb believed that the U.S. government was behind exaggerating the danger of the Brethren to the Egyptian government. See also footnote 43.

[29] Khālidī, *Quṭb,* pp. 137-38. The weekly *Al-Liwā' al-Jadīd* was founded in 1944 and edited by Fatḥi Raḍwān; *Al-Balāgh* was the journal of the Wafd founded in 1923; *Al-Risālah* was founded and edited by Aḥmad Ḥasan al-Zayyāt and since 1963 it has been controlled by the government; *Al-Da^{c}wah* is the journal of the Brethren, established in 1951 by Ṣalah ^{c}Ishmāwī, a leader of the Brethren.

[30] *Ibid.,* pp. 138-94. Barakāt argues that Quṭb joined the Brethren in the late forties and Khālidī states that Quṭb joined the Brethren in 1951, but Quṭb himself gives the date 1953 as the actual time when he became a member of the organization and after his disagreement with Nāṣir. *"Li-Mādhā 'A^{c}damūnī?",* pp. 3-4.

[31] Khālidī, *Quṭb,* pp. 134-5.

[32] *Ibid,* pp. 138 & 144; Balīhī, *Turāth,* pp. 48-49; and see Ishaq M. al-Husainī, *The Moslem Brethren* (Beirut: Khayāt's College Book Co., 1956), p. 23. Also, see, on the events of arrest, release, and then arrest, Quṭb, *"Li-Mādhā 'A^{c}damūnī?",* p. 4.

[33] Richard Mitchell, *The Society of Muslim Brothers* (London: Oxford University Press, 1969), p. 188. Also, Quṭb was the ultimate arbiter of the

works that constituted the ideology of the Brethren. According to Mitchell, the propagation section delineated the intellectual and spiritual direction for the Brethren and collected the work of Ḥasan al-Bannā and added new material. And Quṭb was working on a series called "This is your message." But this activity stopped due to the dissolution of the movement and jailing of many of its members, (*Ibid.* 187-88). But Quṭb rejects the claim that he was the head of this section (see, Quṭb, *"Li-Mādhā 'A^cdamūnī?"*, p. 4).

34 Miṭchell, *Society,* p. 189. Quṭb was a very important opinion maker. Mitchell and Husainī, both authorities on the Brethren, make use of Quṭb's thought to explain the ideology of the Brethren.

35 *Ibid.*, p. 103.

36 The officer's testimony can be found in *Kalimat al-Ḥaqq* (The Word of Truth), 1st. year, no. 2, May 1967, pp. 37-39 as quoted in Khālidī, *Quṭb,* pp. 140-43. Quṭb states that his resignation from the directorship was due to difference in thought and because the line followed was different from what was agreed upon; Quṭb wanted to propagate Islam and impose Islamic law, Nāṣir did not. (Quṭb, *"Li-Mādhā 'A^cdamūnī?"*, March, no. 6, p. 7).

37 The French quotation in the text is Carre's in *"Le combat,"* p. 682. Nāṣir attempted to woe Quṭb, even while he was in prison in 1956. Quṭb was offered the Ministry of Education on the condition that he seek public pardon from Nāṣir, (Hasan, *Milestones,* pp. 9-13). Also, see Quṭb, *"Li-Mādhā 'A^cdamūnī?"*, Feb. no. 2, p. 4.

38 Khālidī, *Quṭb,* p. 143; Mitchell, *Society,* p. 107 and *passim;* and, Husaīnī, *Brethren,* p. 131.

39 P.J. Vatikiotis, *The History of Modern Egypt* (London: Weidenfield and Nicolson, 1969), p. 384; and Husaini, *Brethren,* p. 131.

40 Mitchell, *Society,* pp. 136-37.

41 *Ibid.*, p. 148.

42 *Ibid.*, 137-40; and Hussein, *Islamic Movements,* pp. 8-11.

43 Hasan, *Milestones,* pp. 8-11 and *passim;* also, see Vatikiotis, *Modern History,* p. 326. But Quṭb attributes the falling-out between the Revolutionary Council and the Brethren to "the agents of the United States" because some of Nāṣir advisers like Dr. Aḥmed Ḥusayn, Dr. Muḥammad Ṣalāh al-Dīn and others who had close relations with the U.S. influenced and exaggerated Nāṣir's fears. (Quṭb, *"Li-Mādha 'A^cdamūnī?"*, Feb. no. 2, p. 4).

44 Hussein, *Islamic Movements,* p. 91 and Hasan, *Milestones,* p. 8. Quṭb was sentenced in absentia due to his illness, arthritis, and heart trouble; while in prison, Quṭb had two heart attacks. Throughout his imprisonment Quṭb was sick and had major surgery. On this topic and on torture see also Barakāt, *Turāth,* p. 7; and, Khālidī, *Quṭb,* pp. 145-47; and Carré, *"Le*

combat," p. 681. See Hasan, *Milestones,* pp. 7-8. See also, Quṭb, *"Li-Mmādhā 'Aᶜdamūnī?",* March, no. 6, p. 9.

45 *Ḥamūdah, Sayyid Quṭb.* pp. 60-61.

46 Shades refers to his understanding of the Qur'ān. See *Writings.* See also, al-ᶜAẓm, *Ra'id al-Fikr,* p. 187.

47 Barakāt, *Khulāṣah,* p. 19. Khālidī, in *Quṭb* (p. 147), states that Quṭb was able to establish good relations with his jailers and was called "the judge of the prison." Also, throughout his jail term he was able to publish his books because the government wanted to deny the charge of torture and oppression.

Quṭb himself did not deny the charge that he was establishing an organization within the Brethren. Its basic goal was educational because he believed that a new society could not be established unless people were educated in their religion first. Also, he admitted that he was building a military organization around 1962-64, but he insisted that its purpose was not to overthrow the government but to defend the Brethren in case the government attempted again, as it did in 1956, to repress and torture the Brethren. In other words, according to Quṭb, the military option was only the last measure and defense. *("Li-Mādhā 'Aᶜdamūnī?",* March, no. 4, pp. 6-7, and no. 6, p. 9.) But, a more important issue is not whether the Brethren took arms against the government but whether the government was legitimate and representative of the people. Also, in dealing with the Brethren one needs to address the question whether the government was just: because if the government was not just, taking arms would be warranted. In short, what I am saying is that people can and, sometimes, should fight an unjust government because no body needs to or is obliged to yeild to tyranny. And for someone to decide whether the Brethren acted correctly, one needs to decide first other issues like legitimacy, social justice, and freedom. See also Ḥamūdah, *Sayyid Quṭb,* pp.129-131.

48 Barakāt, *Khulaṣah,* p. 19; and Khālidī, *Quṭb,* p. 149. See also, Quṭb, *"Li-Mādhā, 'Aᶜdamuni?",* pp. 42-44, 53-55, 59-60.

49 *Brakāt, Khulaṣah;* and, Hasan, *Milestones,* p. 10.

50 Hasan, *Milestones,* pp. 30-31.

51 Anwar al-Sādāt, *In Search of Identity,* p. 66. In the beginning of the trials, it was announced that the proceedings would be public and televised. But when the Brethren pleaded not guilty and related the episodes of their torture, the televising of proceedings was stopped. (See, Hasan, *Milestones,* p. 11 and *passim*).

52 The book is discussed in *Writings* and is used extensively in the study. Also, on these charges, see Hasan, *Milestones,* p. 33.

53 *Ibid.,* pp. 37-38. Also, see Khālidī (*Quṭb,* p. 151) where he mentions that in

Moscow in 1965 President Nāṣir announced a plot by Quṭb and others to overthrow his government and to assassinate public officials.

54 *Chronology of Arab Politics,* published by the Political and Public Department of the American University of Beirut, Lebanon, Vol. IV, 1966, p. 296. For more details, see also, Hasan, *Milestones,* p. 12; and Hussein, *Islamic Movements,* p. 10.

55 *Al-Ahrām,* founded in 1876 by Salīm and Bishārah Taqlā, is a daily newspaper controlled now by the governemnt but is usually described as "semiofficial. *Al-Balāgh* was the newpaper of the *Wafd* and was founded in 1923; *al-Liwā' al-Miṣrī* was a daily newspaper for the National Party and was founded in 1922.

56 For more information, see al-Balīhī, *Turāth,* pp. 28-30.

57 For instance, a well-known writer, Muḥammad Quṭb, not related to Sayyid Quṭb, first admired Sayyid Quṭb when he read *al-Madīnā al-Mas'ḥūrah* (The Enchanted City); Quṭb, *al-Shahīd al-'A^{c}zal,* p. 15. Also, many writers praised and were influenced by him; for specific names, see Khālidī, *Naẓarīyyat,* pp. 114-17; and Barakāt, *Khulāṣah*, pp. 5-6. Many statements that distinguish Quṭb from others can be found; for instance, Hamid Enayat in *Modern Islamic Political Thought* states that what distinguished *fiday'yn-i-Islam* and the Muslim Brethren is that the former did not produce "protagonists either of the political perspicacity of Hasan al-Banna or intuitive gifts of Sayyid Qutb..." Fiday'yin-i-Islam (The Devotee of Islam) is the Iranian counterpart of the Brethren in Egypt. It became active during the Second World War and was founded by Sayyid Mujtaba Navvab Safavi (d. 1956), and was one of the movements that toppled the Shah of Iran in 1979.

58 Khālidī, *Naẓarīyyat,* pp. 5-14 & 274. This is the author's M.A. thesis in literature.

59 This topic is explained in *Chapter II.*

60 For criticism of Sayyid Quṭb on the matter of repudiating existing Muslim societies, see Barakāt, *Khulāṣah,* pp. 198-220. The reasons why Quṭb drifted from al-^{c}Aqqād is the latter's co-existence with and not speaking against unjust government and his neglect of emotions in his writings. (See al-Nadawī, *Sā'iḥ,* pp. 88-89; see also, Enayat, *Islamic Political Thought,* p. 115; and Khālidī, *Quṭb,* p. 109.

61 An instance of scholar's dissatisfaction with Quṭb's diversion from traditionalism is the article "Al-Mu^{c}tadūn 'alā al-Fiqh al-Islāmī" (Aggressors on Islamic Jurisprudence) by Dr. Wahbah al-Zahili published in *Majallat al-Ra'y al-Islāmī* (The Journal of Islamic Opinion) and republished in *Majallat al-Fikr al-Islāmī* (The Journal of Islamic Thought). For more details on some of these characteristics as seen from a partisan point of view, see Barakāt, *Khulāṣah,* pp. 17-18 & 30-62; and, Khālīdī, *Quṭb,* pp. 187-91.

62 Al-Afghānī, and ᶜAbdūh, Iqbal, are Muslim modernists; al-Mawdūdī and Asad are fundamentalist thinkers. They are well-known reformers who focused their attentions on reviving Islam as a modern force. They exerted tremendous influence on the Muslims, especially in Egypt. Their writings are discussed in the Comparative Sections in *Chapter II* and *III.*

63 Mālik Ibn Anas (d.785) was a founder of one of the four authoritative schools of law in Islam. Al-Imām al-Bukhārī (d. 870), author of *Saḥiḥ al-Bukhārī,* and al-Imān Muslim (875), author of *Saḥih Muslim,* have been accepted as authorities on the collection and transmission of the *Ḥadīth* (The Prophet's Sayings); the two books are collection of the Prophet's Traditions. Al-Mawardī (d. 1058) was a jurist and judge and taught in Baghdad. His most famous book is *al-Aḥkām al-Ṣulṭanīyyah,* (Sultanic Rules), a very important treatise on the theory of government in Islam. Ibn Taymīyah (1262-1328) was one of the most famous Sunni jurists in Islam. Some of his books are *al-Sīyāsah al-Sharᶜīyyah* (Political Rule) and *Minhāj al-Sunnah* (The Method of the [Prophet's] Traditions).

64 Plato (427?-347 BC) and Aristotle (384-322 B.C) were the two well-known ancient philosophers. Martin Luther (1483-1546) was a German theologian and the leader of the Protestant Movement. Rene Descarte (1596-1650) was one of the founders of modern thought. Some of his works are *Meditation* and *Discourse on Method.* Charles Darwin (1809-1882) was the controversial British biologist and the author of *The Origins of the Species.* Karl Marx (1818-1883) was revolutionay philosopher of the 19th century who laid down the foundations of Marxism. Some of his work are *Capital, A Contribution to the Critique of Political Economy,* and The *Communist Manifesto.* Henri Bergson (1859-1941), a French philosopher of evolution, was the winner of the Nobel Prize in Literature. Some of his work are *Time and Being* and *Introduciton to Metaphysics.* T.W. Arnold (1864-1930) was the author of *The Caliphate* and *The Preaching of Islam.* Bertrand Russell (b. 1872) was a philosopher and the author of *Principles of Mathematics, Philosophical Essays,* and *A History of Western Philosophy.* Robert Briffault (1876-1948) was the author of *Breakdown, The Collapse of Traditional Civilization in Europe, The Days of Ignorance,* and *Europe and Limbo.*

65 Facts of publications are taken from the books themselves. When that is not possible because a book is out of print or has no date of publication, I use information from Barakāt, *Khulāṣah,* and Khālidī, *Quṭb,* pp. 219-61, and ᶜAẓm, *Rā'id al-Fikr.*

66 In English, it is published under *Social Justice in Islam* (New York: Octagon Books, 1970) and (Washington, D.C.: American Learned Society, 1956). Quṭb gave his permission for the latter. The Society's Near East Translation Program translates significant wroks from Near Eastern Languages into English in order to further understanding of other cultures.

67 Published in English as *Islam and Universal Peace* (Indianapolis, American Trust Publications, 1977).

68 Hasan, *Milestones,* pp. 20-21.

69 See the Introducation by Muhammad Quṭb to Sayyid Quṭb, *In the Shades of the Qur'an* (London: MWH. 1979), p. vii.

70 Published in English as *This Religion of Islam* (Delhi: Markazi Maktaba Islami, 1974).

71 Publised in English under *Islam, The Religion of the Future* (Delhi, Markazi Maktaba Islami, 1974); and, under *Islam the Religion of Future* (Kuwait: I.I.F.S.O., 1971).

72 published under *Milestones,* Hasan.

73 Moreover, Quṭb has about twenty nine unpublished works. The books numbered 1-21 belong to the literary stage; and, from 22-29, to the Islamic.

1 "Muhimmat al-Shāᶜir fī al-Ḥayah" (The Poet's Reponsibility in Life), part.

2 "Dirāsah ᶜan Shawqī" (A Study on Shawqī). Ahmad Shawqī (1869-1932) was a very famous modern Egyptian poet. He introduced tragic love into Arabic poetry and developed the dramatic form of poetry into opera performance. He is best known for his tragedy *Maṣraᶜ Kilīobatrā* (The Death of Cleopatra) and *Majnūn Lāylā* (Layla's Madman) or lover.

3 "al-Murāhaqah: Akhṭāruhā wa-ᶜīlājuhā" (Adolescence: its Dangers and Treatment), poetry.

4 "al-Mar'ah lughzun Basīṭ" (The Woman, a simple Mystery), poetry.

5 "al-Mar'ah fī Qiṣaṣ Tawfīq al-Ḥakīm" (Woman in the Stories of Tawfīq al-Ḥakīm). Tawfīq al-Ḥakīm (b. 1899) was a writer. Among his well-known novels are *ᶜAwdat al-Rūḥ* (The Return of the Soul) and *Ahl al-Kahf* (The People of the Cave).

6 "Aṣdā' al-Zamān." (Echoes of Time), a collection of poems.

7 "Dīwan al-Shiᶜr al-Thālith lahu. (His Third Poem), a collection of poems.

8 "al-Ka's al-Masmūmah" (The Poisoned class), a novel.

9 "Qāfilat al-Raqīq" (The Slave's Caravan), a novel.

10 "Ḥilm al-Fajr" (The Dawn Dream), poetry.

11 "Min ᶜAmāq al-Wadī" (From the Depths of the Valley), a novel.

12 "Al-Madhāhib al-Fannīyyah al-Mu'āṣirah" (Contemporary Artistic Methods), literary studies.

13 "al-Ṣuwar wa al-Ẓilāl fī al-Shiᶜr al-ᶜArabī" (Images and Shades in Arabic Poetry, literary studies.

14 Shuᶜrā' al-chabāb (The Poets of the Youth), a study on some contemporary poets.

15 “al-Qiṣah al-Ḥadīthah” (Modern Story), a critical study of writing modern stories.

16 “^{c}Urabi al-Muftarā ^{c}alayhī” (Urabi, the falsely defamed), a biography of Aḥmad ^{c}Urabi (1839-1911), minister of war under the Khedive Tawfīq and Leader of the Egyptian revolt in 1882. He was exiled to Ceylon but returned to Cairo at the beginning of this century.

17 “Laḥaẓāt ma^{c}a al-Khālidīn” (Moments with the everlasting heroes. It is a collection of poems composed by modern poets and includes Muhammad Iqbal.

18 “al-Qiṭaṭ al-Ḍālah” (Stray Cats), a novel.

19 “al-Qiṣah bayna al-Tawrāt wa al-Qur’ān” (Story-telling in the Torah and the Qur’an).

20 “al-Qiṣaṣ fī al-Adab al-^{c}Arabī (Stories in Arabic Literature), literary studies.

21 “al-Namādhij al-Insānīyyah fī al-Qur’ān” (Human Personality-types in the Qur’ān), literary studies.

22 “al-Mantiq al-Wijdānī fī al-Qur’ān” (Consciousness in the Qur’an), literary studies.

23 “al-Asālīb al-Fannīyah fī al-Qur’ān” (Artistic Methods in the Qur’an), literary studies.

24 “Ma^{c}ālim fī al-Tarīq” (Signposts on the Road), a second collection.

25 “Fī Ẓilāl al-Sīrah” (In the Shades of the *Sīrah*); *sīrah* is the life of the Prophet Muḥammad.

26 “Fī Mawkib al-Imān” (In The Procession of Faith).

27 “‘Awwalīyāt Hādhā al-Dīn” (Prerequisites of this Religion).

28 “Hādhā al-Qur’ān” (This Qur’an).

29 “Taṣwibāt fī al-Fikr al-Islāmī al-Mu’aṣir” (Corrections in Contemporary Islamic Thought).

For more details, see Khālidī, *Quṭb,* pp. 256-61.

CHAPTER II

THE IDEOLOGICAL DISCOURSE OF SAYYID QUṬB

An evaluation of any particular ideology, belief or thought, including Islamic fundamentalism, should be centered on general premises. Such premises are not self-evident, and their justification must be an important issue for thoughtful persons. Because Sayyid Quṭb questions the principles and standards of ancient and modern philosophers, Muslim and non-Muslims, he attempts to provide us with specific arguments about the truth and validity of Islam. This *Chapter* is divided into three sections: the first deals with the definition of Islam as a *manhaj* (method) and a *niẓām* (system) and the universal Islamic concept (*al-taṣawwur al-Islāmī*)- itself consisting of seven characteristics. In the second part, a comparative analysis of Islamic fundamentalism and Islamic modernism is made in order to analyze and contrast basic concepts such as reason and religion; and the third is made into an evaluation of the foundations of Quṭb's thought. Throughout this exposition, I expound and develop Quṭb's arguments first, then make substantive comments on these arguments by pinpointing their logical adequacy or inadequacy and elaborating their implications.

1 - The Universal Islamic Concept *(al-Taṣawwur al-Islāmī al-Kawnī)*

Quṭb builds his ideological discourse on a peculiar view of Islam:

Islam is not only rituals performed, an ethical call, a mere system of government, an economic system or a system of international relations... All these are some of the several aspects of Islam, not the whole of Islam.[1]

The core of Islam is its *taṣawwur* (concept) of life and the universe which constitutes the infrastructure for all the aspects of Islam, social, economic, political as well as personal, psychological, and otherwise. For Quṭb, the importance of the Islamic concept can be seen first in the Muslims' need for a comprehensive interpretation of existence; an interpretation that brings closer the nature of great truths which includes divinity, the universe, life, and man. Secondly, the concept channels to man the knowledge of his position and goal in the universe which leads him to the knowledge of his proper role. For knowing man's place, goal, and role in this universe helps man to define his proper social and political approach and method *(al-manhaj)* in life. Consequently, the political *niẓām* (system) that rules over human life becomes, for its validity and correctness, dependent on the comprehensive interpretation of the Islamic concept and its values.[2]

This conceptual centerpiece, *al-taṣawwur,* is composed of seven characteristics which are, in Quṭb's opinion, necessarily connected; for the understanding of *al-taṣawwur* is imperative for grasping the essence of Islam. These characteristics are (1) *al-tawḥīd* (oneness of God), (2) *al-'ulūhīyyah* (divinity), (3) *al-thabāt* (fixity), (4) *al-shumūlīyyah* (comprehensiveness), (5) *al-tawāzun* (equilibrium), (6) *al-'ījābīyyah* (positiveness), and (7) *al-wāqiᶜīyyah* (realism).

1 - *Tawḥīd* (oneness of God): It is, according to Quṭb, the basic fact and component of the Islamic creed as well as one of the characteristics of the Islamic concept. *Tawḥīd* is a characteristic of Islam as well as the other two monotheistic religions, Christianity and Judaism. Islam means submission to God alone and necessitates following God's *manhaj* alone in all affairs of life, prostrating oneself before God alone by obeying his method, laws, and order, and worshipping Him alone in matters of religion and organization of life. Positively, submission to God means that there is only one God; negatively, it indicates the falsehood and unnaturalness of submitting to others, people and principles. From this first premise, other substantial rules follow. For instance, man should organize his life and society in accordance with the divine will and revelation, since the Muslim should believe that there is no ruler except God, no legislator except God, and no organizer of man's life and relations and connections with the universe, beings and his fellow man except God. And as a dominating theme in Quṭb's political thought, it makes him believe that the Islamic concept guarantees coherence in character and energy in the entity of the Muslim individual and society and prevents destruction, split personality, and dissipation that are caused by other creeds and concepts.

> *The Islamic taṣawwur makes a total separation between the nature, the place and the characteristics of divinity and those of humanity. The two are neither changeable nor mixed; for the Islamic concept shows conclusively God as the divine and the created as his servants.*
>
> *Divinity is one, not multiple; it is the divinity of the Almighty God. Anything besides Him belongs to [the realm of] the created...*
>
> *The truth of this belief constitutes the basis of the creed of the Muslims and leads to a concept.*[3]

Quṭb grounds this belief in Qur'anic textual authorities:

> *You have no god other than He;*
> *truly, I fear for you the chastisement of a dreadful day;*
> *said the council of his [Noah's] people,*
> *'We see thee in manifest error?'*
> *Said he, 'My people, there is no error*
> *in me; but I am a Messenger from the Lord of all being'.* — VII: 59
>
> *Hast thou received the story of Moses?*
> *When he saw a fire, and said to his family, 'Tarry you here; I observe a fire.*
> *Prehaps I shall bring you a brand from it,*

or I shall find at the fire guidance;
when he came to it, a voice cried, 'Moses,
I am thy Lord;
put off thy shoes; thou art in the holy valley, Towa. I Myself have chosen thee;
therefore give thou ear to this revelation. Verily I am God; there is no god but I;
therefore serve me, and perform the prayer of My remembrance.— XX: 9-14

And when God said, 'O Jesus, son of Mary,
didst thou say unto men, "Take me and my mother as gods, apart from God"?
He said, 'To thee be glory!
It is not mine to say what I have no right to.
If I indeed said it, Thou knowest it, knowing what is within my soul,
and I know not what is within
Thy soul;
Thou knowest the things unseen.
I only said to them what Thou didst command me:
"Serve God, my Lord and your lord".
And I was a witness over them,
while I remained among them; but when thou didst take me to Thyself,
Thou wast Thyself the watcher over them;
Thou Thyself art witness of everything.
If thou chastisest them, they are Thy servants;
if Thou forgivest them, Thou art the All-mighty, the All-wise;
God said 'This is the day the truthful shall be profited by their truthfulness. — V: 116-118

And We sent never a
Messenger before thee except that we revealed to him, saying,
'There is no god but I; so serve Me'.— XXI: 25

Dividing systems of thought, life, and action into God-given and man-made, Quṭb classifies the individuals who regulate their life and behavior in accordance with the divine creed as the followers of the divine religion. But those individuals who derive their system from a king, a prince, a tribe or a people constitute followers of the man-made religion; be it the king, the prince, the tribe or the people, respectively.[4] His argument is grounded in the following verses:

That which you serve, apart from him,
is nothing but names yourselves have named, you and your fathers;
God has sent down no authority touching them.
Judgment belongs only to God;
He has commanded that you shall not serve any but Him. That is the right religion; but most men know not. — XII: 40

Or have they associates
who have laid down for them as religion
that which God gave not leave?
But for the Word of Decision,
it had been decided between them.
For the evildoers there awaits a painful chastisement.- ILII: 20
They have taken their rabbis and their monks
as lords apart from God, and the Messiah,
Mary's son- and they were commanded to serve but one God;
there is no god but He,
glory be to Him, above that they associate....— IX: 31
We have sent down to thee the Book
with the Truth so worship God, making thy religion His sincerely.
Belongs not sincere religion to God? And those who take protectors- apart from Him-
'We only serve them that they may bring as nigh in nearness to God'-
surely God shall judge between them
touching that whereon they are at variance. — XXXIX: 3-4

Thus, perceiving religion as a *niẓām* of life which includes a metaphysical *taṣawwur* and is accompanied by a social order leads Quṭb to postulate the equality of every system of life with religion; religion is derivative from the system regulating life, and is unlimited by abstractions, metaphysical doctrines, emotions or beliefs. Fundamentally, it is the culture or the system that disciplines the behavior. This is the reason for Qutb's view of communism as a social system as well as a metaphysical concept based on material contradiction, and ultimately, as a religion.[5] Because any concept that regulates life- and every life is necessarily regulated by a concept whether the individual is aware of it or not- is a religion, the result is that there is a synonymity between religion and consistent behavior. Here, Quṭb's definition of religion in terms of not only concepts and principles but, more importantly, in terms of behavior and culture necessitates the conclusion that the religion of a group, a people or a nation is not a result of their claim or belief but is a manifestation of their behavior and culture. Thus, professing Islam but indicating by their behavior partial or total adherence to other systems of government and life (like the adherence of some contemporary Muslims to Western values and philosophies) leads people to enter *al-jāhilīyyah.*

It is apparent that Quṭb's interpretation of religion differs from most other Muslim or non-Muslim interpretations. Accordingly, this interpretation of religion sheds light on Quṭb's and other fundamentalists' insistence on action- action being the barometer and the outer manifestation of inner belief- and on their repudiation of other fellow Muslims whose outlook and life-style are Western. In other words, Quṭb's definition of religion in this manner serves the fundamentalists to achieve two objectives: as a device to propel Muslims to view life as a totality and as a criterion for rejecting partially and totally other religions, ideas, and political systems. Thus, viewing communism as a religion allows Quṭb to contrast it with Islam in order to reject it.

Though correct in viewing religion as a system that regulates man's life and as something which must affect politics and society insofar as it demans compliance with its moral and political values, Quṭb seems to go too far. Because of his identification of religion with behavior and culture in general, the distinction between what is personal and what is public becomes blurred. Both, the public and the personal, are subject to legal prescriptions and are regularized by the same concept, *tawḥīd.* In fact, the organization of personal life becomes part of the organiztion of public life; and, insofar as the personal or private life affects society it is not personal or private any more. What becomes actually important is not whether an act is personal or public but whether that act is in conformity with the Holy *Qur'ān* and the divine law (the *sharīᶜah*) whose fountainhead is *tawḥīd.* Submission to God, therefore, is not a personal or public act but is the focal point which engulfs the Muslim society in its legislation, governance, and life. Cónsequently, the distinction between the personal and the public is replaced by the distinction between the religious and the irreligious or the non-religious. But this is precisely Quṭb's contention; that is, in Islam everything is subordinated to God. Believing in God requires that the individual view his action from a religious perspective, not from a public or a private one.

Though Quṭb's exposition of religion is enriched by his insistence on the totality of Islam, his exposition of *tawḥīd* is impoverished. His refusal to enter into the discussion of God's essence and attributes as the philosophers and theologians do and his denial of man's capability of correct speculation on these matters empty his concept of any philosophical or theological depth, though *tawḥīd* is not, in principle, a thing to be seen but is to be conceived. For *tawḥīd* belongs to the realm of the metaphysical and does not belong to the physical, especially in Islam where nothing is like God. Notwithstanding this, Quṭb insists on the oneness of God for the correctness of any system of thought and shelters himself behind the Holy *Qur'ān* in considering it as the ultimate and only proof on all metaphysical, moral, and political issues. In fact, Quṭb's view of *tawḥīd* amounts to denying not only the authenticity and the legitimacy of commonly held opinions from any historical, philosophical or theological schools but also of knowledge itself.

In attempting to make his definition conclusive and complete, Quṭb views knowledge as something that exceeds mere understanding. Knowledge, is complete *fahm* (comprehension) and *tafāᶜul* (interaction) with this comprehension in the *aᶜmāq* (depths) of the soul and conscience, then, followed by harmonious *ᶜamal* (action).[6] Put differently religion does not reduce knowledge to categories of understanding but turns our knowledge into a movement *(ḥarakah)*. Revelation, or true knowledge, requires its transformation into immediate action; every revealed case represents a response to or a motive to a real situation. Knowledge for its own sake is not an Islamic *manhaj*. Knowledge is revealed for the sake of activism; science for the sake of action; and creed, for the sake of life.

The justification used by Quṭb centers around the following Qur'anic texts:

> *As for those in whose hearts is swerving,*
> *they follow the ambiguous part,*
> *desiring dissension, and desiring its interpretation;*
> *and none knows its interpretation, save only God.*
> *And those firmly rooted in knowledge say,*
> *'We believe in it; all is from Our Lord';*
> *yet none remember, but men possessed of minds.*
> *Our Lord, make not our hearts to swerve*
> *after that Thou hast guided us;*
> *and give us mercy from thee;*
> *Thou art the Giver.* — III 6-8
> *Say:' God-He originates creation,*
> *then brings it back again;*
> *so how are you perverted?'*
> *Say: Is there any of your associates who guides to the truth?'*
> *Say: 'God-He guides to the truth;*
> *and which is worthier to be followed*
> *He who guides to the truth,*
> *or he who guides not unless he is guided? What then ails you,*
> *how you judge?*
> *And the most of them follow only surmise,*
> *and surmise avails naught against truth.* — X: 36

From the above definition, one can discern the following points. First, for Quṭb, knowledge is not mere understanding but primarily, a state of mind, i.e., comprehension; or the first state that leads to mental understanding of a thing or being. The second state is psychological and spiritual interaction, i.e., acceptance by the soul and conscience. All this requires, and should be followed by, action. Complete knowledge is thus composed of the three states: of the mind, of the soul and the conscience, and of the body, corresponding respectively to comprehension, interaction, and action.

Of course, this definition of knowledge leads Quṭb (and will lead anyone else) to question man's ability to attain true knowledge of God. Since knowledge involves comprehension and interaction in the soul and the conscience, no man is capable of having complete or certain knowledge of God's manner of existence or of His nature.[7] The unknowability of God stems from man's inability to interact spiritually, consciously, mentally, and physically. And this definition makes it natural for Quṭb to object to the philosophic claim that God is thought thinking itself. For him, if true knowledge depends on true knowledge of God, and if the knowledge of God is not possible, it follows that true knowledge is unattainable. And this is exactly where Quṭb is leading us. Thus, Quṭb's definition of knowledge whose fountainhead is the knowledge of God is strict and unattainable by definition and leads to more questions than answers. But this is no problem to Quṭb, for God in the *Qur'ān* has alluded to the inability of man to understand the essence of God.

But because God's existence is a given and the starting point of Quṭb's system, he makes no attempt to prove His existence or attributes; for he entertains no doubt about God's creation of this universe, and, as such, of His true knowledge of the creation. Believing that God's revelation, the Holy *Qur'ān,* is the only valid constituent in the foundation of any metaphysical truth, anything else is viewed as amounting only to speculations having no claim to knowledge.

In fact, the issue at hand, or Quṭb's thought, is not an attempt to prove metaphysically or physically the existence of God, but is an invitation to the Muslims to follow religion and to oppose those philosophies and ideologies that are not in harmony with Islam or that do not include divine revelation as its fountainhead. To do this Quṭb explains Islam and its implications and, then, attacks harshly any system that is contrary to his version of Islam. His writings, therefore, are of two natures, expository and polemical- and I will concern myself with the exposition of Islam and refrain from polemics.

To understand why Quṭb perceives human knowledge as only speculation and Islam, or religion in general, as knowledge, we need to understand Quṭb's conception of Islam and religion. He argues that the superiority of Islam as well as religion in general results from its *manhaj* of treatment of the various kinds of truth. Part of the superiority manifests in the *manhaj* of addressing the being of humanity in

> *a way characterized by vitality, tone, direct touch, and allusion. It is allusion to the great truths which are not represented by words but alluded to by words. Moreover, it is characterized by addressing the being of humanity in all its aspects, energies, and avenues of knowledge. And thus it does not only address thought in the human being. [On the other hand], philosophy is another manhaj, for it tries to limit truths by words. But since the kind of knowledge that it encounters cannot be limited by semantical structures and since many aspects of these truths are beyond the scope of human thought, philosophy ends up inevitably in complication, confusion, and dryness whenever it attempts to deal with the issues of the creed.*[8]

From this statement we can derive some very important assumptions: (a) religion, as opposed to philosophy and science, addresses the whole and inner being; (b) the great truths, i. e., questions of the essence of God, soul or life and death and the like are unknowable to man; and (c) religion offers, and, for that matter, our knowledge is composed of, allusions *('īḥā'āt)* to the truths. Precise and total knowledge is not within human capacities. Our knowledge through divine religion is accurate and true but only as an allusion to the truth. For instance, man feels and is capable of realizing the idea of God's existence, but God's manner of existence and essence are incomprehensible by thought or any other means. Quṭb can reasonably hold this view, for he believes that man has not been able, historically or substantively, to understand God's or even man's essence. For him, philosophy is composed of speculations that although logical, yet cannot be proven.

His concept of religion as being composed of allusions to the truth is fundamentally different from medieval and classical thought on more than one point. First, whereas the medieval thinkers thought of religion as the language of the common- i.e., the unphilosophic- people, Quṭb views religion as composed of true allusions to the truth inaccessible to both, philosophers and non-philosophers. Secondly, although religion is only composed of allusions to the truth, it is the only credible and possible path to knowledge, to a well ordered life, and to the satisfaction of humanity in its most important aspects. Not only is Quṭb's concept of religion opposed to the classical and medieval notions but also to traditional, theological, and contemporary modernist Islamic thought. The Holy *Qur'ān* has been conceived as a complete book containing metaphysical, moral, and political doctrines. Although Muslims (philosophers and theologians) accept the possibility of true knowledge in principle, Quṭb and the fundamentalists stand alone in advocating the unattainability of knowledge by any intellectual pursuit- religious, philosophic or scientific. For one thing, Quṭb does not accept the notion that the finite (man) can understand the infinite (God).

The problem with Quṭb's exposition is not so much in the nature of its opposition to medieval and contemporary thought as in its fragmentary and contradictory nature. For Quṭb's limits on knowledge extend not only to philosophy and science but, more importantly, to religion itself. If religion is nothing but allusion to truth, our knowledge is in fact nothing but fragments (i.e., allusions) which do not constitute a unified or comprehensive body of knowledge. But Quṭb's argument stands up on the ground that religion offers mankind a unified knowledge composed of allusions. Pushing his argument to its logical limits, however, produces a contradiction; namely, a complete religion yet fragmented. Because of the fragmentary composition of human knowledge and nature, complete knowledge by religion or by philosophy, becomes a theoretical impossibility. However, Quṭb has no problem accepting the fragmentary nature of human knowlegde since it is what he perceives as reality.

2 - *Al-'Ulūhīyyah* (Divinity): The second characteristic and component of the Islamic concept is *'ulūhīyyah,* which indicates its unchangeability and impossibility of development. However, this does not preclude mankind's development within its framework and advancement in understanding and responding to it. *Al-'ulūhīyyah's* total, absolute, eternal and everlasting nature is beyond the scope of the partial, limited, made, and disconnected human nature. It is enough for man to realize what regulates the divine concept, what corrects his thought, what straightens his conscience, what organizes his life, and what leads him to his proper role. This idea of *'ulūhīyyah* indicates the following:

(A) The source of the Islamic concept itself is God and not the Prophet or anyone else. Any human expression of the truth and human *manhaj* cannot explain the Qur'anic texts in any final manner. Hence, the text should speak for itself, the understanding of which requires direct experience and interaction. The function of the Prophet Muḥammad or any other prophet, according to Quṭb, is not law-giving but "only the precise transmission [of revelation] and honest preaching, and not mixing revelation" with any human thought. This is because the Prophet Muḥammad never claimed to be a philosopher, a scientist or a law-giver. He presented himself only as a prophet and offered a divine message.[9] Quṭb assigns this role to the Prophet by citing some verses, among which are:

> *Muhammad is... the Messenger of God,*
> *and the Seal of the Prophets;*
> *God has knowledge of everything* — XXXIII: 40
> *Have they not reflected?*
> *No Madness is in their comrade (Muhammad); he is naught but*
> *a plain warner...* — VII: 183
> *Say: 'I give you but one admonition...*
> *He (Muhammad) is naught but a warner unto you,*
> *before a terrible chastisement.'* — XXIV: 45

Quṭb's denial of any special or greater understanding of truth to humans- even to the Prophet, who is after all a human- means that divine knowledge or revelation surpasses human knowledge insofar as the divine authority surpasses the human source of knowledge. Quṭb's argument is made in order to deny any special or more authentic understanding of religion by a group of people- the philosophers, the theologians or the jurists. Practically speaking, because no one can have a better understanding, this means that individuals are capable of understanding revelation and, as such, are eligible to become (if other conditions are met) rulers and founders of good states - a theme that will be discussed in the following *Chapter*. Thus, Quṭb's rejection of elitism in its intellectual as well as political manifestations, provides an opportunity for people to establish an Islamic state without waiting for the appearance of a mystical figure, the philosopher or the prophet, but through the actions of common Muslims.

(B) Being divine indicates also that revelation is distinguished from human thought and its development. The Islamic concept is eternal, but human understanding of that concept may develop and advance. What this means is that it is possible to understand the universal Islamic concept in different lights. Because of changing material, political, and economic conditions among ages, generations, and individuals, the understanding of the Holy *Qur'ān* cannot be limited to a specific understanding of the past or the present. For Quṭb, insofar as revelation is the basis of the concept, there is no better or worse understanding. For the Holy *Qur'ān* itself does not sanction any specific interpretation. But, although he believes that human thought may develop and advance in understanding this concept, he does not provide any criterion for measuring this development or advancement except the revelation itself.

But, if different interpretations of revelation are allowed Quṭb's, total rejection of the philosophers' or the theologians' interpretations of Islam seems unwarranted. By accepting their methods as individual interpretations, he could have argued for the rejection of their conclusions without the need to disavow philosophy or theology altogether, but only the ideas that contradict Islam clearly and legitimately. For the Muslim philosophers and theologians attempted to understand God and Islam in their own ways and according to their means.

Moreover, Quṭb's rejection of the philosophical and the theological quests is a rejection of a fundamental human need, i.e., the desire to know, and of rational and logical devices to investigate, measure, and, even, define advancement and development. But Quṭb is unconcerned with the issues of man's natural tendency towards rationalization and investigation. Furthermore, by denying the Prophet Muḥammad any role except the transmission of revelation, Quṭb reduces the status attributed to the Prophet by the theologians, the philosophers, and, even, the traditionalist- for instance, for correct understanding of revelation- and, also, forfeits another yardstick for measurement and development.[10] The Muslim philosophers, for instance, assign to the prophet-philosopher a crucial role: he is the central figure and foundation of knowledge, truth, happiness, and the virtuous city.[11] Thus, whereas the philosophers, for instance, do not allow every individual to create his own understanding of Islam but insist on following religion for the unphilosophic, Quṭb reverses the picture and claims that the Prophet has no understanding of his own, though the unphilosophic may enjoy different understandings and interpretations of the revelation.

Hence, it appears that the authorized version of religion for the philosophers is the Prophet's, but, no authorized version, besides the revelation itself, exists from Quṭb's perspective. Actually, Quṭb's argument is a mechanism that allows the rejection of the past; if anyone's interpretation is as good as another's, contemporary Muslims can interpret religion in terms suitable to their modern conditions. And the equality of all Muslims in terms of their capacity to understand revelation is ultimately directed towards political ends.

On yet another level, the notion of ancient and medieval thinkers on the division of mind and soul in a hierarchy is rejected in favor of a commonsensical understanding of Islam in particular and religion in general. For instance, whereas reason is represented by al-Fārābī as the ultimate pathway to truth by attaining the level of the active intellect and by partaking of its immortality, truth comes about, according to Quṭb, by the whole being and not only by one aspect. Furthermore, while al-Fārābī, Ibn Sīnā, Ibn Ṭufayl, and Ibn Rushd consider, for instance, true happiness as reserved to the philosophers and, as such, see nature as limiting the number of people who can attain happiness, Quṭb, on the other hand, considers any person as capable of attaining happiness if that person understands- not necessarily philosophically- the Islamic concept and interacts with it.

(C) Insofar as revelation is distinguished from human thought, Quṭb distinguishes it from imagination. Imagination is basically apparent in paganism, but Islam, as opposed to other religions, is free of distortion, additions, and interpretations derived from paganistic beliefs which are, in turn, based on emotions, imaginations, fantasies, and human concepts. Being divine precludes imperfection, ignorance, and whim. These characteristics accompany every human action and are embodied in concepts arrived at initially by humans from paganism and philosophy.[12] Quṭb justifies his position by quoting the following verses:

And recite to them the tiding of Abraham
when he said to his father and his people,
'what do you serve?'
They said, 'we serve idols, and continue cleaving to them.'
He said, 'Do they hear you when you call,
or do they profit you or harm'.
They said, 'Nay, but we found our fathers so doing'.
He said, 'And have considered
what you have been serving,
you and you fathers, the elders?
They are an enemy to me,
except the Lord of all Being
who created me,
and Himself guides me,
and Himself gives me to eat and drink,
and, whenever I am sick, heals me,
who makes me to die, then gives me life,
and who I am eager shall forgive me
my offence on the Day of Doom.

My Lord, give me Judgement,
and join me with the righteous,
and appoint me a tongue of truthfulness
among the others... — XXVI: 69-89
Say you: 'We believe in God,
and in that which has been sent down on us
and sent down on Abraham, Ishmael, Isaac and Jacob,
and the Tribes, and that which was given to Moses and Jesus
and the Prophets,
of their Lord;
we make no division between any of them,
and to Him we surrender.'
And if they believe in the like of that you believe in,
then they are truly guided,
but if they turn away, then they are clearly in schism;
God will suffice you for them;
He is the All-hearing, the All-knowing; the baptism of God;
and who is there that baptizes fair than God?
Him we are serving.
Say! would you then dispute with us concerning God,
who is our Lord and your Lord?
Our deeds belong to us,
and to you belong your deeds;
Him we serve sincerely. — II: 130-133

Also, Quṭb rejects the claim that Western culture and philosophy, ancient and modern, can be part of Islamic thought because they do not enjoy a correct understanding of God. One thing is clear; it can sufficiently be argued that the Muslim philosophers attempted to rationalize Greek thought in Islamic terms. By arguing that reason and revelation are not contradictory, they did not aim at highlighting the importance of religion per se but of philosophy since religion at their time was the dominant factor anyway. Their impressive goals manifested in preserving Greek thought and harmonizing philosophy and religion. Reason, God, religion, and happiness were perceived in a manner identical to that of the Greek; but what the philosophers had to deal with, which their predecessors did not, was the Holy *Qur'ān* and its claim to being the truth.[13] But for Quṭb, Islamic philosophy, and, for that matter, theology are un-Islamic; they are shades of Greek philosophy and theology. In fact, the "paganism of Greek thought," as opposed to the monotheism of Islam, constitutes, for Quṭb, the first foundation of Western thought as well as the first justification for its rejection.

Quṭb's criterion in rejecting ideas because of their Greek or Persian origins seems unwarranted; for ideas can be Greek and of monotheistic origins such as Artistole's unmoved mover. Hence, the proper criterion in the selection of an idea or system should rest on its coherence and reasonableness, on the one hand, and its utility to Islam, on the other. A notion such as God's knowledge of particulars, universals, or both should not be rejected or accepted because the Greeks said so, but should be studied on its own. Whether God knows only universals depends on whether God is limited in His knowledge and whether His mode of knowledge is voluntary or involuntary-such issues are relevant for tackling the concept of God's knowledge. And the correctness of the answers given to these questions is not dependent on being Greek or Arabic but on a more basic elements- consistency, proof, and logic.

For truth does not rise or fall because of its Greek or Islamic origin but supersedes localities and cultures. Virtues, morality and principles are neither restricted to a specific culture nor to one way of life but can be human universal. Islam has itself endorsed and allowed some customs, habits, principles, and rituals from the pre-Islamic period. The *Ka^{c}bah* itself, which the Arab pagans held in high esteem and made the center of their pilgrimage, was purified of idols and made the most revered place in Islam. Because Islam does not aim basically at destroying what people love and cherish but aims at turning them into more positive instruments in society and in worship, it separates and derives the good from evil. Of course, Islam does not tolerate idols, but not every idea or notion unaccounted for by Islam is paganistic or polytheistic. The Arab's love for the family and the tribe is an example; for this pre-Islamic kind of love was not obliterated, but qualified for the interest of a higher level of organization, i.e., the'*ummah*.[14] And because Islam is not restricted to the Arabs, a similar method of adopting what is just, true or useful and of denying what is unjust, untrue or harmful can be followed with other cultures.

Now, if philosophy and theology are inadequate tools for the attainment of truth, the important issue is concerned with the alternative. The alternative, for Quṭb, is a new and fresh interpretation of Islam from its original sources, i.e., the Holy *Qur'ān* and the Traditions. By rejecting theology and philosophy, Quṭb advocates direct, personal and intuitive understanding of revelation. His whole thought is dominated by the optimistic belief in the ability of man to know by simply looking within himself and by the notion that if man is left alone to his own conscience and soul with the help of religion, he will be able to acquire an adequate understanding of the universe.

The human mind cannot be the origin of the correct *muqawwamāt al-taṣawwur al-Islāmī* (components of the Islamic concept). It can only receive the concept from its divine origin. Its reception is correct when it is devoid of any previous preconceptions, individual or ideological. Because the human mind cannot act as a judge of the validity or invalidity of the concept, its judgement is restricted to textual interpretations in accordance with the idiomatic or linguistic exegesis of the text. Hence, human minds must surrender to textual authority whether it produces familiar or unfamiliar notions.[15]

Because Quṭb perceives that Islam is in conformity with innate human constitution *(fiṭrah)* and, more importantly, in conformity with the whole universe, he argues that we are part of this universe. Hence, our happiness results from the harmony between the part and the whole; unhappiness and misery, on the other hand, are the consequences of the conflict between man-made, undivine system and the universe. Therefore, knowledge and happiness are based on their correspondence and harmony with nature. In ***Al-Mustaqbal Li-Hādhā al-Dīn*** Quṭb defines happiness as the conformity to and the fulfillment of human *fiṭrah* in nature itself.[16] Thus, it is apparent that nature for Quṭb plays a fundamental role in the foundation of knowledge as well as existence itself. Consequently, any definition, say of social justice or beauty, is defective if it is not based on an accurate and correct understanding of nature itself. Hence, he argues in ***Al-ᶜAdālah al-Ijtimāᶜīyyah*** that

> *the nature of social justice in Islam cannot be realized in a comprehensive manner unless the Islamic concept of divinity, universe, life, and man is realized. Social justice is nothing but a branch of the wider origin [oneness of God] that all Islamic teachings are derived from.*[17]

Quṭb's perception of Islam as a true system *(niẓām),* because of its conformity to nature, leads him to postulate such conformity as a prerequisite for true knowledge, happiness, and good societies. His insistence on conformity to nature is a derivative from the notion of God's creation of man and nature. And, as understood from the above, no social or political principle can lead to happiness unless it is founded on and is not isolated from nature. This is, again, a result of believing that everything is created and given by God; what conforms to and fulfills the divine law is what leads to happiness.

It is obvious that Quṭb follows the ancient and medieval philosphers in perceiving happiness, knowledge, and good society as being dependent on a correct understanding of nature. For instance, in the ***Republic,*** Socrates shows us that the city would not be well-ordered and happy unless it was ruled by philosophers who are versed in metaphysics- metaphysics being the study of true nature. For Socrates, the ultimate goal is the contemplation of the Good,[18] which corresponds to Quṭb's obedience to the Creator, God. Because of its centrality, Quṭb states that when there is no harmony between the metaphysical concept and the social order, the consequence is assuredly misery regardless of material gains; those systems that separate man from nature lead to man's misery and unhappiness.

However, religion replaces reason and philosophy from Quṭb's point of view. Whereas the ancient and medieval philosophers show the good city, knowledge, and happiness as dependent on correct metaphysics attained and justified by reason, Quṭb grounds the good state, knowledge, and happiness on correct doctrines harmonious with nature. By linking the correctness and the ability of any political order to produce and promote happiness to that order's conformity to nature, Quṭb produce an argument on the need of political and social orders for a solid basis: a correct concept that takes into account the fulfillment of the purpose of human existence; a fulfillment that requires a correct understanding of nature. Thus, religion is made into the only system that is capable of providing a true and correct understanding of nature and, more specifically, of human *fiṭrah.* For Quṭb views Islam as much as a part of nature as the stars are. Therefore, religion, or the divine system, as distinguished from human systems, can provide a social system that does meet and fulfill human *fiṭrah.* Consequently, any social order not meeting and fulfilling human *fiṭrah* is unnatural, unjust, and disharmonious with the movement of man and with the movement of the universe.[19] This view Quṭb grounds in the following Qur'anic verses:

Say: 'Everything is from God.'
How is it with the people?
They scarcely understand any tiding. —IV: 82
And to Him belongs whatever inhabits the night and the day;
and He is the All-hearing, the All-knowing.
Say:'Shall I take to myself as protector other than God,
the originator of the heavens and of the earth,
He who feeds and is not fed?'
Say: 'I have been commanded to be
the first of them that surrender';
be not thou of the idolaters. —VI: 12-13
The unbelievers say,
'Why has a sign not been sent
down upon him from his Lord?'
Thou art only a warner and a guide to every people.
God knows what every female bears,
and the womb's shrinking and swelling...
God changes not what is in a people,
until they change what is in themselves...
To Him is the call of truth,

and those upon whom they call, apart from Him,
answer them nothing ...
To God bow all who are in the heavens and the earth,
willingly or unwillingly...
Say: Who is the Lord of the heavens and of the earth?
Say: 'God.' — XIII: 8-16.
... To him belongs the Kingdom of the heaven and the earth;
He gives life, and He makes to die, and He is powerful over everything.
He is the First and the Last,
the Outward and the Inward; He has knowledge of everything.
It is He that created the heavens and the earth in six days.
Then seated Himself upon the Throne.
He knows what penetrates into the earth,
and what comes forth from it,
what comes down from heaven and what goes unto it.
He is with you wherever you are;
and God sees the things you do. — LVII: 1-5
So set they face to the religion, a man of pure faith- God's original [fiṭrah] upon which he originated mankind.
There is no changing God's creation.
That is the right religion;
but most know it not. — XXX: 30
We shall assuredly urge thee against them
and then they will be thy neighbours there only a little.
Cursed they shall be,
and wheresoever they are come upon
they shall be seized and slaughtered all-
God's wont with those who passed away before;
and thou shall find no changing the wont of God. — XXXIII: 62

At this juncture, we can distinguish the following points. First, the validity or invalidity of any social order or, for that matter, any concept or doctrine depends on its ability or inability to fulfill and to meet the needs of human nature. Secondly, injustice and similar concepts result from a failure in meeting and fulfilling the needs of human nature. Thus, thirdly, justice and happiness are possible only when man lives according to nature and the fulfillment of his nature which is in harmony with the universe. Quṭb's argument is made in order to conclude that human systems, philosophies, and sciences are defective in the sense of wasting the various positive, spiritual, emotional, physical, social, and political energies of human life. As such, Quṭb uses this "defectiveness" as a means for rejecting philosophy and other man-made methods of knowledge as normative statements about truths.

But, why does Quṭb reject reason and espouse human nature *(fiṭrah)* as the only criterion for happiness and truth? For reason is also part of human nature. And Quṭb does not explain the reason for adopting the *fiṭrah* as a more credible yardstick for happiness than reason. Quṭb does not entertain the idea that if the psychological state of man is capable of attaining hints concerning truth, it may seem more reasonable to assume that that rational part which is capable of forming thoughts is more legitimately endowed to arrive at those hints of truth. Or, it might be that, for Quṭb, truth is different from one person to another depending on their psychological or spiritual readiness, but this also applies to the rational part. Also, Quṭb is unaware that if the correctness of thoughts is difficult to ascertain notwithstanding logic and dialectics, it is more difficult to ascertain the correctness of emotional and natural states. For Quṭb's rejection of philosophy, because it does not offer a unified system, can be equally applied to naturalism, emotionalism or spiritualism; individuals do enjoy different and diverse experiences and tastes concerning spiritual attainment. In other words, if differences among philosophers negate the usefulness of philosophy, so do the varying feelings that people experience. Hence, the yardstick used by Quṭb in arriving at happiness and knowledge suffers from the one-sidedness of which he accuses the philosophers. If a good society needs a correct metaphysical understanding that is harmonious with nature, Quṭb should have provided us with a specific mechanism that helps in making the decision on what nature is or is not and what happens when people feel differently about what constitutes nature.

Quṭb's answer might be found in this statement: the correct

signs of the correct approach are the potentiality of the *manhaj* in fulfilling the needs of man. Utility, then, is one sign of correctness, and one aspect of Quṭb's thought is utilitarian. And since these needs are innate in *fiṭrah,* another sign of correctness is being in accordance with nature, and another aspect of his thought is natural. Therefore, the correct method or *manhaj* in arriving at the truth is the method which is natural and utilitarian.

But this yardstick is unclear and imprecise too; there is a problem in Quṭb's terminology relating to the definitions of the "natural", "utilitarian" or "human needs". The term "natural" for instance, is not so obvious as Quṭb assumes. For the term "natural" may mean what man feels or thinks he feels as natural. In fact, it can be said that one person's "needs" are another's "luxuries." Some people perceive "needs" as being the minimum requirements for survival such as food and shelter- actually even people disagree on the term the "minimal." Others view "needs" as those things that are conducive to a virtuous life; even then, it seems difficult to pinpoint these "needs". Some, for instance, consider marriage as a deterrence to man's spiritual advancement; others, as an important step to satisfy a basic need which will help in freeing the human spirit. On yet another level, some might see the possession of castles, apartments, cars, ships, and so forth as needs. At certain level, we cannot but define man's needs, nature, goals, and so forth since the Holy *Qur'an* is not a book of definitions of needs and nature but a book of moral, spiritual, and legal guidance that still requires man to define his environment and his needs. Quṭb fails to notice that the complexity of any science such as Islamic jurisprudence indicates the complexity of human conditions. However, Quṭb simplifies the issues in terms of clear cut doctrines: "things," "needs", and "concepts" and negates any conceptual or practical ambiguity.

On the other hand, Quṭb's concept of a "method" as a necessary postulate serving all aspects of life in a unified way fails to recognize similar concepts developed by Greek and medieval philosophers who conceived life as a unity as well.

Their attempts pointed in that direction; not only did they view life as a unity but a unity that is organized in a specific manner. Therefore, his conclusion that all human philosophies and concepts have not led to a comprehensive and meaningful life but to unsettling disruption in the soul and the conscience of man should be restricted to modern Western thought.[20] Actually, his argument that the substitution of human thought for the divine system leads to catastrophic repercussions and that any interference of human thought in the divine system can result in very unfavorable outcomes is an overstatement as well as a misunderstanding of the divine message. For religion speaks to human reason which is responsible for understanding and applying its stipulations. Errors are to occur, but it is part of human nature to err since man is imperfect. But the alternative to human reason is nothing but the absence of investigation and study which results in catastrophic outcomes in religion and life in general. In fact, the important issue is not whether man interferes but whether his interference is warranted. Among other things, man did interpret the revelation by turning the anthropomorphic Qur'anic verses into symbols of love and power.

Furthermore, if Islam, according to Quṭb, is a religion that does not depend for its validity on miracles or reason but is based on contemplation and human nature *(fiṭrah)*, we are at loss in our attempt to distinguish revelation from mere imagination or in knowing what contemplation is. Though he defines contemplation in his book ***Fī al-Tārīkh... Fikrah wa-Minhāj*** (On History: an Idea and a Method) as being comprehensive or an attempt to comprehend the nature of the universe or human relations and as an assurance of a relation between the Creator and the created, it is sought by neither theology, philosophy nor, even, Sufism.[21] Quṭb's concept of contemplation aiming at seeing the universe as a single whole is assured from the outset; for a correct contemplation is the comprehension of the true relations between the different parts of the universe, including mankind. And as such, it is not substance but relations which are the object of contemplation.

Since no philosophy, theology, science or miracles separated or joined together can be the bases of the validity of religion, contemplation, and the Holy *Qur'ān,* one doubts whether any man is capable of reaching the contemplation defined by Quṭb. How one comprehends true relations is not obvious unless man is born with it. But if man is born with it, he should not deviate from it. Quṭb's definitions smack of subjectivity and negation of the authority of reason and philosophy, and, even, of nature and human *fiṭrah.* In fact, if *fiṭrah* exists at all, it should not be hard to prove; man does not insist, for instance, that he has a face or a heart or, for that matter, reason: he knows they are part of him. But men differ on the plausibility of the existence of such a thing as *fiṭrah* unless it means man's potential feeling, thinking, and reasoning. But, Quṭb's exposition of the existence of *fiṭrah* makes it more in need of proof than any other human faculty.

However, Quṭb insists on the affinity of Islamic revelation and nature. In ***Al-Mustaqbal*** he argues that the Islamic system *(niẓām)* derived from the Holy *Qur'ān* is not a system of a specific historical epoch or a local system for one generation or another or a particular environment or location. It "is a universal reality co-existing with unfolding [generations of] mankind as the permanent law of universe [nomos] or the world...."[22] Quṭb grounds his concept in the following verses:

Surely We sent down the Torah,
wherein is guidance and light; thereby the Prophets who had surrendered
themselves gave judgment for those of Jewry,
as did the masters and the rabbis, following such portion of God's Book
as they were given to keep and were witnesses to...
And therein We prescribed for them:
A life for a life, an eye for an eye...
And we sent, following in their footsteps,
Jesus, son of Mary, confirming the Torah before him;
and we gave to him the Gospel,
wherein is guidance and light...
And we have sent down to thee
the Book with the truth, confirming the Book that was before it,

and assuring it.
So judge between them
according to what God has sent down, and do not follow their caprices,
to forsake the truth that has come to thee.
To everyone of you
We have appointed a right way and an open road. — V: 48-51

What is important here is that what he describes as natural is in fact to be found in the Holy *Qur'ān;* naturalness is not what exists in man's nature but is actually what the Holy *Qur'ān* depicts as such. We can say that all man's actions can be considered natural, but, only those that the Holy *Qur'ān* recommends are natural. For in the absence of injunctions from the Holy *Qur'ān*, man cannot even, in Quṭb's view, know what is natural. Therefore, the ultimate yardstick is not human nature but the Holy *Qur'ān*.

Not only does Qutb relegate the validity of knowledge to its conformity to innate human nature but he also does not consider reason as an essential part of that nature. Consequently, although religion aims at contemplation which is the discovery of the relations between different parts of the universe, ultimately man cannot understand these relations since they are beyond his grasp. Thus, what happens by espousing this notion is that man's contemplation is indeed frustrated, and the goals of religion are unattainable; for Quṭb's concept of divinity leads to the obstruction of man's vision of true relations in the universe, of innate human nature, of miracles, of intuition, and of reason. And what we are left with is a vicious circle where we know neither where to enter nor to exit.

3 - ***Al-Thabāt*** (Fixity): From the second characteristic, divinity, all other charactersitcs follow. For the divinity of the Islamic concept fixes its bases and essence and conceptual underpinnings and excludes any change or development. Quṭb cites as examples truths given in the Holy *Qur'ān:* the truth of God's existence, immortality, oneness, dominion, and managing of the creation; the truth that the whole universe is God's creation; the truth that the goal of man's existence is the worship

of God; and the truth that the real human bond is creed and is not color, race, country or class.[23] Acceptance of these notions, without questioning, is a must for the correct *manhaj* and *niẓām*.

Quṭb quotes the following verses in order to support his position:

> *Even so we have revealed to thee a spirit of Our bidding.*
> *Thou knewest not what the book was, nor belief;*
> *but we made it a light,*
> *whereby We guide whom we will of our servants. And thou, surely thou shalt guide unto a straight path-*
> *the path of God, to whom belongs whatsoever is in the heavens, and whatsoever is in the earth. Surely unto God all things come home.* — XLII: 52-53

On yet another level, Quṭb views the value of the Islamic concept in its function as the regulator of human thought so that it does not swindle "with lusts and stimuli." Consequently, for Quṭb, the fixity of the Islamic concept serves as a regulator of human thought and life in order to ensure the continuation and the safeguarding of a proper human life. An example that shows the necessity of a fixed concept is modern experience. According to Quṭb, mankind is walking in darkness, and nothing is fixed, neither concepts, systems, situations nor customs. Mankind "changes its modes of thought and belief as it changes its fads of dress...."[24]

This leads us to the question of development; for, besides rejecting the idea that man's essence changes or that man has no essence, Quṭb insists that

> *the issue of man does not change because it is the matter of his existence in this universe and his fate, the issue of his relation with this universe and those living, and his relation with the Creator of this universe and the Creator of these living beings. It is a matter that does not change because it is the matter of existence and man.*[25]

Thus, Quṭb's argument is that if man's nature does not change and if revelation is in accordance with that nature, then revelation itself fits all ages. Because the major issues of existence, life and death, love and hate, and body and spirit are fixed features of man, revelation addresses these issues in a way co-existent with human nature itself. But if and when human nature changes- and Quṭb does not believe it did or will- then changes in thought and in viewing the universe become possible and, more importantly, valid and warranted. Keep in mind that he is not talking about whether it is better to travel on a aircraft, a ship, a camel or a donkey but with more basic human issues.

Practically speaking, Quṭb views the fixity of the Islamic concept as a guarantee to the Muslim society of the harmony and tranquility of Islamic thought and life with the universal order (unity), as a protection to the Muslims from submitting to evil concepts and systems, and as a theoretical framework providing a set of principles for both rulers and the ruled. And above all, it provides the basis of a stable and fixed Muslim society that permits the freedom of natural development of emotions and thoughts and of organization and conditions. This characteristic accounts to Quṭb for Islam's persistence throughout time, notwithstanding the turbulent times, blows and attacks from its enemies from within and from the outside.[26]

Apparently, Quṭb rejects first the possibility of change of man's nature and essence because there is no proof to his satisfaction that it does change. Secondly, man is instinctively or naturally oriented towards thinking of issues of this universe. Therefore, those important questions that man has asked himself throughout the ages like "who is he? Where did he come from, and, why?" are ingrained and fixed in the nature of man and are not the product of one society or another or one civilization or another. Here, the reader is puzzled; for if those questions are ingrained in human nature, it seems illogical to reject the philosophical and theological quests which are basically concerned with these questions. In the light of this argument, it appears that the exploration of these questions by philosophers, scientists, and others should be viewed by Quṭb as constituting a natural search to understand what man or nature is. For philosophy is a natural quest after natural questions; Sufism is an attempt made with a view to understand those innate questions. But Quṭb's intention is to argue that since the issues that man deals with are fixed, revelation, which is fixed insofar as it deals with these questions, replaces reason.

In fact, we cannot answer these questions except by a philosophical, theological or spiritual discipline. Quṭb's denunciation of the three as being un-Islamic is unwarranted because in the absence of these three and other methods, we are left with an existential method of interpreting the Qur'anic injunctions on man, universe, and so forth. This method lends itself to mere conjectures that in reality amount to nothing more than preferences. While we look in vain to find answers to these questions of definition in Quṭb's exposition, it seems that Quṭb discredits any personal or general system of attaining the truth that does not accord with his own understanding. In some ways, Quṭb's message is: you are right insofar as you do not contradict my understanding of Islam. Furthermore, Quṭb's disregard and misunderstanding of the schools of Muslim philosophers, theologians, and sufis obscure his understanding of their notions of man's essence and development.

Quṭb complicates the issue of nature by asserting that man's essence does not change, although he does not tell us what man's essence is. For sure, we cannot deny that men have posed similar questions for hundreds of years; an indication of a general interest and a natural tendency in man to question his environment and himself. Those questions, however, are not man's essence but are manifestations of that essence. Thus, it seems that Quṭb's argument lacks basic postulates such as definitions of essence and nature and distinctions between essence and manifestations.

Nonetheless, many of his notions are very similar to those of philosophers and theologians. The view of the Islamic concept as a regulator is a philosophical, juristic, and theological stipulation; the philosophers, for instance, view the essential value of the Islamic concept as lying in its social and political power of organization; it is a regulator of the Virtuous City. That humanity needs a specific fixed system in order to secure a happy and virtuous life is also a remnant of the philosophical traditions of the Greeks and the Muslims; but Quṭb is unaware even that some of the questions he poses and the answers he gives are Aristotelian in nature- for instance, that man undergoes many stages without ceasing to be man, or that man is what his potential is.

Quṭb understands development in the following - Aristotelian- way: "The material of this universe- whether nuclei or simple radiation...- is fixed in its essence. But it moves taking forms that are permanently changing, pivoting and developing".[27] In a similar manner, humanity is fixed although it is in a permanent flux. Consider the following- also, Aristotelian- example that Quṭb provides. First, any human being

> *passes through various biological stages: from being a sperm to old age. And he passes in various social stages, advancing or deteriorating depending on his closeness to or farness from humanity. But all these stages do not rule him out from the fact of his fixed humanity, its inclinations, energies, and faculties that are derived from the fact of being human.*[28]

Seen in this light, the conceptual characteristic of fixity in Islam, does not, in Quṭb's view, necessitate freezing the movement of life and thought but permits its movement within this fixed framework and around this fixed pivot. Thus, fixity by no means indicates rigidity but a well-directed development and advancement. This concept of fixity leads Quṭb to argue that "absolute development is merely a way to justify whatever is wanted," and a justification for licentiousness. First, it can be used by the state for the justification of its action towards individuals; for if there are no fixed principles and values that individuals can take refuge in against the state it follows that no fixed rights can be claimed by people and no references to fixed constitutions can be used. Thus, Quṭb sees that absolute development is a trick made by the state in order to impose on its citizens the concepts of what is right and wrong, i.e., a justification for state control. In other words, this development is the absolute development of the state more than that of the individuals. Individuals become subordinated to what the state considers as right and wrong; for the state defines rights, punishment, rewards, and the like; and, constitutions are the creation of the state to control its citizens. Ultimately, the action and interaction between the state and its citizens, Quṭb argues, boils down to this: "an animalistic emancipation of lusts" of the individuals is exchanged for "a tyrannical emancipation of the authority" of the state.[29]

This kind of emancipation is best illustrated to and by Quṭb in dialectical materialism which proclaims religion as the opium of people and fixity in religion as a service to the ruling classes. Quṭb's opinion is squarely opposed to that of Marx who, in the ***German Ideology,*** argues that God is simply the fantasy image of the repressive powers of the state. Quṭb's argument is primarily directed at communism; for he objects to the principle of dialectics in history on the ground that the dialectical approach does not really account for consequences of events. More precisely, causal sequences that are advocated by Marxism are pre-ordained, unwarranted conclusions; for Marx's descriptions of reality are his prescriptions for the future: Marx made dreams into facts and turned fantasies into goals. Furthermore, Quṭb describes Hegel and Marx's arguments of thesis, antithesis, and synthesis as well as the Marxist conclusion such as the victory of the working class, as unwarranted, unjustified, and unscientific. What puzzles Quṭb is the reason and mechanism by which the principle of contradiction terminates, i.e., the realization of the classless society. In other words, the classless society is a utopia.

In fact, his rejection of man's changeability is directed at the theory of evolution and communism, and, more precisely, Darwinism and Marxism. Quṭb lays many charges against Marxism: First, he accuses Marxism of being based on deep ignorance of the human soul, its nature, and its history because it obliterates the differences between the history of man and the history of animals and portrays all human motives as the result of material conditions, "hunger and the struggle to satisfy that hunger." But if this is true, Quṭb wonders about the sudden change in man that leads him to behave like an angel producing as much as he can but taking only what he needs without any control, government, divine creed or any acceptable reason. He also wonders about the possibility of change when the conditions of the classless society change. Secondly, this "scientific concept" and the theory of history, to Quṭb, are nothing but myths. On a more immediate level, nothing is left of Marxism except the state and its dictatorial, police regimes. The state has not withered away, but people have; and there is nothing left except the state. "Marxism- as a doctrine- is nothing," Quṭb states, "but the unprecedented scientific ignorance."[30]

Furthermore, Quṭb's preoccupation with purity leads to the rejection of Christianity, whose essence has changed by borrowing Greek thought and rituals. This borrowing as well as materialism culminates in his conclusion that ancient and modern Western thought is characterized by Greek paganism and Christianity as well as animosity to religion; a characterization that disqualifies ancient thought and modern Western thought from being included in and from being a ground for the development of modern Islamic thought.[31] Not only does Quṭb consider Western thought in general antagonistic to religion but, more importantly, foreign and alien to the spirit of Islam.

His rejection of philosophy and science which he considers essentially as Western is not only methodological but equally substantive and normative. For him neither philosophy nor science can take the place of religion because the nature of religion and philosophy is different; the philosophical concept originates in human thought and attempts to interpret this existence and man's relation to it. But it stays within the border of passive knowledge *(al-maᶜrifah al-bāridah)*. On the other hand, the doctrinal concept in general is a concept that springs from the conscience, interacts with feelings, and engulfs life. It is a living connection between man and existence or between man and the creator of existence. Any knowledge that cannot be transformed into an active movement is not in accordance with the nature of Islam. Every piece of knowledge revealed in the *Qur'an* demands the immediate action of the receiver. Seeking knowledge as an objective in itself is not an Islamic *manhaj*. In Islam legitimate knowledge is measured primarily by action, true science, work, and, correct creed.[32]

Moreover, Quṭb argues that human knowledge is conditioned, and, for this reason, does not consider civilization in general as a universal human heritage without a country, race or religion- in other words, there are only particular civilizations. But science is exempted when it does not trespass into "the domain of metaphysical and philosophical interpretations" of human soul, history, art, literature and emotions.[33] If anything, this statement reveals Quṭb's awareness of the sociological influence that society has on its people, including its thinkers. Individuals who live in a certain environment under a specific regime and government at a specific time- and every individual is constrained by these limits- cannot totally isolate themselves from their societies. Though Quṭb does not provide any evidence, he insists that individuals are more or less chained mentally, psychologically, and physically to societies. Therefore, their products, especially the intellectual cannot be said to belong to the whole of mankind but to specific ages and societies. This is a necessary postulate for Quṭb in order to put forward the argument that a proper understanding and a correct assessment of the nature of those products require the study and understanding of the role and place they occupied and played within the process of development- which in fact cannot be completely ascertained in numerous cases. This argument provides Quṭb with a justification for rejecting any foreign element, even though it is only an idiom. "Every idiom," Quṭb contends, "has its own history and connotations derived from its history", and thus, cannot be used in an abstract way without its linguistic derivations, objectives, and historical circumstances.[34] Also, as is the case with medieval Muslim thinkers, modern Muslim thinkers committed the error of borrowing concepts and terms from the West. It would have been better for the Muslim thinkers to have developed purely Islamic terms because the Islamic concept has its own terms that are in agreement in the nature of their linguistic derivations, objectives and historical circumstances with the nature of Islam.[35] Consequently, we can derive the following:

As with cultures and concepts, terms and idioms such as "God" and "reason" cannot be isolated and borrowed to a different culture; for every idiom or concept should be understood in its own context. They have to be understood within their own environment because linguistic differences produce cognitive differences. "God" and "Allah", for instance, though used interchangeably, they have been understood differently. For God is usually understood as having a Son who is also worshipped; Allah has no child. But Quṭb does not comment on the Jewish worship of "God", and Arab Christian worship of "Allah."

Quṭb is correct in his emphasis that terms and concepts need to be understood first in their environment before being transported into another language and culture. Thus, it is important to the translator and the philosopher or anyone else who is interested in other cultures to understand their history and semantics. This, however, should not mean that individuals or, for that matter, nations are incapable of understanding other cultures or borrowing terms and concepts. For instance, it is possible for a Muslim to explain his understanding of God to the Christian British. To be sure, humans are constrained by their own culture and environment which imposes difficulties in communication, but this does not warrant the conclusion that people cannot communicate conceptually or cannot supersede their cultures and fathom the philosophies or religions of other people, if there is a conscious attempt to do so. For mankind has the capacity to understand reason in all its meanings, instrumental or philosophical, though many individuals cannot reach that level. This should not culminate in asserting the incommunicability of concepts; for if this is so, how does Quṭb justify the conversion of, for instance, an American to Islam? Does it mean that his conversion is superficial or his understanding inadequate? Of course, Quṭb would not make this claim; for he believes that every individual is capable of understanding and interacting with Islam. Now, if a foreigner is capable of understanding the loftiest ideas of Islam, a Muslim should be able to understand foreign- and, in Quṭb's opinion, lower- concepts. Moreover, if a person cannot understand another culture, why does Quṭb reject a long standing civilization, i.e., the Western? Does it mean that he does not understand that culture but nonetheless discredits it?

Hence, Quṭb's claim of people's inability to understand other cultures rebuts his own refutation of Western and Eastern cultures because refutation involves correct understanding which is not possible. Here, there is an obvious contradiction: Quṭb can understand other cultures and notions such as communism and material contradiction which did not originate in Islam, and thus, can refute them. Other individuals like the Muslim philosophers or thinkers are incapable of doing the same or of understanding the Greeks.

Furthermore, though Quṭb believes that the ultimate truth (God) is ahistorical, he does accept the notion that to know whether a concept is true or false, it is necessary to understand its historical development. Whether there is actually one God, many gods or none at all or whether religion and state should be joined or separated- in short, all metaphysical, ethical, and philosophical statements are not subject for their validity or invalidity to historical development. The existence or non-existence of God is not a historical matter, it is speculative. Whether all nations have believed or disbelieved in God, this does not mean that He really exists or does not exist. This, however, is not a denial of the very important role of history; for history of philosophy, for instance, can illuminate and increase our knowledge of God: How the Greeks or the Muslims have perceived God, reason, and war is not a speculative but is a historical matter. Without information and facts, one can speculate for hundreds of years without knowing how a specific culture understood a specific concept.

Quṭb's attack is not only directed at the Greek or medieval Muslim philosophers but also at any attempt to philosophize. Whereas he regards medieval thought as useless and irrelevant to Islam, he praises the efforts of some modern thinkers, first among whom are Muḥammad ᶜAbduh and Muḥammad Iqbāl. Although Quṭb acknowledges the attempts of ᶜAbduh and Iqbal as great and fruitful efforts to revive Islamic thought, he makes them his target in criticizing modern Islamic thought. He charges that by trying to defend Islam Iqbāl and ᶜAbduh became the victims of deviation from Islam. More to the point, Quṭb takes issues with the two writers, with cAbduh on the validity of reason as a criterion for truth and with Iqbāl on borrowing doctrines and terms from the West.

Muḥammad cAbduh, following the medieval Muslim philosophers, assures us that harmony exists between reason and revelation; and the premise of his thought is that reason is based on and supported by revelation. He considers the message of the prophets to be complementary to reason. Accordingly, man is capable of discovering, unaided by revelation, the moral law. Furthermore, whereas Quṭb isolates science from religion, cAbduh reinterprets some verses in the Holy *Qur'ān* in the light of new scientific discoveries. The problem with cAbduh, according to Quṭb, is that he viewed the mind and revelation as equal, not as one subservient to the other. The role of revelation, for Quṭb, is to rectify and adjust the direction of knowledge; in other words, revelation and reason are by no means equal and "pure reason does not exist in the realm of reality but is an ideal." Since Quṭb also rejects reason as a valid way of attaining truth, his rejection of cAbduh's equation of validity of reason and revelation and basing the latter on the former is consistent.

As in the case with cAbduh, Quṭb does not spare Iqbāl from criticism. But Quṭb justifies Iqbāl's deviations on social and political grounds; Iqbāl lived in "an environment of intellectual aimlessness." Iqbāl, adds Quṭb, wanting to do away with the aimlessness in mind and thought of the Muslims who were facing the West and its thought of positivism and experimentalism, tried to show the experimentalist and positivist bases in Islamic thought. In other words, he tried to base Islamic thought on modern Western thought itself and was mistaken in his "attempts to frame the Islamic concept in borrowed, philosophic modes, derived from Hegelianism, idealistic rationalism, and Comtean positivism."[36]

More importantly, in ***The Reconstruction of Religious Thought in Islam,*** Iqbāl argues that the "Absolute Ego" is "the whole Reality." From the Ultimate or Absolute Reality or Ego (God), egos (humans) proceed; and this leads Iqbāl to ascribe the use of the proper name 'Allah' "in order to emphasize the individuality of the Ultimate Ego."[37] In his work, ***The Secrets of the Self,*** a book originally written in Persian, Iqbāl argues that the order of the universe originates in the Self (God) and that the continuation of the life of all individuals depends upon the Self. He expresses the opinion that life comes from forming desires and bringing them to birth. But the attempt to focus on the self has resulted, Quṭb believes, in exaggeration; for Iqbāl interpreted some Qur'anic texts in a way that goes against their nature and the nature of the Islamic concept in order to prove that death and resurrection do not end in man's final reward and punishment.[38] For Iqbāl heaven and hell are not the end because heaven and hell are states, not localities. Hell, Iqbāl states, is the painful realization of one's failure as man and "is a corrective experience which may make a hardened ego once more sensitive to the living breeze of Divine Grace." For Iqbāl, there is "no such thing as eternal damnation in Islam," and heaven "is the joy of triumph over the forces of disintegration."[39]

Quṭb's criticism is warranted; in Islam, after death and resurrection man is either rewarded or punished for his deeds on earth. Traditional interpretations of the Holy *Qur'ān* maintain that heaven and hell are not corrective experiences but, are respectively punishment and reward.[40] Either reward or punishment or, in other words, experiencing happiness or misery follows death. But the characteristics of the soul are already developed, and energies are spent, and, for this reason, the soul and the body are either rewarded or punished. This traditional view is, according to Quṭb, justified by the text itself:

Then after that you shall die,
then on the day of Resurrection you shall surely be raised up.—
XXIII: 15

... when death comes to one of them, he says,
'My Lord, return me;
haply I shall do righteousness in that I forsook'.
Nay, it is but a word He speaks;
and there, behind them, is a barrier
until the day that they shall be raised up. For when the trumpet is blown,

that day there will be no kinship anymore between them,
neither will they question one another.
Then he whose scales are heavy...
they are the prosperers.
And he whose scales are light...
they are lost in Gehennam dwelling for ever,
the Fire smiting their faces the while they glower there. — XXIII: 101-105

Also, Quṭb's criticism of both ᶜAbduh and Iqbāl for their attempt to base contemporary Islamic thought on science is also warranted. And in matters of details, Quṭb is right in his charge that some Islamic concepts are not understood by Iqbāl and ᶜAbduh on their own terms- for instance, that hell and heaven are physical as well as psychological, and that the fruits of reason (science) cannot be the foundations of a new Islamic philosophy.

On yet another level, Quṭb's methodological objections to the expositions offered by modern Muslim thinkers is unwarranted for the following reason: Quṭb's problem resides in his perception of philosophy as monolithic, whereas philosophy is composed of numerous attempts to understand the universe; attempts ranging from ascertaining reality and God's existence to denying reality and God's existence. Hence, to lump together all sorts of philosophies- or for that matter, any other discipline of knowledge- is a sign of a disability in comprehending the diversity or, even, the reality of philosophy and its endeavors. Neither philosophy, science nor religion should take the place of each other; actually they can aid and complement each other in looking for the truth and in rejecting falsehood. If religion seeks what is true, so does philosophy. Of course, there are misguided philosophical attempts but, on the other hand, there are also misguided religious attempts. This is not an endorsement of any philosophical or theological conclusions but is an invitation to distinguish between methods and ideas. For it would be impossible, for instance, for a Muslim to advocate the truths of Islam or to refute the proponents of dialectical materialism or communism by depending only on the Holy *Qur'ān.* Quṭb should not ask them- but he does anyway- to read the Holy

Qur'ān as evidence since its truth is the issue in the first place; and, he cannot say their beliefs do not concern me since the message of Islam is universal. Therefore, another method has to be found; this method cannot be theology or jurisprudence since they are built on Islamic principles which his opponent does not accept. This would be begging the question. Hence, the method has to be a rational one, which can fathom and undermine the opponent's philosophy on the one hand, and which can explain and validate his philosophy, on the other. Hence, a religious argument can be made not only to study philosophy but also to establish one- especially if Islam is comprehensive and offers an intelligible interpretation.

4 - ***Al-Shumūlīyyah*** (Comprehensiveness): The fourth characteristic, the comprehensiveness of the Islamic concept, is derived as well from the second characteristic, divinity. What characterizes the Islamic concept is its comprehensiveness whereas man's concepts and thought in general are partial and limited. Temporal and spatial limits of man is one of Quṭb's persistent arguments. Man's limitations in knowledge, experience, and understanding and his weakness, inclinations, lusts, and wishes are made up for by the Islamic concept which provides mankind with an intelligible interpretation of the beginning of the universe and of every subsequent motion, and above all provides an intelligible interpretation of the appearance of the phenomenon of life from the inanimate matter. Consequently, Quṭb perceives divine, (i.e., revealed) religion as being neither restricted to conscience nor isolated from reality, nor merely rituals, nor only interested in personal matters, nor only concerned with the after-life. More importantly, it is the religion that offers to humanity the comprehensive interpretation of existence and of man's relation with his Almighty Creator, place and purpose in this existence.[41] If this is correct, it follows that a human system is not needed. On this opinion, he uses the *Qur'ān* as the foundation.

Pharaoh said, 'Who is your lord,
Moses?' He said 'Our Lord is He
Who gave everything its creation,

then guided it.' Pharaoh said,
'And what of the former generations?'
Said Moses, 'The knowledge of them
is with my Lord, in a Book;
my Lord goes not astray, nor forgets.' — XX: 50-54
Surely We have created everything in measure.
Our commandment is but one word,
as the twinkling of an eye. — LIV: 49-50

God knows what every female bears,
and the wombs' shrinking and swelling;
everything with Him has its measure.
The knower of the unseen and the visible,
the All-great, the All-exalted. — XIII: 8-9
Surely your Lord is God,
who created the heavens and the earth
in six days – then sat Himself upon the Thrown,
covering the day with the night it pursues urgently-
and the sun, and the moon, and the stars subservient, by His command.

Verily, His are the creation and the command. — VII: 54
And We have sent down to thee
the Book with the truth, confirming the Book that was before it,
and assuring it. So judge between
them according to what God has sent down;
and do not follow their caprices,
to forsake the truth that has come to thee.
To every one of you We have appointed a right way and an open road...
And judge between them
according to what God has sent down,
and do not follow their caprices,
and beware of them lest they
tempt thee away from any of what God has sent down to thee.
But if they turn their backs,
know that God desires only to smite them
for some sin they have committed;
surely men are ungodly.
Is it the judgement of pagandom [jāhilīyah]

then that they are seeking?
Who is fairer in judgment than God.— V: 48-50

One might wonder about what Quṭb means by this interpretation. If Islam's interpretation is intelligible, it indicates the possibility of its understanding and investigation, or else what does intelligible mean? For we know that God has ordered the Muslims to think about the universe and its constitution. And the fact that Quṭb's interpretation is based on the notion that God created this universe and that by His own will everything takes place- a fact that constitutes an essential component of the Islamic concept- is not discredited when man attempts to understand factually and philosophically the essential elements of the creation. Quṭb's suggestion[42] that the only possibility of bridging the distance between ideas and actions is by transcending that distance and by attributing the distance to the creative will of God suffers from the negation of intelligibility. For "intelligibility" indicates man's ability to comprehend the "distance", or dimension, and, surely, man can attribute the distance to God or to anyone else but doing so requires knowledge, not its absence.

Thus Quṭb's argument about the comprehensiveness of the Islamic concept, as an attribution of the direction of the universe, life, and man to one comprehensive will and to its dealing with all essential truths of divinity, of the universe, of life, and of man, should not necessarily prevent man from attaining a first hand and direct knowledge of truth. The Muslims should not dismiss the question of rational investigation since the Holy *Qur'ān* in its discourses presupposes man's rationality as well as his power of discernment to ascertain the Holy *Qur'ān's* claims. For God orders the Muslims to look within themselves and into the universe in order to ponder over the wonders of creation; and whenever truth is involved, God questions man's unfounded and traditional beliefs and actions. Accordingly, if for Sayyid Quṭb unity underlies all kinds of truth,[43] the individual should be able to ascertain philosophically and factually this notion. Anyway, Quṭb's opinion of the limitation on human knowledge is opposed to ancient thinkers and medieval Muslim and non-Muslim philosophers and is directed at modern thought. It is, in fact, in harmony with most modern thinkers as well as Marxism, liberalism, positivism, and, in general, modern Western thought. Ironically, Quṭb's attempts to discredit modern Western principles for their partiality, like the inadequacy of human thought, lead to similar outcomes, like the relativity of knowledge.

But Quṭb is correct in his perception that the ultimate goal of creation as a whole and man in particular is the worship of God by seeking unity between man and man and the universe. Therefore, man does not realize the goal of his existence by worship alone but also by achieving unity in all aspects of life. Qutb's rejection of any divorce of politics from religion and of the totality of the diverse aspects of life as belonging either to economics, society, politics or any other aspect comes as a result of his belief in the existence of a strong relation between the nature of the social order and the nature of the metaphysical or doctrinal concept. Not only this, but, more importantly, the social order itself is derived from the metaphysical concept;[44] hence, the compartmentalization of human life prevents an accurate understanding of man and the universe. But what marks the superiority of religion in general and Islam in particular, according to Quṭb, is its totality.

The realization of man's existence, however, should not be limited only to human *fiṭrah,* as Quṭb contends; it should also involve the whole being - the philosophical included. And Qutb's declaration, for instance, that the division of Islamic jurisprudence into civil and religious branches is a technical matter but in Islam all these aspects are parts of worship, should have been extended to other disciplines of knowledge.[45] For if Islam is comprehensive, it should link all aspects of life to the regulations of the Islamic concept. But "all aspects" should have included truely all aspects like the physical, the social, the scientific, the philosophical and so forth.

Furthermore, if the division of human activity is incorrect for the attainment of a comprehensive understanding of life and the universe and for happiness, it would seem impossible to disregard human activities, like the theological and the philosophical, without endangering the essence of happiness and comprehensiveness. The Prophet himself acknowledges the higher status of the worshipper who attains knowledge over the one who does not, and considers seeking knowledge a form of worship. Secondly, the notion that the nature of the metaphysical order influences the social system is correct, for it seems unlikely to create a good state on false assumptions. But Quṭb has not rejected this idea thought it is philosophical. For this notion had been espoused by the works of ancient and medieval philosophers (like in Plato's ***Republic*** and al-Fārābī's ***Virtuous City***). Their insistence on the need for the good city had led them to found it by a philosopher-king or a philosopher-prophet who was well versed in metaphysics. For they aimed at creating a total and comprehensive social, political, and metaphysical system. It appears, again, that Quṭb's insistence on the indivisibility of human activity should have included all, philosophy and otherwise. Of course, there are good and evil human activities; and the former are to be accepted, the latter to be denied. But the criterion used for acceptance or rejection, depending on whether an activity is material, metaphysical or spiritual, is inadequate since there are spiritual activities that are harmful or deceptive, and material activities that are useful. A better criterion for classification might reside in the outcome of a specific activity whether it is good, evil, useful or harmful, and, above all, whether it is warranted or not. In fact, philosophy and science- like many other activities- can be likened to an instrument, such as airplane, which may be used positively or negatively.

5 - ***Al-Tawāzun*** (Equilibrium): The fifth characteristic, the equilibrium of the Islamic concept in its allusions to the truth and its components, comes forth from comprehensiveness. Because the Islamic concept is secured from speculations and exaggerations existing in philosophy and other religions misconstrued by the interference of human thought, an equilibrium, argues Quṭb, is made. More to the point, the equilibrium of the Islamic concept is due to its balancing of two aspects: the known and the unknown. The aspect of human

existence which surrenders to God and seeks Him is balanced by another, the known. The unknown, like the nature of God's existence or the existence of the day of judgement, has to be believed in and surrendered to; an aspect that Quṭb considers part of the *fiṭrah*. Since man possesses a natural inclination to submit to the unknown, Islam meets this inclination through addressing man's consciousness. Also, since man possesses an inclination to the known and needs intelligible and manageable objects, Islam meets this inclination by exhorting study and research into natural science, medicine and other sciences and by providing a clear logic, comfortable to the mind and heart with proofs that the *fiṭrah* receives with approval and resignation. But since the human mind cannot comprehend all the secrets of existence, the Muslims should accept the teachings and orders of God without questioning.[46]

To support his arguments, Qutb quotes the Holy *Qur'an*. The Holy *Qur'an,* he tells us, poses many challenging questions to mankind which are ultimately unanswerable but which converse with the human *fiṭrah* and help understanding and thinking about the essential issues of life. Consider the following verses[47] cited by Quṭb.

> *Or were they created of nothing? Or are they themselves the creator?*
> *Or did they create the heavens and the earth?*
> *Nay, but they have no sure faith.*
> *Or are thy Lord's treasuries in their keeping?*
> *Or are they the registrars?*
> *Or have they a ladder whereon they listen?*
> *Then let any of them that has listened bring*
> *a clear authority.* — LII: 35 - 39
> *Or have they taken gods out of the earth who raise the dead?*
> *Why, were there gods in earth and heavens*
> *other than God, they would surely go to ruin;*
> *so glory to God, the Lord of the Throne,*
> *above that they describe!*
> *He shall not be questioned as to what he does, but they shall be questioned.*
> *Or have they taken gods apart from Him?*

Say: 'Bring your proof! This is the Remembrance
of him who is with me, and the Remembrance
of those before me. Nay, but most
of them know not the truth, so therefore they are turning away.
— XXI: 21-24
Is not He, who created the heavens and the earth, able to create
the like of them? Yes, indeed;
He is the All-creator, the All-knowing.
His command, when desires a thing, is to say to it
'Be,' and it is! — XXXVI: 81-82
Has not man regarded how We created him of a sperm-drop?
Then lo, he is a manifest adversary.
And he has struck for Us a similitude
and forgotten his creation;
he says, 'Who shall quicken the bones
when they are decayed?'
Say: 'He shall quicken them, who originated them the first time;
He knows all the creation... — XXXVI: 78-79

It is apparent that Quṭb is correct in seeing these and other verses as providing man with proofs that ask the mind to consider and to reflect on God's signs. And in so doing, the human *fiṭrah* finds what it longs for from the known and the unknown. But one of the important meanings in these verses, which Quṭb neglects, is that God, by questioning people's concept of gods, life, and death, is asking them to bring forth proofs for their beliefs. For instance, the verses "*Or were they created of nothing? Or are they themselves the creator? Or did they create the heavens and earth? Nay, but they have no sure faith?*" include the invitation to the following:

1 - To reflect on the origin of creation. To do this, man has to investigate whether he is created from nothing, i.e., by himself or whether there is a creator.

2 - If there is a creator, is it man or something else?

3 - If it is man, did he create the heavens and the earth?

4 - Surely, it is not man who created the heavens and earth since man knows he did not.

5 - If it is not man, is it nature or the gods (as the Arabs used to believe)? Whatever your opinion, provide a sure faith (or clear authority). Obviously, sure faith is not only a mere belief but one with a proof; for the Arabs had a belief or faith in gods and in nature. Thus, a sure faith or clear authority is equivalent to evidence; and, those who want to assert something need to produce some kind of evidence. But the Arabs did not have a sure faith- all they had was what their fathers and forefathers taught them. On the other hand, these verses cannot be taken to mean do not philosophize or reason because the addressees are those who can reason and can be persuaded not by emotions but by thought. And the objections are directed not at the thougthful believers but at the pagans who say what they cannot prove. In other words, these verses cannot be used to prohibit philosophy and speculation since they are not directed at philosophy, theology, and science but at paganism.

What is important here is that God's knowledge of human nature requires men to provide evidence since He knows that the emotional states (beliefs, customs, traditions and so forth) cannot change just because someone wishes them to change. Therefore, Quṭb, in disclaiming the validity of evidence in human discourse, is overlooking a very important methodological part of the Qur'anic discourse, which the Muslims view as the hightest achievement in human eloquence and truth. The logic of the Qur'anic discourse, which aims at penetrating human rigidity and ignorance, presents the Muslims with a precedent for questioning and answering. The Qur'anic verse: *"He shall not be questioned as to what He does....."* which Quṭb understands as indicating the inability of man to think about God's action, is not a prohibition of thinking but directed against the arrogance of man who, because of his ignorance, complains about God's actions instead of attempting to understand them. And the proof for this interpretation is that the verse ends in *"but most of them know not the truth, so therefore they are turning away,"* and not by "But most of them believe not."

As to Quṭb's statement that the proof is being in conformity with *fiṭrah*, the Holy *Qur'ān*, which defines *fiṭrah*, does not speak only, or its "clear logic" is not related only, to emotion but also to reason. In fact, those individuals whose judgements are immature (like children) or impaired (like mad individuals) are not subject to legal and moral prescriptions and are not even required to pray or perform other duties.

Another aspect of the equilibrium of the Islamic concept is the balance between the absoluteness of the divine will and the stability in the observable universal laws and rules. What have been considered as the laws of nature are, for Sayyid Quṭb, still laws but dependent for their beginning, continuation, and end on the divine will. Like al-Ghazālī before him, Quṭb sees that cause-effect relationships are not necessary (except that God ordained them to be so). Al-Ghazālī argues in ***The Incoherence of the Philosophers,*** Problem Seventeen, that a cause-effect relationship is not a necessary or a permanent relation, or that one follows from the other. Whereas, for instance, in the burning of a piece of cotton at its contact with fire, the philosophers before and after al-Ghazālī argue that fire alone is the agent of burning, al-Ghazālī denies that.[48] But Averroes argues that the denial of the cause-effect relationship and the insistence on ascribing an effect to the will of the Creator which itself has no particular well-defined course lead to the inability to know or to observe facts. An interesting example that Averroes gives is that a man may persuade himself that, in front of him, there are ferocious animals and that he fails to see them because God did not create in him the sight of them.[49] Whereas for Averroes and other philosophers there is a necessary order that God cannot break or transform, for al-Ghazālī and Quṭb the order is created by God, and, as such, is under the will of God. Qutb argues that the divine will ordained that the universal laws appear to man as such in order that man can "observe, realize, and adjust their [people's] life accordingly and to deal with the universe accordingly."[50]

The ultimate benefit of the equilibrium of the Islamic concept, according to Quṭb, is that in the fixity of the universal laws (*sunnah*) and the absoluteness of the divine will, the conscience stands on stable and solid grounds so that man works and knows and, at the same time, is free from enslavement to nature due to his knowledge that all things are ultimately dependent on God's will. For instance, there is an equilibrium between man's being the servant of God and his dignified position in this universe. Being a servant of God is a valve that prevents and prohibits men from being slaves to each other regardless of their positions and offices in this life. Thus, man should worship and should be governed only by God and not by any human individual, group or institution. Therefore, in Islam, there is no need to diminish God's position and character in order to pay tribute to man and to announce man's control over and effectivity in the universe. Man and God are not opponents or warriors, where if one wins the other loses.

In one sense, Quṭb subscribes to Socrates's opinion in the ***Republic*** about the proper manner of education. In the ***Republic,*** Socrates sees as harmful the effects of teaching people that the gods are ruthless and insists that the youth in the virtuous city should be taught to respect the gods and to think of them positively. But Socrates does not see all myths as harmful; he himself sanctioned some myths. On the other hand, all kinds of myth, for Quṭb, are like poison; and, society should be built on true concepts.[51]

Furthermore, Quṭb views the truth of Islam as stemming from its harmony with nature. Islam (the revelation of God) is in harmony with the laws of the universe and the nature of existence and human *fiṭrah*. And, as such, Islam is not only a religion but is also an integral part of the universe and its laws and the articulation of the universe and its laws - all of which are created by God. On the other hand, humanity has been unable for centuries to find a comprehensive thought regarding universal and human forces and has been separating material forces from spiritual forces. This inability as well as instability is due, according to Quṭb, to three basic problems: invention, ignorance, and the unreliability of science.

Invention is not embodied in inventing machinery and the like but is the result of the interference of human thought in the divine concept as manifested in, for instance, rationalism and positivism. But Quṭb does not consider the problem as much the outcome of human interference in God's system but as the neglect of modern philosophy of that system which is either relegated to the realm of personal preferences or denied altogether.

Ignorance resulting from not understanding nature. Philosophers cannot even agree on the definition of the nature of nature and the nature of the universe. Here too, Qutb is unaware that the problem is not the existence of many definitions of nature or that the philosophers cannot agree but is mainly due to assigning to God very little influence or no influence at all.

The unreliability of science is due to its changeability. For instance, what was certain a hundred years ago is now rejected as unscientific. This, however, does not lead Quṭb to reject all science but to qualify its acceptance. Science, pure and applied, is accepted on the condition that it does not exceed its limits by trying to interpret philosophically what is found.[52]

6 - ***Al-'Ījābīyyah*** (Positiveness): The sixth characteristic of the Islamic concept is positiveness which operates in the realm of the relation between God and the universe, life, and man. According to Quṭb, the divine qualities of Islam are not negative; God, for instance, is not the divine perfection portrayed in the negative manner of Aristole: Aristotle perceives God as a thought thinking itself. Neither is God's perfection, Quṭb adds, restricted to some aspects as the Persians argued: the god of light and the god of evil. Nor is God's perfection limited to any degree of being (thought) as Plotinus argued. Nor is He the God portrayed by the people of Israel where He is the God of only one people. Nor is He what some Christian sects perceive as having his perfection mixed with an other entity (Christ or the Holy Spirit). Above all, divine perfection is not the non-existence of God as in materialism.[53]

But, in Islam, Quṭb contends, the oneness of God is the embodiment of positiveness. In order to make his point, Quṭb quotes the following verses:

Surely your Lord is God,
who created the heavens and earth in six days-
then sat Himself upon the Throne,
covering the day with the night it pursues urgently-
and the sun, and the moon and the stars subservient,
by His command.
Verily, His are the creation and the command.
Blessed be God, the Lord of all Being. — VII: 54

Say: 'O God, Master of the Kingdom,
Thou givest the kingdom to whom thou wilt
and seizest the kingdom from whom Thou wilt, Thou exaltest whom Thou wilt,
and Thou abasest whom Thou wilt;
in Thy hand is the good;
Thou art powerful over everything.
Thou makest the night to enter into the day
and Thou makest the day to enter into the night,
Thou bringest forth the living from the dead
and Thou bringest forth the dead from the living,
and Thou providest whomsoever Thou wilt
without reckoning. — III: 25-26

God knows what every female bears,
and the womb's shrinking and swelling;
everything with Him has its measure —.
The knower of the unseen and the visible,
the All-great, the All-exalted:
Alike of you is he who conceals his saying,
and he who proclaims it,
he who hides himself in the night,
and he who sallies by day;
he has attendant angels,
before him and behind him
watching over him by God's command.
God changes not what is in a people,
until they change what is in themselves.
Whatever God desires evil for a people,
there is no turning it back;
apart from Him, they have no protector.

It is He who shows you the lightning,
for fear and hope, and produces the heavy clouds; the
thunder proclaims His praise,
and the angels, in awe of Him.
He looses the thunderbolts,
and smites with them whomsoever He will; yet
they dispute about God,
who is mighty in power. — XIII: 8-13

Hast thou not seen that God knows
whatsoever is in the heavens and whatsoever is in the earth?
Three men conspire not secretly together,
but He is the fourth of them,
neither five men, but He is the sixth of them,
neither fewer than that, neither more,
but He is with them,
wherever they may be;
then He shall tell them
what they have done,
on the Day of Resurrection. Surely God has knowledge of every thing. — LVIII: 7

Thus Islamic oneness is distinguished- say, from Aristotelian or Neoplatonic oneness- in that it entails action; Muslims seek to establish Muslim societies. Thus, ultimately, it seems that the value of this characteristic as well as the others, for Quṭb, is social and political. This conclusion can be made clear by the example that Quṭb gives of the effect of the oneness of God: the first community of Muslims was a community created by believing in the oneness of God. The effect of oneness was not only metaphysical but it resulted in creating an Islamic community. Accordingly, the Islamic concept is not a negative (i.e., inactive) concept living in the realm of the conscience, satisfied with existing theoretically in an idealistic picture or in the spiritual realm but is, above all, a design to create a situation where the oneness of the creator and unity of mankind are preserved. In other words- and this statement is replete with political implications that will be discussed in *Chapter III*- the positiveness of the Islamic concept can be seen in two ways: first, as a motivating force in the life of the individuals to create a Muslim *'ummah* (personal motive), and, secondly, as a design for the creation of the good *'ummah* (Political, communal motive). The design itself that guides peoples to their proper and good life, i.e., Islam, requires its own fulfillment, i.e., the creation of an Islamic state.

Thus, the value of Islam cannot be appreciated and realized except in the Islamic state, for those individuals seeking Islamic goals and values, the existence of the state becomes essential without which Islam does not survive in its best forms, i.e., the political. For this reason, Quṭb tells us that action is the "practical translation of belief".[54] Moreover, the meaning of *shahādah* (acknowledging that there is no god but Allah and that Muhammad is His messenger), for Quṭb, is not only doctrinal, philosophical or metaphysical but equally political. For, the *shahādah* entails and requires, first, that the Muslims live all aspects and details of their life in accordance with Islam; secondly, that they call other individuals to Islam; and, thirdly, that they act in order to establish the political regime that is conducive to the realization of the Islamic concept and to erect the life of humanity on the Islamic order- elaborated in the following *Chapter*. It is not enough for Quṭb that Islam resides in the conscience and heart or serves as an ethical code, but he insists on seeing Islam as

> *a creative movement aiming at establishing a human life unknown before it or to any other system... This creative movement stems from a specific concept of life in all its values and relations... It is a movement born in the depth of the conscience, then establishes itself in the world of reality. The movement is imperfect until it materializes in the world of reality.*[55]

According to Quṭb, as a creative and active movement, Islam has many functions. First, it occupies the human being with energy and work and in the conscience and behavior and "does not leave man to emptiness that will result in anxiety and perplexity or to aimless contemplation that results in nothing but images and contemplation."[56] It stipulates certain functions, spiritual and material- like prayer, fasting, almsgiving. Though one of its most important aspects is its engagement of the mind, soul, conscience, and body, Islam, after furnishing basic foundations and principles, frees the mind to pursue the sciences and to conduct research into the universe. In this sense, the Islamic concept allows the human mind and science to pursue the vast domain of the universe.

Secondly, Qutb views the ultimate function of Islam as the elimination of worshipping any human, physical or metaphysical entity except God. This elimination is a fundamental quest for freedom and liberation. The liberation of man, or "the birth of man", is the liberation from submitting to human laws, legislation, and authority. Before this liberation takes place, the complete and free man is not possible, let alone Nietzsche's superman. And what makes liberation a necessity is that throughout the ages and specifically in our time humanity lives in a vicious circle and is in need of a new experience in life: an experience that goes on delivering mankind from slavery to man to the worship of God alone.[57] The significance of this characteristic, besides the doctrinal, is political and social which requires activism and motivation- two themes discussed in the following *Chapter*.

7 - ***Al-Wāqiʿīyyah*** (Realism): The Islamic concept deals, Quṭb argues, realistically with the world. It does not perceive the world in abstract terms or idealistically. He bases this idea on the following verses:

> *So glory be to God*
> *both in your evening hour and in your morning hour.*
> *He is the praise in the heavens and earth,*
> *alike at the setting sun and in your noontide hour.*
> *He brings forth the living from the dead,*
> *and brings forth the dead from the living,*
> *and He revives the earth after it is dead;*
> *even so you shall be brought forth.*
> *And of his signs is that He created you of dust;*
> *then Lo, you are mortals, all scattered abroad.*

And of His signs is that He created for you,
of yourselves, spouses, that you might repose in them, and
He has set between you love and mercy.
Surely in that are signs for a people who consider.
And of his signs is the creation
of the heavens and earth and the variety of your tongues and hues.
Surely in that are signs for all living beings.
And of his signs is your slumbering
by night and day, and you seeking after His bounty.
Surely in that are signs for a people who hear.
And of His signs He shows you lightning,
for fear and hope,

and that He sends down out of heaven water
and He revives the earth after it is dead.
Surely in that are signs for a people who understand.
And of His signs is that the heaven and earth
stand firm by His command;
then, when He calls you once and suddenly,
out of the earth, lo, you shall come forth.
To Him belongs whosoever is in the heavens and the earth;
all obey His will.

And it is He who originates creation, then brings it back again,
and it is very easy for Him.
His is the loftiest likeness in the heavens and the earth;
He is the All-mighty, the All-wise. — XXX: 17-27
Say: 'Praise belongs to God,
and peace be on His servants
whom he has chosen.'
What, is God better, or that they associate?
He who created the heavens and earth,
and sent down for you out of heaven water;
and We caused to grow therewith
garden full of loveliness
whose trees you could never grow.
Is there a god with God?
Nay, but they are a people who assign to Him equals!
He who made the earth a fixed place

and set amidst it rivers and appointed for it firm mountains and placed a partition between the two seas.
Is there a god with God?
Nay, but the most of them have no knowledge.
He who answers the constrained,
when He calls unto Him,
and removes the evil and appoints you to be successors in the earth. Is there a god with God?
Little indeed do you remember.
He who guides you in the shadows of the land and the sea
and looses the wind, bearing good tidings before His mercy.
Is there a god with God?
High exalted be God, above that which they associate.
Who originates creation,
then brings it back again,
and provides you out of heaven and earth.
Is there a god but God?
Say: 'Produce your proof, if you speak truly.' — XXVII: 59-64

From these verses, Quṭb claims that the Islamic *niẓām* (system)- mentioned above- is realistic because it is possible. In some ways, Quṭb confuses realism with "possibility." Realism for Qutb does not mean that he accepts what exists but that what he accepts (for instance, the Islamic state or a Muslim community) can exist. Thus, the Islamic concept, Quṭb contends, is both *al-wāqiᶜīyyah al-mithālīyyah* (idealistic realism) and *al-mithālīyyah al-wāqᶜīyyah* (realistic idealism.) Idealistic realism means that the concept deals with facts, divine, universal, and human; with this world as it is manifested; and with man as a real being having special characteristics, and not as an abstract supposition. For Islam does not conceive of man as an absolute mind or spirit; unlike rationalism, it does not deal with stipulations that do not pertain to reality, but, unlike material positivism which takes nature as God that created the mind, it is balanced.[58]

This leads us to the second quality. Being realistically idealistic is in relation to the Islamic method given to mankind. Though Islam takes into consideration the abilities and faculties of mankind, Quṭb argues, Islam can uplift humanity to the highest level and the utmost possible human perfection. It is realistic in its demands of man in his life, society, and doctrines, but does not accept life as it is and aims at the advancement and development of human existence. This is so because the crux and axis of "development in Islamic thought is the development of the entire mankind" and opening the doors before it to creativity. Islam does not degrade human pain but it does not use, for instance, "class hatred to cure pain since hatred itself is considered an obstacle" to the progress of mankind.[59]

A corollary to this is that, in order for mankind to advance, it should not dwell on its weaknesses but should instead try to transcend them and to channel its energy towards creativity. Therefore, arts in general and literature in particular, and, for that matter, any social or political thought and system should have positive effects or should be directed in a way that results in positive and useful conclusions.

To clarify this more, in ***Fī al-Tārīkh,*** Quṭb views the arts, for instance, as

> *an expression of living values that the conscience of the artist interacts with. These values may differ from one individual to another. But, in any way, it is derived from a specific concept of life and of relations between man and the universe and between man and man.*[60]

To Quṭb, arts in general should not be studied, performed, and treated only as personal expressions of genius or individuality but also as expressions of values and principles of society. Thus, for instance, if people were to succeed in isolating and studying literature apart from society, they would only find "empty words." Conscious of it or not, individuals are affected by the values they hold in their arts which are, in turn, influenced and derived from people's concept of life. Quṭb concludes, therefore, not only the uselessness and futility of separating arts from the concept of life but also the importance of subjecting arts to the Islamic concept. And because Islam furnishes a specific value system, it is natural that the expression of its arts follows a specific direction in serving the values of Islam.

Furthermore, Islamic arts should not falsify human personality or reality or highlight human life in an idealistically exaggerated way. The Islamic arts that are acceptable to Quṭb are the ones that aim at the truth whether in describing the potential and actual faculties in man or the goals proper to humans. What this means is that Islamic literature and arts are directed not in the compulsory direction suggested by materialistic interpretations of history but are and should be the adaptation of the human soul to the Islamic concept of life.[61]

In fine, Quṭb's argument is, first, that the arts or any other social or political activities should primarily serve the positive values and concepts of a society. Secondly, art is not value-free and should not be considered as such or used as being representative only of individuals or their dreams. Thirdly, Islam prescribes a course that should be followed in all aspects and activities of life, including the arts.

But, in fact, Quṭb's exposition of the arts is not only a prescription for arts but also for any activity: journalism, writing and so forth. Consequently, the arts and the society that Quṭb is advocating will have to be controlled by the state because only the state can enforce those limitations or goals. This control gives the state the liberty to define what Islamic art or writing is, and indirectly, the right of censorship. Though the arts should serve society, Quṭb does not consider that their direction, if controlled by the state, can be very unfruitful. And although the state should encourage the arts that glorify Islam, it should not impose its concept on the individuals. Also, his argument that art is not value-free and therefore is not only representative of individuals and their dreams is not evidence that the artist is chained by his society and cannot produce values that are not new or, even, unacceptable to his society. If that was the case, society would have stood still and no advancement whatsoever could have been made.

2 - A Comparative Analysis of the Philosophies of Islamic Fundamentalism and Islamic Modernism

In order to understand Quṭb's thought, it is important as well to see his place within modern Islamic thought. In dealing with philosophy, science, morality, and religion, Quṭb is reacting to long standing arguments made by his predecessors, fundamentalists and modernists. Quṭb adds to, adopts, and sharpens many of the fundamentalists ideas advocated by al-Mawdūdī and al-Bannā, and rejects many of the modernist ideas as advocated by ᶜAbduh and Iqbāl. For this reason, I will analyze in this section three main sets of principles that make up the intellectual foundations of both Islamic fundamentalism and Islamic modernism. These sets of principles are reason and morality, philosophy and science, and religion. Also, comparing and contrasting these principles reveal the different conceptions of both movements; in fact, the different conceptions of these principles distinguish one movement from the other.

To begin with, notwithstanding its insistence on the existence of moral principles in human nature, fundamentalism emphasizes man's inability to arrive at them by reason. This necessitates the existence of revelation in order that man has an example to follow. For Abū al-'Aᶜlā al-Mawdūdī and Quṭb, innate human intuition or *fiṭrah,* the recipient of revelation, is nothing but the obedience to dominant forces that created the law which is controlled by God for the well-being of this universe. Although the function of *fiṭrah* is to direct man to the good, they view man as having diverted his natural drive and forgotten the *fiṭrah* and replaced them by will and choice. For man has involved himself in a domain (philosophy) that, although supported by reason and argument, has led him to wrong conclusions symbolized in his worship of stars, gods, ideals, idols, abstract ideas, and world forces. Nonetheless, they assert that man looks by nature for God; and, as much as he seeks water and shelter, he does also seek God. Put simply, moral laws, residing in the *fiṭrah* are intuitive and are as natural as physical laws. For instance, al-Mawdūdī contends that humans agree that a society that is well-administered, enjoys cooperation, mutuality, consultation, social justice, and equality is a good society; also humans agree that theft, adultery, murder, spying, jealousy and so forth are evil.[62]

Modernism, on the other hand, maintains the existence of natural and moral laws in nature. These laws, the moral and the natural, are authentic and can be demonstrated by reason. ᶜAli Sharīᶜatī, for instance, argues that, contrary to Marxism which equates moral law with social customs and relates them to social and economic materialism, Islam attempts to attribute moral laws to the primordial nature of man.[63] This means that it can be found by reason. Jamāl al-Dīn al-Afghānī insists on the existence in man of an urge to rise above bestiality or lust and to improve his life. This does not take place by following *fiṭrah* only but primarily by the pursuit of knowledge and cultivation of those arts and skills which have been the works of civilization. In particular, the Muslims should pursue progress which is manifest in the study of science; for solid moral and religious grounds require not only religion but also solid knowledge.[64]

The difference between the modernists and the fundamentalists can be summarized in the following statement. Whereas Quṭb and al-Mawdūdī consider the secrets of human nature as known to God only, Al-Afghānī, ᶜAbduh, Iqbāl, and Sharīᶜatī consider man as capable of attaining some, if not all, of those secrets. This difference is due to their conception of reason. For the concept of *fiṭrah* which is interwoven with the concept of reason manifests itself in al-Mawdūdī's, al-Bannā's, and Quṭb's argument that the Muslim should submit to God in everything. Those individuals who do not submit but ask God for logical proofs and do not obey when dissatisfied with the proofs are infidels. This is so because Islam, for the fundamentalists, means total submission with or without logical proof and satisfaction. Belief in the day of judgement, for instance, should be adhered to whether a logical proof can be found or not. Although Islam is not opposed to reason, a logical proof should follow belief and not vice versa.[65] For Ḥasan al-Bannā, logical proofs and syllogisms are accepted because the mind is spoken to in the Holy *Qur'ān*, but their service is the defence of religion against myth and distortion. But, more importantly, God's existence is in need of no proof; it is intuitive. And the question "who created God" is a misguided question- for humans are incapable of understanding themselves, let alone God. Belief is by definition the heart's submission and tranquility with certainty.[66]

The modernists agree that religion is intuitive more than volitional, but perceive that reason and religion are in harmony. According to Muḥammad ᶜAbduh, the Muslims in general have agreed that some issues in religion cannot be believed in except through reason as in knowing, for instance, God's existence and God's ability to send messengers. Also, the Muslims have agreed that religion forwards high principles that man cannot understand easily; but religion does not forward principles that are opposite to reason. For instance, man can prove that God exists but reason cannot understand the essence of God. This stems from man's inability to understand himself. Thus, Islam is the religion of oneness, and reason is one of its strongest helpers.[67]

Religion, according to ᶜAbduh, is the strongest factor in morality and one of the greatest human forces; for it influences the majority more than reason does. More importantly, reason is the source for the knowledge of religion and for using it; but once belief is attained, the Prophet should be followed.[68] Similarly, for Iqbāl, while religion starts with feeling, it has never taken itself as a matter of feeling alone and has constantly striven after metaphysics. Religion is not a compartmental affair, mere feeling or mere action, but is an expression of the whole man. In Islam, the ideal and the real are not two separate or opposite forces but Islam attempts to bridge the gap between the ideal and the real where the ideal absorbs eventually the real.[69] Similarly, Sharīᶜatī defines Islam as a profound spiritual, idealistic, intelligible, and logical interpretation of the universe fully attuned to earthly reality and to divinity.

The major difference here is that whereas the fundamentalists preceive Islam as a comprehensive system that is self-proven and self-contained and, thus, requires no logical proof, the modernists accept the principle of arriving at truth by proof, i.e., philosophy. Thus, ᶜAbduh allows individuals to seek proofs, but once attained the individuals need to submit to the Prophet's teachings. Put differently, the fundamentalists disclaim the ability of human reason to arrive at any metaphysical truth without the aid of revelation, while the modernists find that reason can arrive at moral and metaphysical truths by reason (and by the whole being).

The explanation for this opposed understanding is related to the difference in the modernists' and fundamentalists' conceptions of *tawḥīd* and the purpose of Islam. For instance, al-Mawdūdī and Quṭb define Islam as a program of life according to the rule of nature given by God and as the expression that aims at constructing the superstructure for the whole of humanity on the *ḥākimīyyah* or governance of God. Viewing *tawḥīd* as the fundamental component of Islam and not only as a religious creed but, more importantly, as the elimination of systems based on the basis of human independence on earthly affairs from the governance of God, it should lead to complete transformation in the life of individuals and societies. Also, it indicates that God is the creator, the governor, and controller, of this universe and negates the government of man, class, and race.[70] Thus, an essential part of the fundamentalists' conception of *tawḥīd* is the negation of and opposition to any man-made system and order or to *al-jāhilīyyah*. Their perspective, moreover, denies any meaningful search or research in this universe since they believe that everything is clear and given.

But viewing *tawḥīd* in a more constructive way, the modernists make it their starting point to seek fulfillment and understanding. Because not everything is given, man has to exert himself, they do not use *tawḥid* as an instrument of negation and opposition but as, to paraphrase Iqbāl, a working force for the establishment of equality, solidarity and freedom. Iqbāl even considers the state as no more than an attempt to establish these principles into a definite organization.[71] For Sharīᶜatī *tawḥīd* means viewing the whole universe as a single living and conscious organism that possesses intelligence, will, purpose and feeling.[72]

Iqbāl and Sharīᶜatī's definitions of *tawḥīd* allow and even encourage the principle of philosophizing, but do not accept every philosophy. For instance, Sharīᶜatī argues that the method of attaining truth is to invent "a method of investigation" useful for the discovery of truth. Although, according to Sharīᶜatī, Plato's philosophy is more sophisticated than Descartes', the latter was a more useful one.[73] Iqbāl, for example, contends that the birth of Islam is anti-classical and that the Muslim philosophers did not understand Islam, which they read in the light of the Greek thought. For Islam asks its adherents to use their sense perception and mind to understand the world, while the philosophers despised sense-perception. Furthermore, Islam encourages empirical approaches to knowledge, but science has a sectional character and is unable to furnish a complete knowledge. Thus, the concept of mechanism is inadequate for the analysis of life. But still Iqbāl believes that the religious and the scientific, although they follow different methods, aim at the real.[74] His rejection is directed at materialism and speculative philosophy, not at every intellectual or spiritual pursuit.

In fact, modernist Muslim thinkers perceived philosophy essentially in terms of science. For instance, ᶜAbduh's argument that Islam cannot contradict reason means that it cannot contradict science. For he believes that the domain of reason is not speculation but the scientific field. Although reason and revelation are compatible, those thinkers who tried to harmonize revelation and philosophical proofs about God's existence and essence went too far; their speculations cannot be ascertained. But science, on the other hand, can be ascertained; therefore, when ᶜAbduh says there is harmony between reason and revelation, reason is equivalent to science.[75] Al-Afghānī as well makes science the ultimate judge not only when the *Qur'ān* is obscure or controversial but also when the *Qu'rān* contradicts science. Because the *Qur'ān* provides very general principles, it should not contradict "the stipulation of reason and the achievement of science. Interpretation is the method to solve the contradiction between science and the *sharīᶜah.*"[76]

Fundamentalism views science differently. For instance, al-

Mawdūdī asserts that Islam does not prohibit benefiting from human experiments, but experimental science is biased and is not pan-human. Science, which was started in the West, is directed towards nationalism, moral confusion, and atheism.[77] Although al-Bannā and Quṭb agree with some of his conclusion (like the direction of science), they view science as pan-human and accept its benefits; for they believe that the Muslims have contributed to it.

In one way or another, and notwithstanding some objections, the modernist thinkers accept modern Western thought based on science by subjecting the interpretation of the Holy *Qur'ān* and religion in general to scientific discoveries; thus, for instance, *al-jin* becomes equivalent to the modern scientific term "microbes." Their rejections of medieval thought should be viewed in this manner; for they subject medieval and ancient philosophy as well as Muslim theology and thought to science. The modernists replace speculative philosophy, which the medieval thinkers depended on for the exposition of their ideas, with philosophy of science. But in fact, they erect a very unstable criterion for the interpretation of revelation which reflects the inadequacy of their understanding of science; they could not see that science is of tentative nature and that what is a correct theory today may be obsolete tomorrow. If the theory of modern science is based now on atomism, perhaps the future will produce another theory; and, thus, it seems unreasonable to change our understanding of revelation with the change of science. Iqbāl, for instance, suggests the rewriting of Islamic theology on the basis of science. One of the particulars he gives is the verse in the Holy *Qur'ān* where God is likened to light. Usually, this verse has been used by some scholars to mean omnipresence, but Iqbāl thinks that, because of the discoveries in physics, it should be interpreted as absoluteness. His argument runs as follows: Modern physics teaches that the velocity of light cannot be exceeded and is the same for all observers. Since light is the nearest approach to the absolute, the metaphor of light as applied to God must be viewed as a suggestion of absoluteness of God and not of his omnipresence.[78]

The modernists' emphasis on science for the validity of

interpreting revelation leads to the rejection of the traditional, theological, and philosophical understandings and to the acceptance of new philosophical and theological interpretations that are based only on science. And, in a way, their arguments strengthen the influence of secular leaders and thinkers who attempt to erect society on science which they perceive as the only method for progress. In another way, moral philosophy and religious precepts are weakened insofar as they have to seek the authority of science. But, science, assuming its correctness, is incapable of providing morality and metaphysics. Knowing that from an Islamic viewpoint God is neither a body nor in a body, it does not make a difference whether the metaphor of God as light is interpreted as absolutenss or omnipresence. For the moral obligation to obey God's teachings does not change or affect the theory of light which has nothing to do with a metaphysical understanding of God. Whether the light travels in particles or in straight lines has no bearing on God's essence and attributes or even moral laws. In Islam, God simply does not exist in any spatio-temporal locality.

Consequently, because science constitutes an essential part of the modernists' new theology that judges the correctness of Islamic teachings and principles, their thought is partly based on a very unstable premise. On the other hand, the Muslim fundamentalists disclaimed any instrumentality or validity for science as a theological or exegetical or interpretive power over scripture. They were more aware of the damage that science can cause if considered as a criterion for interpreting revelation. But their alternative is an impoverishment; an impoverishment resulting from denying not only science for a correct understanding of revelation but also of philosophy, theology, and, even, history which is important for understanding the scripture itself. For it seems illogical to deny, for instance, the imporance of history for understanding the Holy *Qur'an* since the actual writing and the transmission of the *Qur'ān* as well as their accuracy depend on historical accuracy. Also, discrediting history leads as well to the weakening of the Prophet's *sunnah* since its validity depends as well on historical transmission. But the fundamentalists accept both the accuracy of the *Qur'ān* and the *sunnah;* a notion that underscores their inability to perceive the danger of denying the importance and validity of diverse disciplines of knowledge.[79]

Furthermore, how could Islam be understood if important disciplines of knowledge (like history and philosophy) are neglected? The fundamentalists answer, "human nature" *(fiṭrah)*. But it is not a credible criterion since its definition is channelled through a vicious circle: human nature guides man to the right things, but will and choice divert him from the true nature. If *tawḥīd* is in human nature, there would be no atheists. But since they argue that some individuals are guided and others misguided, they should have insisted that the knowledge of the constitution of true nature needs to be derived from the Holy *Qur'ān* without reference to human nature. The fundamentalists would have been correct if they said that man had the potential to follow the true nature that was to be found in the Holy *Qur'ān*. In other words, they should have made the *Qur'an* the only definitive exposition of good nature.

The modernist concept of *tawḥīd* is more adequate than the fundamentalist since, although they reject traditional theology, they still accept the principle of philosophizing. At least, they understand that the problems in contemporary Islam do not stem from the existence of philosophies and theologies but from their underdevelopment or absence in the Muslim world. Thus, they attribute the backwardness of the Muslims to the neglect of innovations in thought and science. But the problem with the modernists' exposition of Islam is their inability to formulate new theories; they are content with general comments and teachings. The two thinkers who attempted to write philosophy, Iqbāl and Ali Sharīᶜatī, have only written philosophical treatises that do not amount to a coherent system or a systematic philosophy.

3 - The Evaluation of the Foundations of Quṭb's Thought

Apparently, to Sayyid Quṭb the ultimate source of knowledge is God. But God's essence and manner of existence can neither be comprehended nor understood by human thought. The validity of human knowledge depends on its conformity to nature. But the true essence of nature cannot be known either. All our knowledge, according to Quṭb, is the knowledge of facts; and questions of the "why" and the "how" are not answerable by humans; the alternative is the acceptance of God's revelation. Because of God's knowledge of man's inability to comprehend the ultimate truth, revelation is no more than allusions to truth; the most attainable by humans. Revelation is validated by its conformity to nature which is not known in its entirety. Therefore, Quṭb has recourse to *fiṭrah* to argue for the validity or invalidity of any idea or system. But the norms of *fiṭrah* are to be found in the Holy *Qur'ān*. This is Quṭb's most important argument for attaining and verifying the truth. But, the circularity of this argument denies its components (revelation, nature, and *fiṭrah*) any possibility of verification. In following this argument, one is struck by one's inability to find a meaningful and solid starting point. One time, man's *fiṭrah* is treated as the source of verification of truth; but, another time, it is distorted because it has failed to arrive at truth. In other words although it functions as repository of truth, *fiṭrah* is not true unless it finds truth. But it seems, as a matter of fact, that truth cannot be ascertaine

Quṭb pronounces his sentence of the unproductivity of and the impossibility of knowledge by philosophizing. Philosophy, he states, is not for man; the proper field of study for man is what is practical. The philosopher, Quṭb believes, has put himself in a place where there is no light except what God has given him. But this light, i.e., reason, should not be used in philosophizing but in the fields of useful knowledge. Quṭb's view on the impossibility and unproductivity of philosophy is the result of his understanding of philosophy as that branch of knowledge that tries to tell us why things happen as they do as opposed to science that can tell us how things happen. But Quṭb is unaware that the whole endeavor of philosophy is viewed by some philosophers such as Hume and Wittgenstein as a mistaken or untenable pursuit.

If philosophy is concerned with relationships between eternal entities which are, for Plato, the only entities about which it is possible to have knowledge, then Quṭb who first rejects the concept of eternal entities and, secondly, does not believe in the ability of man to attain that knowledge if it did exist, is justified in rejecting philosophy as an adequate or proper method of attaining truth. But in fact, the notion of the unknowability of God by reason is not alien to philosophy. On the contrary, if one looks carefully one will find that this notion is very familiar to and adopted by some philosophers. Furthermore, philosophy is not one unified discipline which one might think of when reading the philosophies of Aristotle, al-Fārābī, and Averroes, which are essentially rational and critical, with logic as their crux. There is another kind of philosophy which is openly- as Quṭb is- hostile to speculative analysis and professes to arrive at general conclusions by a direct, personal intuition or other means.

Notwithstanding his rejection of philosophy, not only has Quṭb philosophized but his thought is influenced by modern Western philosophers. Many of his ideas suggested to revive Islam are nothing but the products of Western thought, like historicism or positivism- as manifested in his understanding of the relation between ideas and history. It would have been unthinkable for those ideas to have originated in the Muslim world due to its stagnation. And although he would argue that his ideas are taken from the Holy *Qur'ān*, its seems that those ideas are liable to different interpretations (which actually happened in the history of Islam). But his interpretation is distinctly influenced by Western historicism and positivism and filtered through Islamic criteria. Quṭb would have done better if he did not announce that his ideas are taken completely from the Holy *Qur'ān* since he himself believes in the dependence of ideas on historical circumstances.

Quṭb believes that there are some parts of nature that are inaccessible to human thought, i.e., the unknowable, because man's realization is limited by nature. Recalling Quṭb's definition of knowledge and comparing it with empiricism and rationalism, we find that what is missing from rationalism and empiricism is a comprehensive and conclusive definition of knowledge or truth; as such, Quṭb argues, they are deficient. They are deficient because thought is not the only instrument that receives the divine concept of oneness of God and unity of the universe, but, more importantly, the entire being. Hence, neither empiricism nor rationalism can be satisfactory for Quṭb as the proper instrument or an adequate expression of knowledge. On the other hand, the function of the human mind and reason should be restricted to being a "valuable and great instrument" for realizing the characteristics of the Islamic concept and "as a judge in matters and values concerned with this concept." It is an instrument of receiving, understanding, adapting, and implementing the divine concept. It follows that for Quṭb reason's function is instrumental in attaining and as a receptacle of what exists. Instrumentality is very central in Quṭb's thought. In the absence of Qur'anic injunctions, Quṭb falls back on the effects of ideas and institutions for discerning their validity or invalidity. Quṭb argues, for instance, that progress is part of nature; but the kind of progress he accepts is not whatever is labelled progress but what is conducive to a virtuous life. Thus, ideas are not important as such but in terms of utility. For instance, the science of a time is those stipulations that turn out to be those ideas that can withstand criticism, and thus appear to us as certain. But these are nothing more than approximations to truth. These approximations vary from one age to another, and thus, Quṭb rejects the founding of religion on science or the sifting of the former by the latter. But still science is perceived as an instrument of force and power which the Muslims should seek.

Quṭb has attempted to bring two disciplines together: the religious experience of believing and the practical experience of science as the underlying basis of the new Islamic society: the religious principles provide the unchangeable foundations of the society, science, the practical and changeable needs of society. Consequently, science cannot lead to the sources of moral and metaphysical knowledge but should concern itself with testable things. In other words, though scientific theories are hypotheses and not indubitable knowledge, they can be used to pursue progress. Also, for Quṭb, the rationality of sciences is not only their critical and progressive character but also their in being directed toward serving the underlying principles of a society. Pure epistemology is not pure as one might think but is the outcome of preconceived notions.

For Quṭb, there is no presuppositionless knowledge; all knowledge presupposes a prior understanding of the whole. Quṭb criticizes the ideal of objectivity and insists on the historical character of all understanding; for understanding is conditioned by time, space, environment, and culture. Thus, for instance, claims that the Holy *Qur'ān* permits man to be the lawgiver are rejected by Quṭb who argues that there is no verse to support this. In other words, this is not a different interpretation of the Holy *Qur'ān* but is a total disregard of the *Qur'ān*. But if someone claims, for instance, that the Qur'anic concept of freedom is the freedom from lusts and human laws and, if someone else claims that freedom in the *Qur'ān* means the absence of riches and accumulation of wealth and so forth, Quṭb would argue that their understanding is different- and not necessarily better, except insofar as they help maintain or destabilize society.

Although Quṭb disregards the possibility of understanding the ultimate source of knowledge, God, he nonetheless believes in His existence; for our comprehension of the real source of knowledge is unattainable by observation and accumulation of facts and data because our ignorance is infinite. And though the truth of God's existence has to be justified to an extent, it is ultimately above human authority. Paradoxically, this unattainable knowledge, i.e., the unchangeable and divine knowledge, is the foundation of the Islamic state.

Moreover, Quṭb veiws knowledge as understanding, interaction, and application, but this is only human knowledge. Objective knowledge, truth, and the divine knowledge are not possible. For Quṭb, the two kinds of knowledge, the divine and the human, are not the same except incidentally, for understanding (or human knowledge) is subjective and can and does change with time, place, and social environment. On the other hand, true or divine knowledge is objective, but is unattainable. This is so because, for Quṭb, all understanding is grounded in language and is rooted in a situation; thus, situatedness and historicity and the finitude of understanding underlie all human thought. Revelation is not human, it is divine. The conclusion is that the divine, i.e., revelation, does not change, but the human, the understanding of revelation, changes with time and the situation.

For Quṭb, "the distinction between theory and praxis, thinking and doing" is basically theoretical more than practical. Understanding, for him, is not only for reflection but also for perception and experience (the three stages of knowledge, mentioned above). A proper understanding of the past for Quṭb requires standing in a still operant history. This is to say that historical consciousness is imperative for understanding the past as well as the present; for this reason, he charges that the medieval and modern Muslim thinkers did not understand Western thought. Quṭb contributes and shares with contextualism; he insists that understanding is relative to circumstances. Rational interpretation for Quṭb does not end with personal preferences, but the interpretation has to be justified within the context of the original as well as the new context. But since no context is permanent, different interpretations become possible.

Now, since understanding is conditioned by preunderstanding, Quṭb's argument itself has a conditional character. Therefore, we see that Quṭb allows the possibility of different interpretations if they are based on the text i.e., the Holy *Qur'ān*. But his acceptance of the changeability of interpretation is not to make everything conventional or arbitrary. Quṭb's hermeneutic theory does justice to both the historicity of interpretation and to the experience of truth in understanding. It is important to keep in mind that Quṭb is not necessarily disputing that there are facts; he is disputing certain claims made about those facts. Scientific and historical facts per se are not under attack. What is rejected is the unhistorical methodology or the possibility of a viewpoint outside history.

Quṭb believes that more than a mere subjective assertion of

belief is needed to make an interpretation true but it must take into account the intersubjective conditions of something to be true. Instead of being actually attained- and we know for Quṭb it is not attainable- truth is considered as necessary. This regulative concept (the universal Islamic concept) allows the possibility of inadequate present knowledge and of criticism- which Quṭb has done. At the same time, it allows the possibility of meaningful assertion that an interpretation is true. Consequently, interpretation is not the representation of a thing in itself but a function of social agreement. For this reason, Quṭb insists on the existence of the ideal community for the existence of truth. The ideal community will adhere to the inherent moral order based on universal law that is taught in the Holy *Qur'ān*. But we must remember that the only way to know this inherent order is to follow the Holy *Qur'ān* and is not a matter of speculation or experimentation.

Quṭb's insistence on the application (action) of understanding means that the interpreter must apply his understanding consciously to a present situation. Quṭb's hermeneutic theory does not make criticism impossible. The movement of interpretation or, what Quṭb called, "evolving understanding" requires awareness of the shadows on the text of old interpretations. But because understanding is always partial, each interpretation sheds light on a portion of the text. Therefore, the real force of Quṭb's hermeneutic theory is the necessity of the existence of evolving understanding; and this results from criticism. Consequently, Quṭb's and other fundamentalists' deviation from the norms of society is not necessarily an evil action since the norms themselves are in question. Quṭb's method is a call for a methodological self-reflection on the part of individuals; his attack on science is interpretive and is not antiscientific. But constant criticism would give-and has given-a negative picture of fundamentalism.

Finally, because philosophy for Quṭb is a reduction of the possibility of truth, Quṭb emphasizes truth rather than validity and transforms aesthetics into hermeneutics. For instance, when art was discussed above, Quṭb's interest was not in whether a specific art is well-ordered or beautiful but in the conditions by which the work came to be understood and interpreted. Moreover, Quṭb argues that knowledge should have practical effects and should aim at action. His rejection of philosophy, classical or modern, whether rationalism or positivism, is motivated by his insistence that true knowledge should, first, lead to action and, second, meet the spiritual as well as the material needs of mankind. He tells us that "from knowledge we seek action, we seek to transform this knowledge to a momentum in order to achieve its meaning in reality;"[80] the Muslims do not seek passive knowledge.

Attempting to untangle what has just been said shows the following points. First, Quṭb calls knowledge derived from sense experience passive and perceives that will and understanding are one. Consequently, the passivity of knowledge is the result or a sign of the inadequacy of our ideas and concepts. Activity on the part of the mind and the body is a sign of the adequacy of the idea or concept. Thus, in connecting truth or adequacy and activities together Quṭb underlines the importance of action and its relation to truth- a theme much advocated by the fundamentalists. Secondly, for Quṭb, thought is for the sake of action. The ultimate emphasis in Quṭb's thought is obedience and conformity to God's laws and nature- which requires action- and is not contemplation or deliberation.

Footnotes:

1 Quṭb, *Fī al-Tārīkh: Fikrah wa Minhāj* (On History: an Idea and a Method), (Al-Qāhirah: Dār al-Shurūq, 1974), p. 22, (hereafter cited as *Fī al-Tārīkh*).

2 Quṭb, *Khaṣā'iṣ al-Taṣawwur al-Islāmī wa Muqawwamātuhu* (The Characteristics and Components of the Islamic Concept), Vol. I (Al-Qāhirah: ᶜIssa al-Ḥalabī, n.d.), pp. 3-4 (hereafter cited as *Khaṣā'is*). For a good discussion on the difference between *manhaj* and *niẓām*, see William E. Shepard's article "Islam as a 'system' in the Later Writings of Sayyid Quṭb", *Middle Eastern Studies,* Vol. 25, No. 1, Jan. 1989, pp. 31-50.

3 Quṭb, *Khaṣā'is*, p. 228; and, see pp. 211-222. See also footnote 46. For an example of how Quṭb uses the Holy *Qur'ān* to justify his own thought, see below, pp. 94-97. The quotation is from Sayyid Quṭb, *Mūqawwamāt al-Taṣawwur al-Islāmī* (The components of the Islamic concept), (Bayrūt and Al-Qāhirah: Dār al-Shurūq, 1986), pp. 81-82; see also, pp. 18, 84, 99, 100, 112, 126, 147-149, 187-192. Translations are cited from *The Koran Interpreted,* lst ed., 1955 by Arthur J. Arberry (New York: The Macmillan Company, 3rd. repr. 1969).

4 Quṭb, *Al-Mustaqbal li-Hādhā al-Dīn,* pp. 12-14, and *Khaṣā'is*, pp. 212-15 where Islam is contrasted with other religions like Christianity and Buddism. Also, see footnote 5.

5 Quṭb, *Al-Mustaqbal,* pp. 15-17.

6 Quṭb, *Fī al-Tārīkh,* pp. 26-27. See also Quṭb, *Mūqawwamāt,* pp. 24-25.

7 Quṭb, *Hādhā al-Dīn* (This Religion), (Al-Qāhirah: Maktabat Wahbah, 4th. ed., n.d.), p. 6; also, pp. 7 & 22-23, Contrast his opinions with al-Fārābī who argues like Aristotle that God is an intellect thinking itself. In Him, the subject and object of thinking are the same; (see, for instance, *Arā' Ahl al-Madīnah al-Fāḍilah* (The Opinions of the People of the Virtuous City), (Al-Qāhirah: Maktabat Muḥammad ᶜAlī Ṣubḥ, n.d.) *Chapter V,* (hereafter cited as *The Virtuous City*). Also, see *Chapter I* where God is described as an intellect; and, on emanation, see *Chapters VII & VIII.* Now, God's description as an intellect is itself, from a traditional and from a fundamentalist point of view, is a presumption of knowing God. See also, Quṭb, *Muqqawwamāt,* pp. 44-48.

8 Quṭb, *Khaṣā'is*, p. 16.

9 *Ibid.,* p. 50; see also, pp., 45-49. Also, see, *Mūqawwamāt,* pp. 187-188, 37-38.

10 In fact, Sayyid Quṭb shows a poor understanding of the role of prophecy. Other individuals (non-Muslims) show a better understanding of the role of prophecy, Kenneth Cragg, *Counsels in Contemporary Islam* (Edinburgh: Edinburgh University Press, 1956), 167-81; on the perception of the *Qur'an*

and the prophet (not only as a mouthpiece), see H.A.R. Gibb, *Muhammadanism* (New York: Oxford University Press, reprint, 1976), pp. 49-59.

11 Muhsin Mahdi, tr., *Al-Farabi Philosophy of Plato and Aristotle* (N.Y.: Cornell University Press. 1969), pp. 45-46; also, see pp. 46, 47. See also al-Fārābī's *The Virtuous City,* chapter 25. For an analysis of al-Fārābī's and others' prophetic theory, see Charles E. Butterworth, "Philosophy, Stories, and the Study of Elites," in *Elites in the Middle East,* ed. William Zartman (N.Y: Praeger Publishers, 1980).

12 On philosophy and knowledge, see Quṭb, *Khaṣā'is*, pp. 9-11, 27 & 49-51, and on imagination, paganism, and religion, see *ibid.*, pp. 52-53 & 66-67. Also, Quṭb, *Al-ᶜAdālah al-Ijtimā ᶜīyyah fī al-Islām* (Social justice in Islam), 7th ed. (Al-Qāhirah: Dār al-Shurūq, 1980), (hereafter cited as *al-ᶜAdālah*), p. 24. On the soul as understood by Muslim philosophers, see Maḥmūd Qāsim, *Dirāsāt fī al-Falsafah al-Islāmīyyah* (Studies on Islamic Philosophy), (Al-Qāhirah: Dār al-Maᶜārif, 4th. ed., 1972), pp. 13-52. On the authority of Islam as a religion of certainty in opposition to human invention, see also the Qur'anic verses quoted in *Khaṣā'is*, (pp. 27-28); for instance, II: 83-85, 92-93.

13 Quṭb does not prove that Islamic philosophy is Greek, but asserts it. But no body can fail to see that the Muslim philosophers followed the line of thinking of the ancient philosophers. See, for instance, *Al-Farabi Philosophy,* pp. 13-5 & 32-3 & 44-48, and compare with the references to Plato, pp. 35, 45, 48. For al-Fārābī's preference for philosophy over religion, see pp. 44-48. See also al-Fārābī, *The Virtuous City,* Part I and *passim.* Also, see al-Fārābī, *Rasā'il al-Fārābī* (The Treatises of al-Fārābī), (India: Maṭbaᶜat Majlis Dā'irat al-Maᶜārif al-ᶜUthmānīyyah, 1926), First Treatise, where al-Fārābī argues that the uncaused existence, the active intellect, the heavenly forces, and the human souls are not in a body, do not die or become corrupt, comprehend essences, and enjoy non-material happiness. For an attack on the subjects of immortality, active intellect, and the destiny of the soul as understood by the Muslim philosophers, see al-Ghazālī, *Tahāfut al-Falāsifah* (Incoherence of the Philosophers). For a rebuttal of al-Ghazālī's attacks on the philosophers, see Averroes, *Tahāfut al-Tahāfut* (Incoherence of the Incoherence). For a secondary source, see, for example, Charles E. Butterworth, "Elites," and on Averroes's political philosophy, idem, "New Light on the Political Philosophy of Averroes," pp. 118-127 in George Hourani, *Essays On Islamic Philosophy and Science* (New York: State University of New York Press, 1975). On Philosophy, the *Qur'an*, and their interaction, see, Georges Anawati, "Philosophy, Theology, and Mysticism," in Joseph Schacht, *The Legacy of Islam* (Oxford: Oxford University Press, 1974), pp. 350-58.

14 On the Arabs, their societies, political organization and religion before Islam, see Bernard Lewis, *The Arabs in History,* 1st. ed. 1958 (N.Y: Harper

& Row Publishers, 1966), pp. 21-35, and Philip Hitti, *History of the Arabs,* 1st. ed. 1937 (N.Y: St. Martin's Press, 10th. ed. 1981), 23-29. On the role of the Prophet Muḥammad in changing or preserving pre-Islamic traditions, see Marshall Hodgson, *The Venture of Islam,* Vol. 1 "The Classical Age," (Chicago: Chicago University Press, 1974), pp. 103-46.

15 Quṭb, *Mūqawwamāt,* pp. 44-46, and idem, *Al-Mustaqbal,* pp. 57-58; also, see idem, *Al-^{c}Adālah*, p. 196.

16 Quṭb, *Al-Mustaqbal,* p. 13. Also, see, Quṭb, *Hādhā al-Dīn*, pp. 20-22; see also pp. 24-26.

17 Quṭb, *Al-^{c}Adāldah,* p. 24; also, see also pp. 25-29.

18 On the need for a well-ordered society, see, Plato, *Republic,* for instance, 505a-c; 521 a & *passim*.

19 Quṭb, *Al-Mustaqbal,* pp. 11-13 & 57-61. In fact, many other references can be given on the *fiṭrah* and its importance, see, for instance, idem, *Khaṣā'iṣ*, pp. 4, 51, 83, 114, 127, 133, 134, 135, 137, 146-47, 166-67, 206, 207, 210; and, idem, *Hādhā al-Dīn,* p. 11.

20 Quṭb, *Al-Mustaqbal,* pp. 17-18.

21 Quṭb, *Fī al-Tārīkh,* pp. 14-16. Also, see Quṭb, *Al-^{c}Adālah,* p. 18 and *Hādhā al-Dīn,* pp. 4-6.

22 Quṭb, *Al-Mustaqbal,* p. 10; and see p. 11. *Mūqawwamāt,* pp. 61-62.

23 Quṭb, *Khaṣā'iṣ*, pp. 50 & 88. see, also, Quṭb, *Mūqawwamāt,* pp. 30-32.

24 *Ibid.*, pp. 89-90.

25 Quṭb, *Ma^{c}ālim fī al-Ṭarīq,* pp. 24-25. See also idem, *Al-Mustaqbal,* pp. 11, 58; idem, *Hādhā al-Dīn,* p. 11.

26 Quṭb, *Khaṣā'is* pp. 98-107.

27 *Ibid.,* p. 84. Quṭb dismisses Darwinism on the ground that it has been revised and has not proved its thesis.

28 *Ibid.*, p. 84.

29 *Ibid.,* p. 97. See also, Quṭb, *Mūqawwamāt,* pp. 61-62.

30 Quṭb, *Khaṣā'is*, pp. 96-100, and Quṭb, *Al-Mustaqbal,* pp. 58-66.

31 Quṭb, *Al-Mustaqbal,* pp. 32 33 & 13-52, and, Quṭb, *Khaṣā'iṣ*, pp. 13 & 17. Also, idem, *Ma^{c}rakat al-Islām wa-al-Ra'simālīyyah*, pp. 56, 64.

32 Quṭb, *Khaṣā'is*, p. 141, and compare with Herbert Spencer, *First Principles* (New York, 1910), in particular, pp. 56, 103. See also Quṭb, *Mūqawwamāt,* pp. 198, 24-25.

33 Quṭb, *Ma^{c}ālim,* pp. 140-41. Also, see Quṭb, *Mūqawwamāt,* pp. 46, 61-63.

34 Quṭb, *Khaṣā'iṣ*, p. 115, and Quṭb, *Mūqawwamāt,* pp. 50-51.

35 Quṭb, *Khaṣā'iṣ*, pp. 115. In fact, this opinion is well accepted in

sociolinguistics, see, for instance, Peter Trudgill, *Sociolinguistics* (N. Y.: Penguin Books, 1974), pp. 1, 24-25 & 32.

36 Quṭb, *Khaṣā'iṣ*, pp. 20-22, 63, and *passim*. Also, see, Quṭb *Muqawwamāt,* pp. 51-60. For further analysis on Iqbāl and ᶜAbduh, see also the *Comparative Analysis* in this *Chapter;* Butterworth, "Prudence verses Legitimacy," in A. Dessouki, ed., *Islamic Resurgence in the Arab World* (N. Y: Praeger Publishers, 1982); M. A. Zaki Badawi, *The Reformers of Egypt* (London: Croom Helm, 1976), particularly, *Chapter Two,* pp. 57-59; and, Muhsin Mahdi, "Islamic Philosophy in Contemporary Islamic Thought," in *Man and God in Contemporary Islam,* ed. Charles Malik (Beirut: American University, 1972). On contemporary philosophy in Islam, see Mahdi, "Islamic Philosophy", especially, p. 105, Hamid Enayat, *Modern Islamic Political Thought* (Austin: Texas University Press, 1982), especially, p. 15. On al-Afghānī's acceptance of the benefits of the West and of Islam, see al-Afghānī and ᶜAbduh, *Al-ᶜUrwah al-Wuthqah* (Most Tight Bond), (Al-Qāhirah: Dār al-ᶜArab, 1957), p. 10 and Butterworth, "Legitimacy," pp. 87-90, and his rejection of some aspects of Western thought, see Majid Fakhry, *A History of Islamic Philosophy* (New York: Columbia University Press, 1970), p. 372. Also, for secondary sources on the role of al-Afghānī, ᶜAbduh, and Iqbāl, see Cragg, *Counsels,* pp. 15-67.

37 Iqbal, *The Reconstruction of Religious Thought in Islam* (Lahore: Ashraf, 1960), pp. 59 & 63.

38 Quṭb, *Khaṣā'iṣ*, p. 21. Also, See Quṭb, *Al-Mustaqbal.* pp. 2-13.

39 Iqbal, *The Reconstruction of Religious Thought in Islam,* p. 123 and *passim.*

40 Quṭb, *Khaṣā'iṣ*, pp. 15-16.

41 Quṭb, *Al-Mustaqbal,* pp. 16-26; and Quṭb, *Khaṣā'iṣ*, pp. 107-9.

42 Quṭb, *Khaṣā'iṣ*, pp. 110-125.

43 *Ibid.*, p. 126-27.

44 Quṭb, Al-*Mustaqbal,* pp. 12 & 17.

45 Quṭb, *Khaṣā'iṣ*, pp. 113, 127-30 & 134-39.

46 *Ibid.*, pp. 134 & 140-41.

47 *Ibid.*, p. 136.

48 Al-Ghazālī, *Tahāfut al-Falāsifah,* trans. Ahmad Kamali (Lahore: Pakistan Philosophical Congress, 1963), p. 19. Also, see idem, *Al-Munqidh min al-Ḍalāl* (Salvation from Error), (Al-Qāhirah: Maktabat al-Jundī, 1973), pp. 46-9. These two books are important for those interested in Islamic philosophy and philosophy in general. See also, Quṭb, *Khaṣā'iṣ*, pp. 10-14. On the same topic, see also Harry A. Wolfson, *The Philosophy of Kalam* (Cambridge: Harvard University Press, 1976), especially, pp. 18-20 & 30-20.

49 For instance, Averroes, *Tahāfut al-Tahāfut* (Al-Qāhirah: Dār al-Ma[c]ārif, 1981), p. 781.

50 Quṭb, *Khaṣā'iṣ*, p. 139.

51 See Quṭb, *Khaṣā'iṣ*, pp. 156-60 and compare with Plato's *Republic* on education and where Socrates disagrees with depicting gods as ruthless or in any negative way (381a-c).

52 On science, see, Sayyid Quṭb, *Ma[c]ālim,* pp. 25 & 140, and *Khaṣā'iṣ,* p. 140; on *fiṭrah,* see, Quṭb, *Al-[c]Adālah,* pp. 30-33, and *Hādhā al-Dīn,* p. 24, and *Khaṣā'iṣ.* , pp. 25 & 50-53; on philosophy, see, Quṭb, *Al-Mustaqbal,* p. 29, and *Khasā'iṣ,* pp. 66-67. See also, idem, *Muqawwamāt,* pp. 51-52, 60, 198, 310-311, 322-324 & 329.

53 Quṭb, *Khaṣā'iṣ*, pp. 170-171.

54 *Ibid.*, p. 183.

55 Quṭb, *Fī al-Tārīkh,* pp. 22-23; also, see pp. 19-28.

56 *Ibid.*, p. 15. Also, Quṭb, *Khaṣā'iṣ*, pp. 4 & 82, and idem, *Al-Mustaqbal,* p. 3.

57 Quṭb, *Al-Mustaqbal,* pp. 8-9 & 66; idem, *Khaṣā'iṣ*, pp. 223 & 229-30.

58 Quṭb, *Khaṣā'iṣ*, pp. 190-210.

59 Quṭb, *Al-Mustaqbal,* p. 3; and see, idem, *Fī al-Tārīkh,* pp. 16-20.

60 Quṭb, *Fī al-Tārīkh,* pp. 11.

61 *Ibid.*, pp. 15-27.

62 Abū al-A[c]lā al-Mawdūdī, *Mafāhīm Islāmīyyah* (Islamic Concepts), (Kuwait: Dār al-Qalam, 1977), pp. 10-22 & 28-29; and, idem, *Nizām al-Ḥayat fī al-Islām* (Islamic Way of life), 1st. ed. n.d., (Bayrūt: Mu'assasat al-Risālah, 1983), pp. 6-7.

63 Alī Sharī[c]atī, *Marxism and Other Western Fallacies,* tr. R. Campbel (Berkeley: Mizan Press, 1980), p. 80.

64 Jamāl al-Dīn al-Afghānī, *Al-[c]Urwah al-Wuthqah* (Most Tight Bond), (Al-Qāhirah: Dār al-[c]Arab, 1957), pp. 60-61; and see al-Afghānī, *Al-A[c]māl al-Kāmilah* (Complete Works), Part II, Political Writings, int. and ed. by Muḥammad [c]Amārah (Bayrūt: al-Mu'assasah al-[c]Arabīyyah li-Dirāsāt wa al-Nashr, 1980), pp. 9-13 & 16-17. (Hereafter cited as *al A[c]māl*).

65 Al-Mawdūdī, *Naḥnu wa-al-Ḥaḍārah al-Gharbīyyah* (Bayrūt: Mu'assasat al-Risālah, 1983), pp. 146-48, 150 & 174.

66 Ḥasan al-Bannā, *Rasā'il al-Shahīd Ḥasan al-Bannā* (The Treatises of the Martyr Ḥasan al-Bannā), (Al-Qāhirah: Dār al-Qalam, 198?), pp. 429-31 & 471-74.

67 [c]Abduh, *Risālah,* pp. 19-20, 31 & 46-51.

68 *Ibid.*, pp. 111-113.

69 Iqbāl, *Reconstruction,* pp. 2, 9 & 22.

70 Al-Mawdūdī, *Manhaj,* pp. 28-34; idem, *Naḥnu,* pp. 267-70; and, idem, *Nizām al-Ḥayāt,* pp. 21-22.

71 Iqbāl, *Reconstruction,* pp. 145-55.

72 Sharīᶜatī, *On Sociology of Islam,* tr. Hamid Algar (Berkeley: Mizan Press, 1979), p. 83.

73 *Ibid.*, p. 63.

74 Iqbāl, *Reconstruction,* pp. 4, 14-15, 42, 54-57 & 196.

75 ᶜAbduh, *Risālah,* pp. 18-19, 28-32, 46-47, 59, 69-70, 180 & 112-32.

76 Afghānī, *Al-Aᶜmāl*, pp. 440-441.

77 Al-Mawdūdī, *Naḥnu,* pp. 13-18.

78 Iqbāl, *Reconstruction,* pp. 8, 63-64 & 70.

79 On the importance of historical accuracy and transmission for the authenticity of the Holy *Qur'an*, see Labib as-Said, *The Recited Koran,* trs. Bernard Weiss, M.A. Rauf, and Morroe Berger (New Jersey: The Darwin Press, 1975), pp. 19-60 & 121-25. Also, on the importance of historical accuracy for understanding the *sharīᶜah,* see Hodgson, *Venture,* Vol. 1, pp. 315-58.

80 Quṭb, *Khaṣā'iṣ*, pp. 9-10.

CHAPTER III

THE POLITICAL DISCOURSE OF SAYYID QUṬB

In the *Second Chapter* I treated the theoretical foundations of fundamentalism as advocated by Sayyid Quṭb. In this *Chapter* I treat the political aspects of his teachings. Throughout this *Chapter,* as in the previous one, it should be remembered that Quṭb's understanding of *tawḥīd* is of paramount importance. Quṭb views Islam's political as well as other aspects of life as being tightly linked to and dependent for their validity on adhering to the concept of *tawḥīd*. Besides being the truth itself, Quṭb believes that the most fundamental consequence of *tawḥīd* is God's revelation, which includes social, political, and economic doctrines. The three most important doctrines are the *sharīᶜah* (divine law) based on *al-ḥākimīyyah, al-ᶜadālah al-ijtimāᶜīyyah* (social justice), and *al-thawrah* (revolution) against *al-jāhilīyyah.* In fact, their radical development constitutes Quṭb's basic contributions to modern Islamic political thought as well as his political theory.

The theme that underlines Quṭb's political thought is that Islam accepts only a virtuous and good society and demands absolute obedience to God's teachings. Because Islam prohibits the domination of man by his fellow man by creating human laws and systems, the domination of human law over mankind illustrates clear and complete infidelity. This is so because humanity should be governed by the divine law. And since the goal of mankind today is not obedience to God's teachings, Quṭb maintains that the existence of a Muslim society is extremely necessary in order to allow the Muslims to live in a comfortable and a natural enjoyment and to practice their religion and enjoy spiritual and social comfort. What makes the existence of the Muslim society more urgent is that non-Muslim or the *jāhilī* societies are not in harmony with human nature, which results in partial solutions and remedies to human problems. Frequently, they remedy one side but damage another.[1]

Whereas many thinkers have considered the state from its beginning as that order which is established to deal with the worldly concerns of the members of a society, Islamic thought in general has considered the existence of political order for far-reaching reasons. Thus, although everyday problems and survival are the concern of the state, almost all Muslim thinkers and philosophers do not see them as sufficient reasons for establishing a political system. The state has been seen by jurists, theologians, and philosophers as the structure that protects and encourages morality. The particular reason that Quṭb cites for the existence of the state is the establishment of a moral society on the basis of God's teachings. For him, politics should be directed at the attainment of the Islamic system *(niẓām)* which aims at the realization of the good and at the attainment of normative principles as well as the application of prescriptive remedies to social problems.

This *Chapter* deals with questions pertaining to the nature and grounds of political obligation, the relation of one state to another, and the relation of individuals with each other and with the state. Also, it investigates questions relating to the manner of election of the ruler and of the form of government. In other words, it focuses on Quṭb's theory of the state and of the organization of society. This study of organization leads to the study of government, law, economy, and other aspects of politics. Furthermore, it will investigate Quṭb's notions of individual freedom and equality within the Islamic constitution (the Holy *Qur'ān*) and the limits of individualism. Quṭb's arguments and the concept of restructuring society focus on and aspire to the creation of the Muslim individual, the Muslim society, and then the Islamic system and state.

This *Chapter* is divided into two main sections: the first, political theory, is subdivided into (1) *sharīᶜah* and *al-ḥākimīyyah*, (2) social justice and political economy, and (3) revolution; the second is a comparative analysis of the main political differences between Islamic modernism as advocated by al-Afghānī, ᶜAbduh, and Iqbāl and Islamic fundamentalism as advocated by Quṭb, al Bannā, and al-Mawdūdī. The comparative section in this *Chapter* shows Quṭb's contribution to political fundamentalism and places him within modern Islamic political thought.

1. Political Theory: The Sharīᶜah and Al-Ḥākimīyyah

Tawḥīd is not only the liberation of men from submitting to each other but should also be the starting point in the formation of ethics and values as well as every human legislation and law. A government or a people have no right to legislate for themselves basic notions of right and wrong and lawful and unlawful because legislation, Quṭb reasons, is a divine matter. This is so because society has an inherent moral order based on universal (divine) laws, prescribed in Holy *Qur'ān*. Since these laws are not human conventions, their application, which is the responsibility of the Islamic government, is natural and is not an imposition of human will on social life. Thus, the alternative to human legislation is legislation based on the principles of the Islamic divine law. For Quṭb, Islamic law is not a social phenomenon but an eternal manifestation of God's will defining the duties and rights of individuals as well as of the state. What this means is that legislation of the basic principles of authority, right and wrong or legality and illegality are set forth and sealed from human consideration. No matter what individuals or societies think, they cannot- or do not have the right to- make what is right wrong or what is wrong right. These principles with their flexibility and comprehensiveness are able to meet the needs of life; and what is needed is to codify legal articles from these general principles in accordance with the changeable needs of everyday society.[2]

Because *tawḥīd* is the basis of the criteria of right and wrong, the lawful and the unlawful, and the legal and the illegal, governance or *ḥākimīyyah*, for Quṭb, belongs only to God and not to the individual. Submission to any human will, be it to an individual person or a group of individuals or to a nation, is *shirk* (polytheism) when it stands in contradiction to the divine message or principles found in the Holy *Qur'ān*. Since *al-ḥākimīyyah* belongs to God in this as well as the other life, legislation belongs to *al-ḥākim,* namely, God. The reason behind this notion is that submission to God takes on a vital significance in the conscience and heart and, more importantly in political matters. The real goal for establishing God's laws on earth is not merely the work for the next life; for this and the other life are two integral parts; and the divine law *(sharīᶜah)* plays the role of harmonizing the two stages. This harmony should be of the entire life of man with the general divine will as revealed in the Holy *Qur'ān;* thus, the Muslim's duty manifests in applying the divine law and in realizing on earth the Islamic system.[3]

Qutb justifies his position by citing the following verses:

Governance [Ḥukm] belongs by God.
He commands that you worship Him only;
this is the right religion but most people do not know. — XII: 40
Those who do not rule in accordance with
what God has revealed are unbelievers. — V: 47
Or do they have partners who have
legislated to them some religion that God did not permit. — XLII: 21
And when it is said to them,
'Come now to what God has sent down, and the Messenger,'
then thou seest the hypocrites barring the way to thee. — IV: 65

Thus, without reference to the divine law, Quṭb distrusts man's ability to create a just human legislation; the reason being that legislation made by an individual ruler, a governing family, a governing class, a governing people or governing race cannot by nature disregard its inclinations and self-interest in opposition to other individuals, classes, races or countries.[4]

Here, Quṭb does not define justice and relies on the divine law for its understanding, forgetting that the divine law itself does not define justice, but prescribes limits and deterrents, rewards and so forth. It orders the Muslims to adhere to *al-ᶜamr bī al-maᶜrūf wa al-nahy ᶜan al-munkar* (enjoining the Good and forbidding the evil). Another important issue that needs to be addressed is the theoretical impossibility of disregarding interest and seeking justice or legislating just laws or whether justice is in any case disregarding the interest of the individuals. Though it is true that many legislations are the products of compromise, interest or both- and it might be that there is no just legislation today- this situation, however, cannot obliterate the theoretical possibility of justice; this should be especially so for Quṭb who believes in the naturalness of laws, moral and otherwise. In fact, Quṭb's argument here is an extension of the argument on knowledge- and the same objections to his analysis are appropriate here. *Al-ḥākimīyyah* is also a key concept developed by Quṭb. "No God but Allah" means that the only ruler is God, the only true *sharīᶜah* is God's and the only authority is God's. Here Quṭb like *al-khawārij* (the seceders) does not make the linguistic difference between *ḥukm Allāh* in its political meaning and its juridical meaning. For Quṭb and the *khawārij* political rule includes both.

Also, Quṭb is affected by al-Mawdūdī's concept of *al-ḥākimīyyah*. Al-Mawdūdī postulates the *ḥākimīyyah* of God as opposed to that of man and the *rabānīyyah* (divinity) of God as opposed to man's servitude and God's *waḥdanīyyah* (oneness) as opposed to depending on any other source in the structuring of society. Thus, al-Mawdūdī describes the characteristics of the Islamic state in three concepts:

1- No individual or group has any role in *al-ḥākimīyyah* because God is the only ruler,
2- No one can legislate but God,
3- The law of the Islamic state is the divine law.

But Quṭb is correct in viewing the problem with non-Islamic notions of legislation as residing in the nature and goal of Islamic legislation. The goal of Islamic legislation is not to satisfy this or that group or to protect this or that possession as such, but it primarily aims at practical objectives that guarantee the formation of a righteous society capable of growing and developing.[5] Thus, though legislation should manifest in practical outcomes, it should clearly aim at the highest possible level of human endeavors, a virtuous society.

> *But where God himself, by supernatural Revelation, planted Religion; there he also made himself a peculiar Kingdom; and gave Laws not only of behaviour towards himself; but also towards another; and thereby in the kingdom of God, the Policy, and Laws Civil, are a part Kingdom of God, the Policy, and Lawes Civil, are a part of Religion; and therefore... the distinction of Temporal, and Spiritual Domination, hath there no place. It is true that God is King of all Earth.*[6]

The speaker here is not Sayyid Quṭb but Thomas Hobbes; for Hobbes the kingdom of God requires a covenant with the people, and here he was particularly referring to Judaism. But for Quṭb the kingdom of God should exist on this earth. Also, Rousseau observes, in the context of exposing civil religion and the division between state and religion, the place of Islam in politics. He states, for instance,

> *Mahomet evinced very sane views, and linked his political system well together; and while the form of government established by him subsisted under the caliphs, his successors, it was undivided; and in that respect it was good. But the Arabs, having become flourishing, learned and polished became also luxurious and effeminate, and were subjected by the barbarians: the division between the two powers then began again; and although this division is less apparent amongst the Mahometans than the Christians, it nonetheless exists, and conspicuously so in the sect of Ali, and in those states such as Persia, where it continually makes itself felt.*[7]

It is very interesting that those two thinkers see Islam as a civil religion; but the good societies that they imagine are not based on religion and are born out of social contracts. Modern Western thinkers like Hobbes and Locke have not denied the validity of religion per se, but doubted its capacity to create a coherent and just society on earth and, instead, relegated the role of religion to personal and moral conduct. Because religion is not seen as a legal obligation, and in the absence of legislation from God on political matters, Locke, for instance, accepts people's legislating for themselves. Thus, legislation, it seems, for Locke and Hobbes, is a necessity because

> *no political society can be, or subsist, without having in itself the power to preserve the property, and in order there unto, punish the offences of all those of that society where every one of the membres hath quitted his natural powers, resigned it up into the hands of the community in all cases that exclude him not from appealing for protection to the law established by it.*[8]

In fact, the main difference between Quṭb and the theorists of the state of nature, Hobbes, Locke, and Rousseau, is in the way they perceived the goal of the state. The fundamental and chief function of the state is for Locke the preservation of property (i.e, life, liberty and estate). He states that civil government is the proper remedy for the inconveniences of the state of nature; and since man would not condemn himself in the state of nature, the existence of a neutral arbitrator is necessary.[9] But Quṭb does not see that this cause is good enough for establishing a government or a society; he does not even believe that human beings without reference to divine law can have just laws. The differences between the two, Locke and Quṭb, goes deeper than the possibility or impossibility of just human legislation; it stems from their opposite understanding of law. Although to Locke, as to Quṭb, law is not "so much the limitation as the direction of free and intelligent agent to his interest, and prescribes no farther than for the general good of those under that law, and that liberty necessitates the existence of law," Locke considers law essentially as grounded in reason;[10] whereas for Quṭb it is grounded in revelation.

Therefore, the state of nature to Quṭb and Locke has a law that governs it; for Locke it is the law of reason which manifests itself primarily in independence and freedom. These two manifestations are common in the state of nature because God, the omnipotent, created all men; thus, man is born free and rational.[11] Although men's equality stems from being God's creatures, Locke argues that when men are born reason becomes the judge of matters of good and wrong. But for Quṭb, though men are created equal and share in reason, reason does not replace God's direct legislation and *fiṭrah;* the state of nature is the primordial creation which includes obedience to God.

Therefore, obedience to God necessitates a different conception for the existence of the state. To be obedient to God, Quṭb holds that the cultivation of virtues becomes necessary. But Locke and Hobbes do not view legislating morality as the domain of the state insofar as individuals refrain from violence. Hobbes maintains that because man has an insatiable desire for power after power that ceases only after death, the institution of a civil society functions as a curb against the lust for power.[12]

Because divine knowledge and law cannot be known independently by men, they are transmitted by revelation; thus, Quṭb postulates a state of nature or *fiṭrah* which is primarily to be transferred into civil societies. From this difference on nature and the role of reason, all other opposed conceptions of the role of the state and law follow.

Quṭb's notion of law, discussed here, is not concerned with regulations or procedures but, more essentially, with the principles of law. Regulations and procedures, which may be called laws, are subject to evolution and change in matters such as the forms of government or election; people can regulate their affairs in accordance with the principles of Islam. Thus, legislation in the sense of regulation is allowed by Quṭb, but legislation in the sense of conceptualizing basic notions such as morality is not allowed.

Moreover, rejecting human legislation does not negate the validity of organizing everyday matters but is directed against the argument that the door of *ijtihād* (independent reasoning) has been closed because a number of Muslim scholars have decided to do so or believed that Islamic thought is not in need of basic restructuring. Here Quṭb is walking on a tightrope. On the one hand, and against the demands of secularists, he argues for the unchangeability of the (political) essence and relevance of religion; on the other, he wants to set Islamic thought free from the rigidity and insistence of men of religion on to the validity of existing jurisprudence. Furthermore, looking at the legislative matters in the Holy *Qur'ān* or its verses that can be construed on legislative and legal issues, we will find, in most cases, that they are of a very broad nature. These are the notions that Quṭb wants to be maintained and taken into consideration in the formulation laws or regulations. At the same time, Quṭb perceives that laws and regulations should reflect the principles, values, ethics and morality of a society. Therefore, a Muslim society should adhere to, or a society is Muslim when it includes, the principles, values, and ethics of Islam. This, however, does not exclude finding solutions to new or old problems. All it means, Quṭb explains, is that when the ruler takes his decisions he has to keep in mind

> *the general goals of religion for the improvement of the individual, the community, and mankind in accordance with the principles set forth by Islam and under the condition of justice.*[13]

To Quṭb, one of the most important functions of the state in its legislation as well as the practical matters of everyday is the propagation of morality; this morality is not man's or the ruler's conception but God's ordinance. Rejecting the notion of state as being a mere aggregate of individuals, he holds the state responsible for the moral and spiritual well-being of society before God and the individuals. Quṭb, like al-Afghānī, is aware that the demoralization of the state leads to the demoralization of the individual and views the state as a mechanism to be used for a higher end- a moral life that leads to happiness in this and the other life.

Since moral life is tightly linked to Islamic law, he emphasizes the importance of obedience to the law by both the governed and the governor and considers non-adherence to Islamic law by any government whether democratic or autocratic as both immoral and unlawful. His perception of the Islamic government as the government of law *(sharīᶜah)* first, and of the governed secondly, leads him to view rulers as servants to Islamic law: the law is the master of government and the government is its slave. The government's function is the regulation of human affairs within the principles of Islam. Hence, though Quṭb obliges individuals to obey the government, obedience to the ruler is neither absolute nor permanent- in the Hobbesian sense of obedience accorded to the Leviathan or in the traditional Islamic conception. Non-adherence to or breaking away from Islamic law becomes a sufficient ground for not only civil disobedience but revolution as well.

Although this conception is old and Quṭb did not invent it, under the conditions of Egyptian society in the late forties and the fifties, revival of this notion was construed as a challenge to the government. But what is new in Quṭb's exposition is the view of the ruler as not possessing any real authority; for the source of authority is God; and authority is delegated to the Muslims in general. The authority of the ruler becomes a matter of delegation or vicegerency from the people and can be withdrawn from the ruler in many cases, first among which is non-conformity to and non-application of Islamic law. And because authority is delegated to the people, the ruler in Islam receives legitimacy only from one source: the will of the governed. Thus, Quṭb acknowledges, for instance, the legitimacy of the first four caliphs in Islam because they were chosen by the people, but denies the Umayyids any legitimacy because they changed this rule and forced themselves on the community.[14]

Put differently, Sayyid Quṭb insists not only on the idea of subjecting governments to the force of law but also on the notion of grounding the legitimacy of governments in their adherence to the law. Though legitimacy is dependent on the choice of the Muslims, its continuation hinges on following and applying the laws of Islam; consequently, the people's duty to obey the ruler stems from the ruler's adherence to the divine law. Here, Quṭb is making the distinction between the function of the ruler as the executive of the divine law and his derivation of authority because of his qualifications. The ruler derives authority and legitimacy only from the people in general; and to keep it, he must obey the divine law. The ruler has no religious authority only derived from heaven or obtained as a divine right or through mediation; he derives the power to exercise authority from "the entire choice and absolute freedom of the Muslims."[15] Quṭb's view is based on the following Qur'anic verses:

> *O believers, obey God, and obey the Messenger*
> *and those in authority among you.*
> *If you should quarrel on anything, refer it to God and the Messenger,*
> *if you believe in God and the last Day;*
> *that is better, and fairer in the issue.* — III: 59
> *And those who answer their Lord,*
> *and perform the prayer, their affair being counsel between them...* — XLII: 38
> *It was by some mercy of God that thou wast*
> *gentle to them; hadst thou been harsh*
> *and hard at heart, they would have scattered*
> *from about thee. So pardon them, and pray*
> *forgiveness for them, and take counsel with them*
> *in the affair; and when thou art resolved,*
> *put thy trust in God; surely God loves those who put their trust.*
> — III: 154

Obviously, Sayyid Quṭb is advocating the legitimacy of representative government or, what he called, "the government of *'ummah*." His understanding of the will of the people is a compromise between popular sovereignty and absolutism. Therefore, in theory, it seems that legitimate authority of the ruler stems from two basic components: the chioce or election of the Muslims and the application of Islamic law, the *sharīᶜah*.

The purpose of this exposition is twofold. First, it is the rejection of many medieval notions on jurisprudence as well as its historical development; for Quṭb does not consider, for instance, that the century-old requirement that the caliph be from *Quraysh* (the tribe of the Prophet) is legitimate or well-founded because the principles of Islam refuse to elevate *Quraysh* over other Muslims; all Muslims are equal regardless of their ancestry. Also, he rejects the Umayyids' (the first ruling dynasty in Islam) and the Abbasids' (the second ruling dynasty in Islam) rule as being un-Islamic because there is no hereditary government in Islam and because any seizure of power is prohibited. Thus, he tries indirectly to argue against the underpinnings of the political theory of medieval thinkers such as Ibn Taymīyyah, al-Ghazālī, al-Māwardī, Ibn Jamāᶜah.[16] In fact, Quṭb quotes the *Qur'an* to counter most of their arguments:

The believers indeed are brothers;
so set things right between your two brothers,
and fear God; haply so you will find mercy.

O believers, let not any people scoff
at another people who may be better than they;
neither let women scoff at women who may be better than themselves.
And find not fault with one another,
neither revile one another by nicknames.
An evil name is ungodliness after belief.
And who so repents not, those- they are the evildoers. — XLIX: 12
Mankind, fear your Lord, who
created you of a single soul,
and from it created its mate, and from the pair of them scattered abroad many men and women; and
fear God by whom you demand one of another,
and the wombs; surely God ever watches over you. — IV: 1
On the day that we shall muster
the god-fearing to the All-merciful with pomp
and drive the evildoers into Gehennam herding,
having no power of intercession, save those
who have taken with the All-merciful covenant.
And they say, 'the All-merciful has taken unto Himself a son.'
You have indeed advanced something hideous.
... None is there in the heavens and earth

but he comes to the All-merciful as a servant;
He has indeed counted them,
and He has numbered them exactly.
Every one of them shall come to Him upon the Day of Resurrection, all alone.
Surely those who believe and do deeds of righteousness-
unto them The All- merciful shall assign Love. —XIX: 88-95
We created man of an extraction of clay
then we set him, a drop, in a recepticale secure.
Then We created of the drop a clot
then We created of the clot a tissue.
Then We created of the tissue bones
then We garmented the bones in flesh;
thereafter We produced him as another creature. —XXIII: 12-14
So let man consider of what he was created;
he was created of gushing water
issuing between the loins and the breast-bones.
Surely He is able to bring him back
upon the day when the secrets are tried,
and he shall have no strength, no helper. —LXXXVI: 5-7

Secondly, these examples and their conclusions are directed at contemporary problems: denying the legitimacy of historical processes (whether the appointment of Abū Bakr of ᶜUmar or the Umayyids' hereditary rule) does not exonerate changes made then and *now* in the principles of Islam because only the Muslim people as a whole have the right to choose the ruler then and *now*. Furthermore, the rejection of the use of force to attain power (as Muᶜāwiyah did) is also directed at contemporary Muslim rulers who seized power. All this means that contemporary Muslims can free themselves from preordained policies not based on consent. People can either confirm or deny a leader's assumption to power; consequently, the Muslims do not have to obey current policies but can change them as well as their rulers. More precisely, and in practical terms, the most immediate goal of Quṭb's exposition is a repudiation of the Egyptian government and a demand for election, a call for freedom, and the repudiation of autocracy and government by force (both of which have been very common in the Muslim world).

Futhermore, at a certain level, Quṭb wants to counter the charge that Islam is a static religion and ideology, and to quell the fears of individuals who think that Islam cannot develop or be an instrument of freedom. Therefore, by differentiating between the principles of the *sharīᶜah* and the historical beginning and development of Islamic jurisprudence, he dispels the notion that deriving laws from Islamic *sharīᶜah* is a past, unrenewable activity. His argument on the differences between theory and practice as the result of ignorance or deterioration leads to the exoneration of Islam from its historical development and the attribution of the shortcomings of the theory to practice. Thus, the correct Islamic political theory is neither what has taken place in history nor what is taking place now. For instance, whereas Islamic jurisprudence, or the elaboration of political theory, is static now, it was not established, did not survive, and was not understood in a vaccum. Islamic jurisprudence

> *was established in a Muslim society to meet the needs of the realistic Muslim life. Moreover, Islamic jurisprudence did not establish the Muslim society but the Muslim society... established Islamic jurisprudence.*[17]

What all this means is that the Muslims can write a new political theory and develop a jurisprudence and can disregard the old without remorse about the past. The Muslims should create the political theory and jurisprudence that suit their needs in every age.

A corollary to this is that before codifying laws, the Muslims should establish a community that is truly based on Islamic principles. Since no Muslim society exists nowadays, Quṭb asserts, to try to legislate for that society is to work in a vacuum. Legislation and jurisprudence should develop from within society and not imposed from the outside. Thus, it is imperative that before legislating, a truly Muslim society should be founded. Apparently, Quṭb considers jurisprudence as a practical science based on a political theory whose objective is the protection of

Muslim societies. But in order to protect a society, obviously, it has to exist first. Practically speaking, this means that the Muslims at this time should consider the priority of establishing a Mulsim state and should relegate the question of jurisprudence till after its establishment- also it means that current societies are not Muslim but *jāhilī*. This argument is not only directed at intellectuals but equally at Muslim scholars, religious and secular. Muslim religious scholars, for instance, have believed that Islamic jurisprudence is capable of coping with modernity and its problems. And accepting the teachings of medieval scholars, they have been resistant to change. Quṭb however, wants to show them and the Muslims in general that there is room for change and that changes in Islamic jurisprudence and other matters are not only within the spirit of Islam but are called for as well. The shortcomings of Islamic jurisprudence should be acknowledged and corrected; and jurisprudence in general requires major development.

Thus, Quṭb's acceptance of the principles of the *sharīᶜah,* the Holy *Qur'ān* and the *sunnah,* as the underpinnings of the Islamic state is an attempt to distinguish between jurisprudence and the *sharīᶜah.* This distinction between *sharī'ah* as God's eternal and unchangeable law and jurisprudence as the human understanding of the *sharīᶜah* within specific historical generations leads to undermining any authority from the present or the past. Consequently, it is transformed into a methodological device allowing him to transcend, for instance, the Prophet's companions whose actions and sayings enjoyed normative and legislative power for the majority of Muslims, the Sunnites. And his rejection of the companions' normative status, because of their liability to human errors and historical limitations, can be easily superimposed on contemporary Muslim scholars and jurists whom he considered inactive, closed-minded, and, in many cases, subordinate to the governing power. Quṭb's rejection does not include everything from the past or everything the companions said but is basically directed at the claim of normative authority.

Nonetheless, Quṭb refuses to make any changes in the jurisprudence that deals with matters of worship and rituals by claiming the unchangeability of man's relation to his Creator. But the jurisprudence that deals with social organization and development should not depend on tradition because man's material as well as social needs are always in flux.[18] But this distinction and the subsequent rejection are unwarranted; for, first, the two kinds of jurisprudence are based on traditions of the companions of the Prophet and their followers *(al-salaf)*; and, secondly, Quṭb himself does not acknowledge the validity of dividing life into different compartments. Thus, his acknowledgement of the need for social and political development reveals clearly Quṭb's intentions and views on establishing new Muslims societies that are unencumbered socially by the past. This is one of Quṭb's revolutionary (or rebellious) teachings, which manifests in his revolt against the authority and teachings of medieval and modern scholars as well as against the governments and conditions of the Muslims of today.

In order to substitute for the rejection of the past in its legal, theological, and philosophical manifestations, Quṭb creates a spiritual device, "the spirit of Islam," which plays a decisive role in the construction of his thought. It is, for Quṭb, that which is

> *entertained by those who follow up the nature of this religion as well as its history and is felt behind its legislations and directions... This spirit is difficult to express in a few words but is revealed in the direction and goal [of Islam], in events, incidents, and in behavior and rituals...*

It is the spirit that

> *draws the high horizon which Islam asks its believers to look up to and try to attain, not only by performing the duties and obligations but also by personal volunteering [to perform] what is more than duties and obligations.*[19]

Quṭb has used "the spirit of Islam" especially to show his appreciation of major events of the past; for instance, the spirit has affected the historical reality of the past by transforming Islam, the abstraction, into living human embodiments and models of correct dispositions and behavior. The Prophet Muḥammad and many of his companions and their followers were the embodiments of that spirit. It is this spirit that made a man like Ibn Ḥanbal, the jurist, stand against and confront an overbearing ruler with the word of truth.[20] Consequently, Quṭb establishes a dialectical relationship between the champions of Islam throughout history and that spirit. Thus, the understanding of Islamic history requires the study of this relationship in addition to the capacities of those individuals who received "the universal emanation" for the understanding of basic facts of life. Only those individuals who really have understood and accepted Islam have been able to perform their duties, obligations, and much more as a sign of comprehending Islam in its fullest meaning.

Yet, Quṭb conceives that the spirit of Islam overrides historical processes whether economic, legislative or otherwise. Those individuals who failed did so because they either did not understand or disregarded the spirit of Islam- an example is Muᶜāwiyah who turned the Islamic *'ummah* into a nation governed by a dynasty.[21]

Here one finds problems in attempting to pinpoint the essence or the function of "the spirit of Islam." If the spirit of Islam made many companions and Ibn Ḥanbal behave in a certain way, there is no need for Quṭb's rejection of their legislations and understandings or their normative status. If their action and thought were not only within but the embodiment of the spirit of Islam, the Muslims should accept their behavior and thought. Logically speaking, the Muslims cannot, as Quṭb wants them to do, look at them as the embodiment of the spirit of Islam, one time, and to reject their understandings of politics, elections of the ruler, forms of government and so forth, another time.

Although the spirit of Islam and its principles play a crucial role in making and evaluating history and should be embodied in a political form, the form of government or political regime based on the principles of Islam is not of vital importance. In theory, it is a matter of indifference, according to Quṭb, whether the Islamic state has a republican or other form of government;

the goodness of the state does not depend on its institutions but fundamentally on its underlying principles. Islamic policy may take many forms but its principles and values are the same. Thus, he states that

> *Islam is not a rigid system, and its specific applications do not stand at any age or environment. All that Islam wants to fix is its basic fundamentals tha' define its divine characteristics and preserve the Muslim society from being absorbed in ignorant [jāhilī] societies and from the loss of ability to lead these societies that Islam came to lead.*[22]

But insisting on the adherence to Islamic principles does not lead necessarily to theocracy: the Islamic system or *nizām* is not realized, Quṭb argues, if men of religion rule because in Islam there are no men of religion or clergy. The Islamic system is realized where Islamic law is executed, where the idea of Islam rules, and where its principles and regulations define the kind of government and the form of society. Sayyid Quṭb's repudiation of theocracy stems from his opposition to the notion of any inherent authority of clergy; for Islam has created a society that is based on law. Quṭb is very emphatic in distinguishing between religion and "men of religion" or clergy: because the clergy do not represent "the idea of God," to call an Islamic government a theocracy is misleading. The rule of clergy should not be taken as the ideal form of an Islamic government; for neither theory nor practice supports this ideal.[23]

Furthermore, Quṭb would have rejected the idea of government by jurists like the one advocated by Ayatollah Khomeini. Ayatollah Khomeini, in his book, ***The Islamic Government,*** argues that only a government by jurists is legitimate. Since the Islamic government is based on jurisprudence, the most qualified men for government are the jurists. Khomeini can make this argument because the jurists are indirect representatives of the Imam and can rule in his absence. Major trends in Shiᶜism believe that only the Imam, the descendent of the Prophet, has the right to legitimately rule.[24] But for Quṭb, if religious government means that a specific group rules or assumes authority, this is abolished in Islam and is un-Islamic. The Islamic government is every government that is built on the basis that authority, which is delegated to the Muslims in general, belongs to God alone and on the execution of the Islamic *sharīᶜah.* Though for Khomeini and Quṭb the *sharīᶜah* is the basis of government, Quṭb perceives the right to rule which is dependent on *sharīᶜah* as a matter of delegation from the people, but, ultimately for Khomeini, from the Imam. And, because Quṭb does not believe in the power of delegation from the Imam, judges and sheikhs become for Quṭb no more than scholars— a Muslim judge is a Muslim skillful in the field of law; this however does not give him more authority and legitimacy in terms of election than other Muslims since both doctrines reside in the Muslims in general.[25]

This notion of Quṭb is aimed against those Muslims who believe only in the legitimacy of the clergy and at those individuals who are frightened at the prospect of instituting a theocracy. Quṭb himself was not one of the clergy and this argument allows him to speak in the name of Islam.

While theocracy is not the ideal government in Islam, Quṭb views the first Islamic period of the Prophet and the first two caliphs as a guide for humanity and the zenith of human achievement on the moral and religious levels. He contends that that period produced great examples and the highest ideals and laid down exemplary principles and concepts, ranging from the true essence of man to political, social, and economic duties and rights. But notwithstanding all this respect and reverence for the past, he is very emphatic in indicating that an Isalmic system does not mean the return to the system of the first Muslim society, but is simply every social system based on the principles of Islam. Therefore, an Islamic system can take many forms depending on and in agreement with the natural development of society, for any form is as good as another if controlled by the general principles of Islam. Quṭb's overriding concern now is not the form of govenment but the existence of the Muslims who have strong beliefs because organizational matters alone are not enough to establish a truly Islamic life.[26] In other words, what reformers should aim at first is the upbringing of committed

Muslims and then turn to the question of organization and institutions.

Quṭb's exposition of the authority of the ruler and his insistence on the choice of the people as the basic components of legitimacy do not leave much room for accepting any form of government except the one elected by the people. In addition to what has been said before on authority and legitimacy, Quṭb proclaims the centrality of the government's adherence to *shūrah* (consultation) in the formation of any state. This notion is a device to solicit people's participation and to demand their right in electing the government. But Quṭb does not acknowledge or chooses to ignore that though God ordered the Prophet to consult the Muslims, and though the Muslims consulted each other, this consultation has never been seen as obligatory. Of course, the Muslim scholars had to approve the selection of the Imam or the ruler, but once elected, the ruler had a free hand within the limits of Islam. He did not have to consult the Muslims every time he decided to perform something. Moreover, Quṭb's argument that *shūrah* is not specifically defined and that its form is an organizational matter depending on the needs of every age has no doctrinal or historical precedent. *Shūrah* has been the domain of scholars who advised the ruler and suggested a certain course of action to be followed. And his suggestion that the forms of conducting *shūrah* and of government are of secondary importance, because each society can better define its needs, is contradicted by his insistence on calling the Islamic government the government of the *'ummah.*

Now, if the institution of a legitimate government depends on the approval of the *'ummah,* and *shūrah* is the principle of political life in Islam as well as the method of exercising a legitimate authority, the government of the *'ummah* can take only one form, the democratic- although for Quṭb the form is not important. It is democratic in form because the Muslims in general- not their scholars and elites- should elect their government. Moreover, if Quṭb rejects intellectual elites, philosophers and theologians, and treats the Muslims on an equal footing, so politically, it seems, this is the logical way to follow. Therefore, oligarchy and autocracy, for instance, cannot be acceptable Islamic forms of government if we take Quṭb's point of view. This position illustrates again Quṭb's anti-elitism whether religious, secular or philosophical. In one way, Quṭb subscribes to the democratic notion in his rejection of the assumption that members of a particular class are superior in judgement to the rest and are, therefore, the nation's natural rulers.

But insisting that what is advocated is the creation of an Islamic state based on the teachings of Islam whose institutions should develop from within the society itself, Quṭb calls the government of Islam the government of the *'ummah* and not, for instance, the democratic, socialist or otherwise government of Islam. Also, with politics, as with philosophy, and wanting terms and notions to be indigenous to the Muslims, Quṭb underlines the necessity that institutions and forms of government be the result of evolution from within, and not be imposed from the outside. Quṭb's purpose here is not only to reject terms and idioms but, more importantly, the West; for what matters to Quṭb is that any government should be based on the principle of Islam and not on imitating the West. The rejection of imitation does not mean that Islam and other ideologies do not have some things in common, but what they have in common is irrelevant when measured against their differences. And, what counts in the final analysis is the fundamental theory and the specific concept of the nature of politics, authority, and legislation. What counts between, say, Marxism and Islam is not that they may share some similar ideas on the distribution of wealth, but what is more relevant is that Islam sees God as the owner and dispenser of wealth whereas Marxism sees the workers as the owners. Liberalism and Marxism are, for Quṭb, two sets of doctrines about metaphysics, politics, power and wealth. Hence Quṭb's repudiation of liberalism as well as capitalism, socialism, Marxism and materialsm does not stem essentially from disliking a specific project or idea but on the grounds that these systems have different metaphysical concepts and starting points from Islam. And those principles that they have in common can be explained in Islamic terms (like the concept of social justice and human dignity); hence, there is no need to borrow either the concepts or their terminology.[27]

It may be worthwhile to mention that although it may not be necessary to borrow a foreign terminology- and, this issue has been treated in *Chapter I*- it seems that Quṭb adopted, notwithstanding his disavowal of democracy, the concept of the necessity of people's choice for the election of a legitimate government. And although Quṭb's concept can be explained in Islamic terms, it does not mean it was reared in Islamic traditions or that it is Islamic in origin; in other words, Quṭb adopted a democratic principle. In reviewing Islamic thought, one fails to find any understanding of *shūrah* as the pivot of government and as a political obligation in the sense that Quṭb attempts to present it; the cornerstone for legitimacy had been dependent on applying the *sharīᶜah* regardless of the choice of the Muslims in general. But, it seems that Quṭb adopted without acknowledgement a Western concept, "democracy," and dressed it in an Islamic garment. This notwithstanding, Quṭb's distinction of Islam from other systems is warranted since the government in Islam aims primarily at obedience to God; other systems either deny God's existence like Marxism or relegate it to the realm of personal preference like liberalism.

As he divided religions into divine and man-made, Quṭb divides the world into two parties or systems on earth, that of God and that of the devil. The party of God (*ḥizb Allah*) is the one that proclaims and acts in accordance with God's teachings; the party of the devil *(ḥizb al-shayṭān*) is simply any sect, group, people, nation or individual that does not follow God's teachings.

A political corollary to this is that Qutb defines a nation as

> *that group of people who are connected by religion, which is its nationality. Or, else there is no [true] nation because land, race, language, and material interests are not adequate for establishing a [good] nation.*[28]

Islam unites people on the basis of religion which is the

foundation of unity and separation; for neither race, language, territories nor cultures alone are proper bases of an Islamic life. Religion is the nationality of or the focal point of reference for the Muslims. Therefore, the Muslims should not be like parrots repeating the Christian notion that religion is the relation between God and the individual only. If the Europeans have the right to separate religion from politics, Quṭb reasons, it is because Christianity does not prescribe for Christians how to deal with civil life and issues. But worshipping God alone in Islam cannot be achieved except under an Islamic system.[29]

To justify his position Quṭb cites the following verses:

How should they have the Reminder,
seeing a clear Messenger already came to them,
then they turned away from him and said,
'A man tutored, possessed!' Behold, We are removing the chastisement a little;
behold you revert!. — XLIV: 13

And He taught Adam the names, all of them;
then He presented them unto the angels and said,
'Now tell Me the name of these, if you speak truly.'
They said 'Glory be to thee!
We know not save what thou hast taught us.
Surely, Thou art the All-knowing, the All-wise'. — II: 30

And others there are who say,
'Our Lord, give us in this world good,
and good in the world to come,
and guard us against the chastisement of the Fire'. — II: 199

And what ever good you expend is for your selves...
Those who expend their wealth night and day,
secretly and in public,
their wage awaits them with their Lord,
and no fear shall be on them, neither shall they sorrow.
Those who devour usury shall not rise
again except as he rises,
whom Satan of the touch prostrates;
that is because they say, 'Trafficking is like usury'.

God has permitted tfafficking, and forbidden usury.
Whosoever receives an admonition from his Lord and gives over,
he shall have his past gains, and his affair is committed to God;
but whosoever reverts— those are the inhabitants of the Fire,
there in dwelling forever.
God blots out usury,
but freewill offerings He augments with interest.
God loves not any guilty ingrate…
O believers, fear your God;
and give up the usury that is outstanding, if you are believers.
But if you do not, then take
notice that God shall war with you,
and his Messenger; yet if you repent,
you shall have your principal, unwronging and unwronged….
—II: 274-81
'Surely this community of yours is one community,
and I am your Lord; so serve Me. —XXI: 92
Thou shalt not find any people who
believe in God and the last Day
who are loving to anyone who opposes God and His Messenger,
not though they were their fathers, or their sons, or their brothers, or their clan.
Those- He has written faith upon their hearts,
and He has confirmed them with a Spirit from Himself;
and He shall admit them into gardens underneath
which rivers flow, therein to dwell forever,
God being well-pleased with them,
and they well- pleased with Him.
Those are God's party;
why, surely God's party- they are the prosperers. —LVIII: 22
So let them fight in the way of God
who sell the present life for the world to come;
and whosoever fights in the way of God and is slain, or conquers,
We shall bring him a mighty wage. —IV: 76

But Quṭb is unaware that nationalism has played a different

role in the West than it did in the Muslim world, and if nationalism, he reasons, is a natural product of the Western conception of religion and politics, why does not Quṭb accept it as such? For nationalism, for instance, unified Europe which was a feudal system into a nation-state system. In this sense, it has had a positive effect on Europe which used nationalism to free itself from the domain of the Church. However, Quṭb's argument is correct in terms of the Muslim nation; the Muslims, who are of different ethnic groups, Arabs, Turks, Persians, Kurds, Berbers and so forth, could have been one state of approximately 800 million Muslims. But, because of the division of the Muslim world by the colonizing powers and then the rise of nationalism and its acceptance of this division, the Muslims have been split into many states. Quṭb and the Muslims in general view this step as a deterioration and a backward step that have weakened the Muslims and left them powerless. Not only do the Muslims live under nation-states but many times those states have fought against each other in the name or Arabism or Islam or other mottos. Also, the attempts of most Arab and Turkish leaders and heads of state have been to relegate Islam to a secondary role and to encourage nationalistic feelings which ultimately are opposed to Islamic teachings. Whether advocating linguistic nationalism or racial nationalism, cultural nationalism or a combination, and although they might have served the countries concerned as an instrument to free their land, their effects in the long run, from an Islamic point of view, cannot be commended or called Islamic. At the least, nationalism considers the duty to land and people over any other duty, even to God.

For this reason, I think, Quṭb maintains the notion that a Muslim society is not that society that calls itself Muslim or the country that includes Muslims while the *sharīᶜah* is not the law of the land. Those societies whether of Muslim or non-Muslim majorities were the *sharī'ah* is not applied are *jāhilī* societies. The *jāhilī* society is that society "where people group for other reasons than their human will," and, I think, he is referring particularly to societies like the Egyptian which were dominated by a military junta advocating nationalism and where people did not choose the government. Those societies that are based on necessity (like survival) or were just founded by necessity (like overthrowing an unjust government) are *jāhilī* societies if they do not proceed to a higher organizing principle. Hence, those societies lacking the will to create a higher system or the society that is established without a conscious effort on the part of the founders are defective in nature. And what is equally essential for the creation of the good society for Quṭb is the object and the goal of the will. The most worthy object of will or the higher principle is religion; hence, mankind should be grouped on the highest possible level, religion, and not on the lowest, i.e., anything besides religion such as interest and race, socialism, liberalism or communism.[30]

This argument is directed at the political conditions of Egypt and the Muslim world. President Jamāl ᶜAbd al-Nāṣir advocated socialism and nationalism and opposed religious movements. Quṭb's discussion of nationalism is especially directed at the Egyptian and other Muslim countries who gave priority to nationalistic goals or, in many cases, gave only lip-service to Islam, if not rejecting outright religion as a dominant force in politics.

2 - Political Economy: Social Justice

Today there are for Quṭb two basic ideologies challenging Islam, communism, on the one hand, and capitalism, on the other; and, Islam is at a crossroad. Rejecting capitalism- because of interest and usury, monopoly, exploitation, and the lack of justice- Quṭb refuses to view capitalism or the capitalist system as the model for the Muslims to imitate and follow. Moreover, this capitalistic system has been tied closely with narrow nationalism where states such as England, France, Italy, and Germany allowed themselves in the name of national interest the right to exploit, invade, and occupy other countries in the Middle East, India, Africa, and Latin America. But in Islam, private enterprise is a social function (a theme discussed below). On the other hand, though socialism and Islam converge on many essential points (as in advocating guarantees of minimum standards of life, work, and housing, and social justice), Islam's economic system is an integral part of Islam and is based on *tawḥīd*.

On yet another level, communism and Islam clash head on. One of them, Islam grounds its system on belief in God, the other, namely, Marxism, on denying God; for dialectical materialism dominates Marxism, whereas the divine concept dominates Islam. Ultimately, the conflict presented in economic terms (capitalist, communist or socialist) is, for Quṭb, the conflict between spiritualism and materialism; the former is represented by Islam and religion in general, the latter by capitalism, socialism, and communism. Marxism is the most advanced level of mechanical and intellectual materialism, and though the two camps, the capitalist and the socialist, disagree and wage wars for their own benefit, their difference is a matter of degree, of organization, and of method. Because the materialistic idea of life underlies all of them, Quṭb predicts the final victory for Marxism over capitalism when the economics of the West reaches stagnation. For communism is nothing but a progressive idea when compared to capitalism; it is progessive because it provides some basic material needs for people living under it and speaks to the exploited whereas capitalism speaks to the governing authorities and the exploiting class. However, the outcome of both ideologies is unjust because in capitialism individuals and their ambitions rule over the community and in communism the state rules over individuals.[31]

The alternative for Quṭb is Islam, which has postulated the principle of equal opportunity but made the basic values in society some other things than economics. Although it has set forth the right of individual possession and has made it the basis of its economic system, it simultaneously imposes limits. The Islamic economic system or notions of economics are, again, neither capitalist nor socialist, they are Islamic.

What is essential in the Islamic economic system and its political economy is social justice, and Quṭb provides two primary guidelines for its attainment: the harmonious, balanced, and absolute unity between the individual and groups as one guideline, and the general mutual responsibility between the individuals and groups as another. The importance of justice stems from being an ethical concept as well as being one of the bases of government in Islam. Entrusted with authority which originally belongs to God, the ruler must manifest this trust in, first, obedience to the *sharīʿah* and, secondly, justice: social and economic as well as political.[32] He cites the following verses in order to support his argument:

> *They will question thee what is permitted them.*
> *Say: 'The good things are permitted you;*
> *and such hunting creatures as you teach, training them as hounds,*
> *and teaching them as God has taught you- eat what they seize for you,*
> *and mention God's name over it-*
> *Fear God; God is swift at the reckoning.'* — V: 8
>
> *Say: 'Come I recite what your Lord has forbidden you:*
> *That you associate not anything with Him,*
> *and to be good to your parents,*
> *and not to slay your children because of poverty;*
> *We will provide you and them;*
> *and that you approach not any indecency outward or inward,*
> *and that you slay not the soul God has forbidden,*
> *except by right. That then he has charged*
> *you with; haply you will understand.'* — VI: 152
>
> *Or have they a share in the Kingdom?*
> *If that is so, they do not give the people a single date-spot.*
> *Or are they jealous of the people for the bounty that God has given them?*
> *Yet We gave the people of Abraham*
> *the Book and the wisdom and We gave*
> *them a mighty Kingdom.* — IV: 58
> *Surely God bids to justice and good-doing*
> *and giving to kinsmen; and He forbids indecency, dishonour,*
> *and insolence, admonishing you,*
> *so that haply you will remember.* — XVI: 90

To guarantee the administration of justice Quṭb identifies three principles: complete liberation of conscience, complete human equality, and mutual social responsibility *(al-takāful al-ijtimāʿī)*.

The Liberation of Conscience

Sayyid Quṭb considers morality as the basic infrastructure for building a stable and coherent society and argues that social justice exists only when supported by, first, an internal feeling of the individual's worthiness and the community's need and, secondly, by a creed leading to the obedience to God and to the realization of a sublime human society. Economic liberation is insufficient by itself for realizing a good society or for the survival of the good individual in society. Furthermore, liberation cannot be guaranteed by laws alone because man is affected by needs and inclinations; what is equally, if not more, important than economic liberation is the liberation of the conscience.

Liberating the human conscience from worshipping others than God can only be attained when mankind is freed from submission to humans but submits to God. To do this, Islam disciplines the conscience by inculcating piety, and, then, entrusts it as the guardian of society; for it makes the human conscience the protector, executor, and supervisor of legislation. This trust is manifested, for instance, in legal decisions; legal decisions which are usually dependent on the conscience of a witness whose testimony can put someone in prison or to death. Nonetheless Islam does not leave the conscience to itself but considers God as the monitor and witness of people's behavior. For this reason, piety is very essential in Islamic life and politics; for if the conscience is liberated from enslavement and submission to man and is full of God's love, the individual will be afraid of no one or of losing his livelihood or office. What ultimately this means for Quṭb is that when the conscience is liberated from fear, which lowers self-esteem, the individual can be trusted.[33] Thus liberation from fear and obedience to anyone but God is one of the cardinal principles for building a socially just society.

Quṭb uses the following verses to indicate the importance of the conscience in Islamic society and the application of law:

And if you are upon a journey,
and you do not find a writer,
then pledge in hand.
But if one of you trusts another,
let him who is trusted deliver his trust,
and let him fear God his Lord.
And do not conceal the testimony;
whoso conceals it, his heart is sinful;
and God has knowledge of the things you do.
To God belongs all that is in the heavens and earth.
Whether you publish what is in your hearts or hide it.
He will forgive whom He will, and chastise whom He will;
God is powerful over everything. — II: 282-83
And those who cast it up on women in wedlock,
and then bring not four witnesses scourge them with eighty stripes,
and do not accept any testimony of theirs ever;
those- they are the ungodly, save such as repent thereafter and make amends;
surely God is All-forgiving, All-compassionate.
Surely thy Lord knows very well those
who have gone astray from His way,
and He knows very well those who are guided. — LXVIII: 4
And when God promised you one
of the two parties should be yours,
and you were wishing that one not accounted should be yours;
but god was desiring to verify the truth by his words,
and to cut off the unbelievers to the last remnant,
and that he might verify the truth
and prove untrue the untrue,
though the sinners were averse to it. — VIII: 7
We indeed created man;
and We know what his soul whispers within him,
and we are nearer to him than the jugular vein...
And every soul shall come,
and with it a driver and witness... — L: 16-19

Another important principle is the liberation from being enslaved to social values. Quṭb is aware that the individual can be liberated from fears but enslaved to social values. Thus, besides the moral and spiritual aspects, liberation has also political and material aspects. This is why, for instance, private ownership is allowed; private ownership provides the individual with financial independence from the state which in turn allows political independence; thus, ultimately, the individual is capable of challenging the state that disobeys the *sharīʿah*.[34]

However, it seems that it is impossible that man can be freed from adopting and adhering to values, social and otherwise. And if this is impossible, how is a virtuous society going to come about? In fact, any society whether virtuous or otherwise is in need of social values. And it seems that liberating society from social values just for the sake of liberation serves no purpose; on the contrary, it can lead to the destruction of that society. What people should reject are the values that are harmful and they should create and maintain useful ones- a judgement that should be decided in each society. And I do not think that Quṭb really means to reject every value, but every social value that is not Islamic because he believes that the Islamic state exists for the sake of the cultivation of values and the promotion of morality. Thus if he stipulates the necessity for destroying every social value, the role of the Islamic state is frustrated. Similarly, when Quṭb wants to liberate society from fear, it is not every kind of fear that is meant. The fear of God should be maintained, which is in fact piety- a characteristic of the Islamic state.

In fact, Quṭb's statement needs qualification: what makes a state just and virtuous is not the mere existence of conscience but the existence of the moral one. On the other hand, although the Holy *Qur'an* gives importance to the conscience, the state is built on the law *(sharīʿah)* and not the conscience because the conscience cannot be measured or observed in the sense that we cannot assign to every action a sign of goodness or evil. Some individuals have the capacity to deceive others by behaving in a way that they do not really believe in; others may behave in a way that they do not subscribe to because of ignorance- an ignorant Muslim, for instance, may believe that God has hands and feet or that God did not provide laws. In other words, it is difficult to decide what a good or bad conscience is; and secondly, if this distinction is possible, there is no certain method of determining whether someone acted with a good conscience or not. This, however, does not mean that the cultivation of a good conscience is wrong or impossible, but such a concept is difficult to employ with certainty in legal, political, and economic matters. Though someone who killed another, for instance, can claim that he meant to save that other person, it does not seem feasible to disregard, from a legal and political point of view, matters of facts and to depend on the conscience in announcing sentences. If this were to happen, chaos could become the mark of society. Moreover, even if the conscience of someone is highly developed, this does not provide an immunity from committing unjust and illegal acts. Also, a Muslim ruler, for instance, may commit an atrocious crime or may pretend that he is applying the *sharīᶜah*- and Muslim societies are abundant in those activities- and pretend to have acted in good conscience. And for this reason, Islam does not only emphasize the conscience in the organization of life but, more importantly, law. For without giving priority to strict laws in creating and maintaining societies, the conscience itself and values are in danger.

Human Equality

If the seeds of equality and inequality are in the conscience, its liberation becomes the more essential in order to eliminate injustice and to cultivate justice. Quṭb believes that the administration of justice depends on the cultivation of conscience. He states that when

> *the human conscience has got a taste of all this [liberation], it finds legal and practical guarantees that assure this feeling [of liberation]. And there will be no need for someone to advocate equality in words, for it [the conscience] has tasted its meaning in its depths and has found it a reality in its life. It will not tolerate existing inequality... It will demand its right for equality, will struggle to establish this right, will preserve it when obtained, and will accept no alternative.*[35]

A very important implication of this statement is that values cultivated initially by conscience are more important than values cultivated initially by institutions; for institutions should be reflections of the values of society. This is not to deny the need for institutions but to affirm the importance of values. Thus, what is required first is the establishment of equality in the soul and then in institutions. Quṭb perceives that the origin of inequality is primarily in the soul or the conscience and not in institutions; therefore, remedies should be directed first at the origin and then at its secondary manifestations.

But we might ask, what should a society do when the cultivation of equality in the conscience is not possible? And why should equality be both moral and legal? A person has the right to treat people unequally or to prefer someone than another. Destroying inequality in the conscience does, not seem the domain of the state or even feasible, though eliminating legal equality is its domain and is feasible. In fact, we do not see, as Quṭb does, why people should be all thought of as being equal when they are not.

To be factual, equality and inequality are partly grounded in the conscience and mind but, equally, in nature itself; for some individuals are born weak, stupid, or both, others are intelligent, strong, or both; yet others are strong but stupid or intelligent but weak. It is unfair to treat all people in the same fashion or even to give them the same rights and duties; it is unfair not only to the intelligent or strong, for instance, but also to the average or weak. It would be unfair to ask a weak individual to lift two hundred pounds as much as it is unfair to ask the stupid to solve a complicated mathematical formula- in fact, there is no point in doing that unless we want to test the intellectual ability of the stupid and the endurance of the weak.

But Quṭb does not touch on the question of reason and treats all individuals as equal in economic and spiritual terms. Quṭb himself acknowledges the inequality of men and argues that in Islam's allowing the right of possession there is the application of justice by rewarding the individuals' efforts, suitability to the possessiveness of human nature and, the motivation of the individual to do his utmost and best. Here, there is an acknowledgement that unequal efforts deserve unequal rewards; it is unjust that people who have different capacities should be treated in the same way; for human faculties, whether spiritual, intellectual or physical are unequal, and to assert the opposite is a "vanity."

But notwithstanding Quṭb's acknowledgement of differences in the faculties and capacities of individuals, he maintains that every individual should have equal opportunity. And though success should only depend on the individual's performance and achievement regardless of race and other characteristics, equality is unreal unless it starts before birth. He states:

> *It is the right of every child born in the [Islamic] nation to be born without congenital diseases as others [healthy children]. The guarantees that are provided to any [rich] parents should be given to other [poor] parents. Health care should be provided to children before they are born or else there is no real equal opportunity [between those who can afford medical care and those who cannot].*[36]

When a child is born, Quṭb contends, he has the right to sufficient nutrition, education, and whatever other children enjoy. A reasons for this is that

> *Islam does not approve those false privileges granted to [rich] children at their birth only because they are born to a [specific] family or house or granted to children because of their fathers' moods.*[37]

What he means here by "their fathers' moods" is that even a father should not discriminate between his children by treating one better than the other or by giving, for instance, the whole inheritance to one child and excluding the others. The quotation is another sign of how Quṭb perceives equality. Neither the state nor the individual (the father or otherwise) can discriminate on the basis of preference of the father or the privileges of a family. Equality, for Quṭb, is not a motto or the possibility of being equal. But equality has to be real from the moment of conception till those born are capable of conducting and providing for their life.

In fact, Quṭb has extended the Qur'anic stipulations on the distribution of wealth to cover all aspects of life, medical education and so forth. He cites the following verses for his deduction about Islam's opposition to the concentration of wealth in a few hands:

Give the orphans their property,
and do not exchange the corrupt for the good;
and devour not their property with your property;
surely that is a great crime. — IV: 2
O believers, consume not your goods
between you in vanity, except
there be trading, by your agreeing together. — IV: 32

The unbelievers, though they possessed
all that is in the earth, and the like of it with it,
to ransom themselves from the chastisement
of the Day of Resurrection thereby,
it would not be accepted of them; for them awaits a painful chastisement. — V: 38
Believe in God and His Messenger,
and expend of that unto which He has made you successors.
And those of you who believe and expend shall have a mighty wage. — LVII: 7
... Then, if you perceive in them right judgment,
deliver to them their property;
consume it not wastefully and hastily ere
they are grown. If any man is rich, let him be abstinent;
if poor, let him consume in reason. — IV: 5
And let those who find not the means to marry
be abstinent till God enriches them of His bounty. — XXIV: 33

... those in whose wealth is a right known
for the beggar and the outcast.... — LXX: 24-25

It is for the poor emigrants,
who were expelled from their habitations
and their possessions, seeking bounty from God and His Messenger;

those- they are the truthful ones.
And those who made their dwelling in the abode,
and in belief; before them, love whosoever has emigrated to them...
and preferring others above themselves,
even though poverty be their portion.
And whoso is guarded against the avarice of his own soul,
those- they are the propsperers.— LIX: 7-8

But if success depends on the individual's effort, Quṭb does not provide a reason why the children of someone who worked very hard in his life should be treated equally as those children of the man who took life easily or did not work hard. And what happens if a rich man gives his newly born baby a million dollars is not clear; for the state cannot give every new born baby in the state a million dollars. Another way of handling this issue is by denying the father the right to dispose of his wealth. But, in this case, justice is not served.

On the other hand, Quṭb does not see why the newly born should be chained to his father's fortune. In fact, if the father is rich there is no problem. The problem arises with those who are born to poor families. In most cases, they are made poor the rest of their life because their fathers were so- especially given the economic structures prevalent in the Muslim world. It might be argued that, though born poor, they can change their lot because society provides equal opportunity. But, to Quṭb, the kind of equality that this equal opportunity is going to lead to- if the rich can obtain the best medical care and the poor can only attain the minimum or none or if the rich can go to the best schools and the poor can only go to poor schools or none- is only theoretical. If people are given at birth unequal opportunities, Quṭb does not view it as possible to achieve later on any kind of real equality.

Here, Quṭb is unaware that there are different claims of freedom and of justice. On the one hand, there is the claim of man's right to be free to obtain and dispense wealth in the manner he sees fit, which leads necessarily to unequal possession, education and so forth. On the other hand, there is the (Quṭb's) claim of man's right to be provided (at least at birth) with equal opportunities in terms of education and possession since their absence will perpetuate inequality. If the argument for freedom is upheld, those who uphold the claim for justice may counter by asking the reasons for a person's consent to the laws of government. If other individuals before us made and consented to those laws, we do not have to follow their steps. And we can possess anything we want whether owned by someone or not; for all rational stipulations like Locke or Hobbes' are made to protect inequality. The Lockian stipulation that mankind own the earth in common and that labor allots what belongs to whom is acceptable to us if there is anything left. But we are born after the whole earth has been owned by states and individuals and after agreeing on who gets what. For us to be as you are we either start at the same level (real equal opportunity) or else we are free to create our own law governing property and so forth. In other words, the social contracts that exist are not binding on us, and Locke's argument that if you enjoy what the state or society offers you consent to the social contract is false, because everyone is nowadays born under a social contract not made by him. For us, a real social contract has to take our interest into consideration.

On the other hand, if the claim for justice is upheld, those who uphold the claim for freedom would counter by asking whether it is just to undermine societies when they do not suit a group of individuals. If there is true justice those who exert themselves should be able to gain more than those who do not. Legally and politically you are our equal though we enjoy unequal possession. Even if we start anew with complete equality, inequality is going to surface again and shortly. The only way to prevent inequality is by injustice, i.e., by treating those who are not equal as equal.

On yet another level, Quṭb accepts the existence of social rights, political rights; and natural rights. Social and political rights as well as duties are the invention of societies. They serve their creators whether a group of individuls, a nation, or an individual, and there is nothing wrong in doing so. But to argue, as Quṭb does, that those laws are natural is unwarranted; to argue, for instance, that freedom of speech is a natural right is to assume that a right exists in the state of nature and to assume the existence of the state of nature- I mean by the state of nature the natural (not the civil or political) conditions that humans find themselves in. Man eats, speaks, sleeps, breathes, possesses, changes, accepts, thinks and so forth. He is born with certain faculties that are not subject to any law except natural laws (or regulations and limits). Each individual enjoys, more or less, the same faculties or capabilities. And because men are capable of doing the same things men are similar- and not necessarily equal, not in terms of rights but capabilities. In the state of nature nobody can claim a right but a capability. You cannot claim in the state of nature- or even in civil society- that it is your right to lift up two hundred pounds, you either can or cannot. On the other hand, if someone can do so, it is not his right but his capability, he either can or cannot. Also, a man cannot claim, for instance, the right to fly (before the invention of planes and other machines). If man could not speak, it would be useless to insist on freedom of speech. Thus, what we call human natural rights are not rights at all but capabilities.

But the frustration of nature or the prevention of human capabilities (like speech and life) is injustice because it goes contrary to the purpose of nature. (Also, I am positing a purpose for nature- or God- because if there is not, everything ceases to make sense and, in fact, there would be no sense in talking about rights and duties or justice and injustice; but even communism and evolutionism attribute a purpose). Consequently, those capacities when transported into society through a social or religious contract or other means become rights and entail duties; thus, man becomes entitled to free speech and movement. It is the duty of the govenment not to obstruct or allows obstruction of free speech. Similarly men acquire the right to live, and it is the duty of the state not to obstruct or end his life. Law, then, comes in for the protection of natural capabilities or "political and social rights," and the complexity of laws reflect the complexity of human conditions.

But- and all this discussion has been made to arrive at this conclusion- those natural capacities or political rights do not cover guaranteeing a good life, though it is the duty of the state to guarantee life. It is not the duty of the government to secure good free speech but its duty is securing freedom of speech. Similarly, it is not the duty of the government to secure a good life for the citizenry- as Quṭb wants- but its duty is to secure life itself. But Quṭb's demand can be justified in terms of social needs and agreements or the Holy *Qur'ān*. A specific society might agree to give, for instance, all its citizens equal education; this becomes a right for the citizens and a duty on the state. This agreement, however, does not make this right or duty natural but dependent and conditioned by the needs and agreement of each society.

On the other hand, Quṭb's conception of right cannot be supported by the Holy *Qur'ān* and the *sunnah* or history. Historically, Islam has allowed the Muslims to acquire as much property and riches as they want. For sure, it has discouraged inequality and accumulation of wealth, but has not abolished them altogether. Instead, it has upheld the doctrine of *al-amr bi al-maᶜrūf wa al-nayh ᶜan al-minkar* and imposed limits and taxes. Furthermore, Quṭb contradicts himself in arguing also that the father's exertion of himself secures a good life for himself and his family, society and state and that inheritance is not bad but benefits all mankind; some, directly like his children, and others, indirectly like when money is used in a proper way (commerce or almsgiving). Moreover, children, Quṭb reasons, have the right to inherit from their parents because children inherit usually their parents' health and diseases, temperment, beauty, and other characteristics.[38] For this reason, the father, for instance, cannot disinherit any of his children or whoever is the legal heir by drawing a will (though he can give his wealth away during his lifetime). The community, when the deceased has no legal heir, has a right in his property and money, and his money and wealth become religious endowments. Though this argument is primarily directed at Marxism which considers marriage as private prostitution and wants to destroy the family, it shows Quṭb's inconsistency: one time children have the right to their father's wealth, another, they do not.

Quṭb's argument is dependent on his conception that the

equality of the human race stems from "its beginning and fate, in life and death, in duties and rights, before the law and before God, and in this and the other life." And this leads him to deny the acquisition of unnatural privileges that are created by society. It is important to note that his conception of right is related to nature, for by "its beginning and fate" he means the origin of man; by "life and death" he means also the natural phenomena of life and death; by "duties and rights" he also means natural rights and duties because he believes that rights and duties are as natural as physical laws. Therefore, Quṭb denies the notion that an individual, a people or a race is naturally superior to another because of origin.

The only privilege that Quṭb allows and which makes an individual or a people superior is piety.[39] For this reason Quṭb quotes the following verses to support his argument:

> *Mankind fear your Lord*
> *who created you of a single soul,*
> *and from it created its mate,*
> *and from the pair of them scattered abroad many men and women;*
> *and fear God by whom you demand one of another,*
> *and the wombs, surely god ever watches over you.* IV: 1
> *O mankind, We have created you*
> *male and female, and appointed you races and tribes,*
> *that you may know one another.*
> *Surely the noblest among you in the sight of God*
> *is the most godfearing of you.*
> *God is All-knowing, All-aware.*— XLIX: 13

Piety is not restricted to a specific race or people, and anyone can become pious or impious; and, consequently, anyone can belong either to the superior or the inferior. Therefore, superiority in this sense is incidental and dependent on what the individual or a people does. Its main element is obedience to God and acceptance of *tawḥīd*. And, also, here this conception is natural because Quṭb believes that man seeks God by nature. Consequently, Islam, as interpreted by Quṭb, adheres to the idea that relations between state and society and between individuals and government are ultimately defined by a law higher than that of the state, i.e., the divine law.

Whereas liberalism believes that the interest of the individual is of primary priority and the driving force behind the actions of the individual, society, for Quṭb, should have a higher interest at which freedom of the individual has to stop. The interest of the community comes first, and the individual himself has a special interest to stop at a certain limit in order not to fall victim to his and others' instincts, lusts, and pleasures. Therefore, his freedom must not clash with the freedom of others or end up in endless conflicts. Those who only seek their self-interest are short-sighted because of the harm they inflict on themselves and others.[40]

On the other hand, for Quṭb, Islam provides individual freedom in its best form and human equality in its precise meaning; the state establishes the responsibility of the individual as well as individual freedom. Besides this, Islam establishes the communal responsibility that includes the individual and the community. This responsibility extends not only to the national level but is between the individual and himself, between the individual and his immediate family, between the individual and the community, between nations, and between one generation and successive generations.

It is obvious that Quṭb does not believe either in the existence of free enterprise as understood in the West nor in the strangling of free enterprise altogether as in the communist and other countries. His understanding of justice is socialist, though he denies that and insists on the Islamicity of his thought because socialism does not build its principles on God's revelation. But to prove beyond doubt that his thought is imbued with socialist tendencies, one only has to follow his reasoning on rights and duties; for instance, free enterprise has to give way at a certain level to the general interest of society. An individual can conduct trade and exercise his interest in an atmosphere of freedom but not at the expense of other individuals- for instance monopoly. Moreover, individuals are not responsible only for and before themselves but also before their families, immediate community, and society as a whole; that is, their responsibility goes beyond the neutral position of not damaging society, and includes positive steps such as helping the poor. The self-interest of the individual should include the interest of the community itself or else this self-interest becomes an animalistic pursuit. This pursuit, in the long run, leads to conflicts and ultimately undermines the interest of the individual. In other words, rationality requires that the enlightened individual should think that his self-interest should be limited and controlled or else people become victims to each other. On the other hand, total equality results in smothering of freedom (communism). The only way in which equality and freedom, two important ethical principles, become compatible is when they are controlled; thus, Islam, for Quṭb- and I do not see why Quṭb should not acknowledge that socialism also does- provides this mean of freedom and equality.[41]

Furthermore, and with the logic of a socialist, Quṭb argues that the rights and duties of the individual as well as those of the state are mutual. For instance, every child born in the Islamic state has the right to a proper life and to preserve his life. Meanwhile, individuals have duties to their God and to humanity; these duties are not only financial but moral as well. More precisely, Quṭb cites education as an example of what he means. Education is not only what people read and learn but is the whole life and includes, for example, *al-'amr bi al-maᶜrūf wa al-nay ᶜan al-minkar* (enjoining the good and forbidding the evil) wherever found in the community and not only in schools or institutions of education. It is fair to say that the state that Quṭb envisions is a welfare state because every member of the community is entitled to minimum standards of living and to employment. These standards are basically to prevent human degradation and to provide the necessary conditions for the well-being of society. But what distinguishes Islam from other systems is that these social guarantees are an indication of mercy and obedience to God- two distinctions from socialism! Mercy, for Quṭb, is a sign and one basis of belief because it is the indicator of the conscience being affected by this religion. For this reason, Islam asks its followers to pay *ṣadaqah* (alms-giving) and others; *ṣadaqah* is not only a charity but is also a purification of the soul.[42] In other words, Quṭb argues that though there might be similarity between Islam and socialism, ultimately Islam performs things not in the name of the people or equality but in God's name- a very important distinction from socialism.

Mutual Responsibility

The following principle is also an illustration of the socialist tendency of his thought. The nation as a whole is reponsible for the protection and alleviation of the life of the weak as well as the poor and the needy. Consequently, the state should train people to work so that their primary needs can be satisfied. In the case of those who cannot find work at all or find jobs but are unable to meet their needs, the state has to step in and help those who are in need. For Quṭb, the state is not a joint-stock company; for the individual has the right to be guaranteed the satisfaction of the basic needs in life. Therefore, Quṭb views Islamic mutual responsibility *(takāful)* as not mere charity or mercy but also as a system of preparing people to work and to produce and of guarantees. Mutual responsibility is not only an individualistic but public duty as well; in other words, it is not only an ethical duty but also a legal obligation on the state. He states:

> *Islam considers acquiring education [with which one can earn and deserve his livelihood] a duty on every individual. The community has responsibility to facilitate the fulfilment of this duty. If the community is incapable of realizing this duty, it becomes the responsibility of the state which is in charge of fulfilling this duty.*[43]

Quṭb cites numerous verses to argue that the well-being of the individual as well as the community is the responsibility of all Muslims:

> *To God belongs all that is in the heavens*
> *and in the earth, and unto Him all matters are returned.*
> *You are the best nation ever brought forth to men,*

bidding to honour, and forbidding dishonour,
and believing in God.
Had the people of the book believed,
it were better for them. — III: 104-105
Let not detestation for a people
who barred you from the Holy Mosque
move you to commit aggression.
Help one another to piety and godfearing;
do not help each other to sin and enmity.
And fear God; surely God is terrible in retribution. — V: 2
And fear a trial which shall surely
not smite in particular the evildoers among you;
and know that God is terrible in retribution. — XIII-25.
It is he that created the heavens and the earth in six days
then seated Himself upon the throne.
He knows what penetrates into the earth, and what comes forth from it,
what comes down from heaven, and what goes up unto it.
He is with you wherever you are;
and God sees the things you do. — LVII: 3
Take him, and fetter him, and roast him in Hell,
then in a chain of seventy cubits' length insert him!
Behold, he never believed in God the All-mighty,
and he never urged the feeding of the needy;
therefore, he today has not here one loyal friend,
neither any food saving foul pus,
that none excepting the sinners eat. — LXIX: 30-37

The responsibility of acquiring education and employment falls first on the individual who is required to educate and employ himself. If this individual is incapable, the community becomes responsible, but if the community fails, it is then the responsibility of the state. What this reveals to us is that Quṭb does not want, in theory at least, the state to step in and to control life and education as well as employment unless other avenues are tried first. But when private institutions and individuals fail in their performance, it is the responsibility, ethical as well as legal, of the state to intervene. Therefore, what Quṭb is advocating is neither liberalism, where the state leaves the individuals to meet their fate, nor communism where the state controls means of education as well as employment. Thus, it seems he is advocating a welfare state; for neither the state nor the individual has complete control over education or employment.

Quṭb stresses the importance of society more than the state; the state intervenes only where the voluntary efforts of individuals and of society fail; therefore, the state, in theory at least, is supplementary to individual and social structures, and as long as individuals and societies can get along without the state, the state should not interfere but step aside.

In order to highlight to the Muslims one of the positive aspects of Islam, Quṭb argues that Islam guaranteed social mutual responsibility and security many centuries ago. Furthermore, Islam's esteem for life is very comprehensive and its stipulations on rights and duties are very precise and conclusive. It has considered the nation as one body, and on this basis, has set up severe deterrents or *ḥudūd* for social crime because co-operation requires the protection of individuals; every individual is responsible for guarding the interests of the community. And in order to highlight the universality and importance of social justice in Islam, Quṭb views social as well as international problems as mostly the outcome of injustice and of not extending true justice to other nations. Thus, to be true and Islamic, justice should be extended to all countries, races, and religions. He states:

> *Islam does not only secure complete social justice in the large Islamic countries for its adherents alone but also serves all its inhabitants regardless of their religion, race, language... And this is one of its [Islam's] humane characteristics which other ideologies do not achieve.*[44]

Quṭb views Islam as exonerated from tribal, racial, and familial loyalties; it has attained a high level of fairness.[45] Quṭb's immediate goal in his exposition of equality is to show his dissatisfaction with the feudal conditions in Egypt before the Revolution of 1952; Egyptians in general were split into a few who had everything, and the majority which did not have much. For this reason he argues that understanding and applying true notions of Islamic justice and economics solve social problems and inequity in the distribution of wealth. And his upholding of justice on the international level is directed against the British and other colonial powers. Quṭb's goal in criticizing the West is the mobilization of the Muslims against the colonial powers and the corrupt political nature of party politics.[46]

Another important issue for the mutually responsible society is the family, which necessarily leads to the issue of the equality of the sexes. Quṭb believes that Islam has guaranteed complete equality between the two, but there are preferences to give men and women different functions and jobs. These preferences do not affect the equality between the sexes but reflect the needs of society and the training and potential of each. If women are responsible for the well-being of the family first and then to society this is not a depreciation of their status. On the contrary, the family is the cornerstone of society, not any society but the society that is mutually responsible. Moreover, the Islamic social system is "a family system," which is natural, naturally constituted, and derived from human nature. Thus, Quṭb explains, children need both parents; the family is the natural place where love, mercy, and mutual responsibility are impressed on and taught to children. Hence, families play a very vital role in the formation of human character; for this reason, he warns his fellow Muslims not to follow the West which is witnessing disintegration in its social fabric due to the neglect of families in the name of freedom.[47] The point here is that Islam would not have given women that function, i.e., the supervision of the family, because they are inferior or superior. But she is more suited temperamentally, psychologically, and physically to perform that job; for instance, men are free from bearing children; and pregnancy, Quṭb contends, develops and intensifies the woman's emotional aspect while man develops his contemplation and thought.

The importance of family structure for Quṭb should not be seen as biological only but, more importantly, as social and political; it serves as being one of the channels of mutual responsibility. For this reason, Quṭb attacks communism for its attempts to destroy the family structure and disagrees with its conclusion that families are a pretext for stimulating selfishness and love of possession and as a prevention of communalizing the wealth and property of individuals. Quṭb reasons that the individual's responsibility to the family, besides being ethically called for, is the bond that keeps the family together. This bond is important because the family is the primary unit for building the Muslim society. Contrary to Marxism, the existence of the family for Quṭb is primarily based on human nature as well as necessity; and in agreement with Marxism, on interest. He states that the existence of family is the outcome of, first, fixed inclinations in the human nature and of feelings of mercy and amicability; secondly, on necessities and interest; and, thirdly, being "the nest where sexual ethics and morality are developed" which are "the ethics of the society that is alleviated from animalistic permissiveness and barbarian anarchy".[48]

Besides the family, a great deal of mutual responsibility is obviously of an economic nature. Quṭb's economic theory is an essential and a very important part of the concept of social justice. In turn, the latter is a part of the theory of politics based on the concept of *tawḥīd.* Since the well-being and prosperity of any society require the existence of an economic structure, Quṭb attempts to provide an alternative to communism and capitalism.

Sayyid Quṭb, as we have seen, argues that the function of the government is the enforcement of the law of nature as advocated by the Holy *Qur'an* and accepts the concept of natural rights which should also be reflected in property. The first principle in the Islamic economic theory is the right of private ownership, but Islam stipulates that ownership is non-existent except by the authority of the lawgiver, i.e., God. The lawgiver bestows ownership, and all rights, including the right of ownership, are not fixed unless the lawgiver grants them because rights are not derived from the essence of things but are derived from the permission of the lawgiver. His reason is that God is the owner of everything, and man is His vicegerent. His vicegerency allows him to acquire private ownership, although the acquisition of private ownership is dependent on labor, physical or otherwise. And any ownership that is not based on the legal prescriptions of Islam and labor is a false possession because Islam does neither acknowledge nor guarantee it. Quṭb derives his ideas from numerous verses, among which are the following:

As for the unbelievers, their riches will not avail them,
neither their children, aught against God; those- they shall be
fuel for the Fire.—III: 8
For those that are godfearing, with their Lord
are gardens underneath which rivers flow…
men who are patient, truthful, obedient, expenders in alms,
imploring God's pardon at the daybreak.— III: 16
Praise belong to God who created
the heavens and the earth and appointed the shadows and light;
then the unbelievers ascribe equals to their Lord.— VI: I
How many a beast that bears not its own provision,
but God provides for it and you!
He is the All-hearer, the All-knower.
If thou askest them, 'Who created the heavens
and the earth and subjected the sun and the moon?'
They will say, 'God.'
How then are they perverted?
God outspreads and straitens His provision to whomsoever
He will of His servants; God has knowledge of everything.
If thou askest them, 'Who sends down out of heaven water,
and therewith revives the earth after it is dead?'
they will say, 'God'.— XXIX: 60-62
'Ah, God outspreads and straitens His provision to whomsoever He will of His servants.
Had God not been gracious to us,
He would have made us to be swallowed too.
Ah, the unbelievers do not prosper.'— XXVIII: 82

Surely God is powerful over everything.
Whatsoever mercy God opens to men, none can withhold
and whatsoever He withholds, none can loose after Him.
He is the All-mighty, the All-wise.
O men, remember God's blessing upon you;

is there any creator, apart from God, who provides for you out of heaven and earth?
There is no god but He: how then are you perverted? — XXXV: 3-4

Therefore, the development of any financial enterprise should be within the framework of Islamic laws; for Islam does not accept the benefits and legality of, for instance, gambling, cheating, monopoly or excessive gain.[49]

Private ownership, Quṭb reasons, is not the possession of the thing itself (like land or money) but the ownership of the benefits. To make this clearer, Quṭb states:

> *In short, the truth about private ownership in Islam is [this]: that the origin of ownership belongs to the community in general. And that private ownership is a function [of dispensation] with conditions and limits. And some kinds of property that benefit all people in common are public, and no one has the right to own, but parts of it can be distributed on specific categories [of people, like the poor] that need this property for their improvement and the improvement of the community along with them.*[50]

We can derive from this statement four points: first, original ownership belongs to the whole community or humanity; individuals do not own things in themselves but acquire the right of using them: in other words, this is a temporary ownership. The owner is an agent or vicegerent who has, first, to acquire ownership by work, and, secondly, to use it properly. On death, ownership is transferred to relatives. Secondly, ownership which is a delegation from the community can be taken back by it if the owner or the agent misuses this trust; for ownership is not permanent but dependent for its continuation on the good us made of it- and here Quṭb does not tell us how this can be conducted. Thirdly, some things, such as water, cannot be owned by individuals because of their vital importance in the life of the community. And, fourthly, the community and the state can (and should) grant those needy and poor some kind of ownership- and Quṭb does not say how- to help them live a decent life because the quality of life is the responsibility of the individual, the community, and the state.

Thus, Quṭb's perception of private ownership is used as a political tool to further a good and virtuous life. Because Islam wants to guarantee a decent life for all of its society and not only a group or some individuals, some laws and restrictions should be imposed on society as a whole. Thus, he puts forth the argument that Islam does not leave the right of private ownership absolute without restraints or limits- as the capitalist system does. It allows private ownership along with other principles that makes it an instrument for achieving the interest of the community; Islamic laws of inheritance are, for instance, instruments of diffusing the riches accumulated through generations; one ownership is transfered to many of the deceased's descendents and relatives, and, thus, in this way, wealth becomes communalized and decentralized. Moreover, if these laws of inheritance are compared with the English law which gives the first male born everything, the justice of the Islamic law is apparent.[51] But the situation is not so simple as Quṭb portrays. The purpose of the old European law was, by granting the eldest male everything, to preserve the family's estate intact. If it is divided up among heirs, then within a few generations the estate has become so fragmented as to become valueless; the estate was the source of power.

However, Islam is not against private ownership but against the accumulation of wealth and, to Quṭb, against the feudal system; consequently, the owner is not free to restrict or spend his money as he wishes without taking others into account. Although, for Quṭb, spending is an individual act, nonetheless, the individual has

> *freedom but within a framework of limits, and there is seldom a personal act that has no relation with others [individuals], although this relation may not be direct or obvious. For this reason, Islam has fixed for the poor- those who do not have the required amount to pay zakāt- a share provided from zakāt to improve their livelihood and not only for survival.*[52]

The immediate impression that one can gather so far is that private ownership is not real possession of anything, but it should be kept in mind that to Quṭb (and most Muslims) everything belongs to God. Quṭb states that money in general is originally the right of the community, and the community is charged with it from God, the only real owner. Although in practice people own their possessions; in theory, they do not. Here, ownership is analogical to authority: as authority belongs to God who has charged people with its dispensation whether in electing the ruler or the form of government, ownership also belongs to God who has charged the community with its dispensation; thus, the community delegates ownership as well as authority to individuals.

It seems that in theory everything belongs to God, but, in practice, the community and the individual dispense ownership as well as authority. The authority of the community gives the community the right to dispossess anyone who does not follow the *sharīᶜah*. Thus, whereas the ruler is dispossessed of authority upon his disobedience to the law or negligence of the community, similarly, the owner too can be dispossessed of the authority to dispense his property or the right of ownership. This is so because man, for Quṭb and in Islam, is the vicegerent *(khalīfah)* of God and should use his vicegerency in a proper manner, and dispossession is only an emergency measure because there are other measures like imprisonment that can be taken first. Thus, for Quṭb, the right of dispensation is contingent on reasonableness and good performance.

Whereas ownership of the means of production in capitalism is held by individuals and in communism by the state, Quṭb argues- again as a socialist would- that some essential means should be owned by the community, others by individuals. Though, it seems, Quṭb encourages market economy to satisfy the needs of society, when necessary, he allows the state to command the economy. Obviously, Quṭb wants neither to abolish private ownership nor market economy nor to allow unlimited private ownership of means of production nor complete command economy. As is the case with many other issues, the state intervenes when necessary. He states:

The theory of Islam on socially mutual responsibility does not make any conflict between the rights of the individual and the rights of society. It [Islam] makes it necessary for the state to protect the individual from themselves when necessary.[53]

Because Quṭb is not only against excessive accumulation of wealth but also against the squandering of money, he allows the state to interfere in people's behavior. For, again, squandering ruins not only the individual but also society. While the individual who squanders his wealth becomes "weak-willed and soft," exploiters, profiteers, and the needy will try to benefit from his squandering. More importantly, the mark of Islamic life is not squandering and extravagance but simplicity.[54] Quṭb's opposition to squandering and extravagance is tied to his understanding of the following verses:

And let not their possessions and their children please thee; God only desires thereby to chastise them in the present world, and that their souls should depart while they are unbelievers.— IX: 86

They also said, 'We are more abundant in wealth
and children, and we shall not be chastised'.
say: 'My Lord outspreads and straitens His provision
to whomsoever He will, but most men do not know it'.
It is not your wealth nor your children that
shall bring you nigh in nearness to Us,
except for him who believes, and does righteousness;
those- there awaits them the double recompense for that they did,
and they shall be in the lofty chambers in security.— XXXIV: 34-35
The Companions of the Left (O Companions of the Left!)
mid burning winds and boiling waters
and the shadow of a smoking blaze neither cool, neither goodly;
and before that he lived at ease,
and persisted in the great sin....— LVI: 41-45

O my people, today the Kingdom is yours,
who are masters in the land.

But who will help us against the might of God,
if it comes upon us?
Said Pharaoh, 'I only let you see what I see;
I only guide you in the way of rectitude, XL: 30-33

Thus far, Quṭb's notion on economics is clearly socialist; for Quṭb attempts to take a position between capitalism and communism: he allows private enterprise but permits the state to control the economy when necessary or to dispossess its citizens when they are unreasonable. But we have some problems in attempting to define reasonableness; for it might mean different things for different people or for the state and the individual. But whatever reasonableness is, the real problem is that the state is empowered to define reasonableness. Does the government have the right to disposses someone who has twenty thousand, two hundred thousand, or a million dollars because it thinks it is unreasonable for an individual to have this sum? And what if the government decides that owning one factory is destructive or an extravagant act? In other words, though Quṭb is right that extravagance and excessive accumulation of wealth are not within the spirit of Islam, it would be more dangerous to allow the state to control people's life and livelihood. Because if this happens, i.e., the right to dispossess someone because of squandering or extravagance or something else, people would neither be secure in their possession nor in any other aspect of life including the political. And though every individual act entails social effects, granting to the state the prerogative of deciding what is reasonableness, means that individuals, whom Quṭb wanted to be free from feudal lords and from tyrants, will be subjected to a feudal and tyrannical leviathan. If this happens, the very things that Quṭb wants to protect, the liberation of conscience and mutual responsibility or social justice, will be put in jeopardy, if not eliminated altogether.

Furthermore, neither Islamic history nor theory warrants Quṭb's conclusions; nothing in the *Qur'ān* and the *sunnah* allows the state or the ruler to dispossess the individual from his ownership. The most that can be imposed on the Muslims legally in financial terms is a kind of tax and reparation for crimes; but this tax, *zakāt* (obligatory tax on Muslims who are financially capable), is not a punishment, and Quṭb is aware of this. *Zakāt,* Quṭb states correctly, is a worship, on the one hand, and a social and devotional duty, on the other. It means purity and growth: "It is a purification for the conscience and probity and purification for the soul and the heart from stinginess and from the instinct of self-love...".[55]

3 - Political Action: Revolution (Al-Thawrah)

Quṭb's ultimate goal is to create a Muslim nation based on the principles of Islam like social justice and *sharīᶜah;* but essential steps should be taken, first among which is revolution. As *tawḥīd* is the basis of Islamic government and Muslim society, it is as well the pivot of revolution, and should be the basis of the propagation of Islam *(daᶜwah)* and of political movement. Because *tawḥīd* is a movement of continuous development of life, Islam neither accepts nor justifies an evil reality as such because its main mission is to eradicate evil and to improve the quality of reality. *Tawḥīd,* according to Quṭb, consists of three principles: first, freedom from subordination to anyone but God, or God's *hākimīyyah*; secondly, revolution against the authority of tyrannical lords; and, thirdly, considering as a crime of unbelief the negation of personality and giving up freedom. It is a crime because, God having created him free, man subordinates himself to a tyrannical president or chief or to *al-jāhilīyyah.* "No god but God," declares Quṭb,

> *is a revolution against the wordly authority that usurps the first characteristics of divinity, and a revolution against situations based on this usurpation and against the authorities that rule by their own laws that are not given by God.*[56]

These ideas Quṭb develops by a reinterpretation of the following verses:

> *Muhammad is naught but a Messenger;*
> *Messengers have passed away before him.*
> *Why, if he sould die or is slain, will you turn about on your heels?*

If any man should turn about on his heels,
he will not harm God in anyway,
and God will recompense the thankful.
Many a Prophet there has been,
with whom thousands manifold have fought,
and they fainted not for what smote them in God's way,
neither weakened, nor did they humble themselves;
and God loves the patient.— III: 139-40
Surely those who disbelieve in our signs-
We shall certainly roast in Fire;
as after as their skins are wholly burned, we shall give them in exchange other skins,
that they may taste the chastisement.
Surely God is All-mighty, All-wise.— IV: 59

And when it is said to them,
'Come now to what God has sent down, and the Messenger',
then thou seest the hypocrites barring the way to thee.
How shall it be, when they are visited
by an affliction for what their own hands have forwarded,
then they come to thee swearing by God,
'We sought only kindness and conciliation?'— IV: 64-65
O believers, take not the unbelievers
as Friends instead of the believers; or do you desire to give
God over you a clear authority?
Surely the hypocrites will be in the lowest reach of Fire;
thou wilt not find for them any helper;
some such as repent, and make amends,
and hold fast to God, and make their religion sincerely God's;
those are with the believers, and God will certainly
give the believers a mighty wage.— IV: 144-45
Alif Lam Mim
God
There is no god but He, the Living, the Everlasting.
He has sent down upon thee the Book
with the truth, confirming what was before it, and
He sent down the Torah and the Gospel aforetime,
as guidance to the people, and He sent down the Salvation.—
III: 1-3

Surely, the worst of beasts in God's sight
are the unbelievers, who will not believe,
those of them with whom thou made compact that
they break their compact everytime, not being godfearing.
So, if thou comest upon them anywhere in the war,
deal with them in such wise as to scatter the ones behind them;
haply they will remember.— VIII: 59
Surely We sent down the Torah, wherein
is guidance and light; thereby the Prophets
who had surrendered themselves gave judgement for those of jewry,
as did the masters and the rabbis, following
such portion of God's Book as they were given to keep and were witnesses to.
So fear not men, but fear you Me;
and sell not My signs to a little price.
Whoso judges not according to what was sent down
they are the unbelievers.— V: 49

That which you serve, apart from Him,
is nothing but names yourselves have named,
you and your fathers; God has sent
down no authority touching them.
Judgment belongs only to God;
He has commanded that you shall not serve any but Him.
That is the right religion, but most men know not.— XII: 40

Thus, revolution occupies a decisive role because, for Quṭb, it is the only credible instrument of attaining social justice and of applying the *sharīᶜah.* A revolution should be a conscious effort to transform current existing societies; it does not force people to adhere to Islam. But it aims at creating the Muslim individual, the Muslim society, and the Islamic state. Because the Islamic revolution aspires as well to the transformation of man's enslavement to man and to matter, it is not directed at a particular society but essentially at those societies that subordinate themselves to anyone but God or the *jāhilī* societies.

A real revolution does not patch up old concepts with Islamic concepts; in fact, it should shake and destroy old structures in order to build new ones. Not believing in the viability of mild change for a society erected on false or immoral fundamentals, Quṭb insists on the necessity of revolution as the only proper remedy for decaying societies. And for Quṭb, all societies are, in one way or another, decaying. *"Zalzalah"* (shaking) or revolution is the word used to describe the first step in the process of building a new society.[57] But this *zalzalah,* though strong, is not violent, in theory at least; it should start with education in a twofold manner: first, expounding and teaching the true meaning of Islam and, secondly, refuting the "fallacies of Western ideologies." Hence, we find that one of the characteristics of Quṭb's writings is unusually harsh attacks on the West and its ideologies in order to discredit their use in the reconstruction of Islamic thought.

Because the road to change necessitates creativity, it requires the development of life but not "patching up." Likening a society to a building, Quṭb states

> *there is a difference between having a plan to construct gradually and patching up a construction based on another plan. In the end, this patching up does not establish a new building for you. Thus, it is necessary to destroy the old system and to build a new one.*[58]

Though wanting the Islamic revolution to be gradual in order to spread through ideological education and to induce a gradual transformation of institutions, on the matters of life and religion, Quṭb's highest aim is a total revolution that sweeps away the governments of his time as well as establishing new Muslim societies unrelated to patched-up, non-Islamic codes of law, local traditions, and un-Islamic customs.[59]

The greatest revolution, led by the Prophet Muḥammad, should be repeated, argues Quṭb; what the Prophet Muḥammad did was to transform tribal, polytheistic, and *jāhilī* societies into a unified and monotheistic nation. Moreover, a revolution is easier to attain nowadays than at the time of the Prophet since, according to Quṭb, Islam has spread and people are becoming more accepting of it. Notwithstanding this acceptance, a revolution is as necessary now as it was before the time of the Prophet because of the Muslims' loss of independence, progress, knowledge, and the real meaning of Islam. Although Muslim leaders should be aware of the reality of the world (as opposed to ideals), reality should not be an obstacle to contemporary Muslims in their aspirations; they should learn from the Prophet Muḥammad who faced and changed all the evil realities and the *jāḥilīyyah* of his age. The keynote for the Muslims' success was- and will be- the result of an Islamic revolution; and because Quṭb is so convinced of the validity of the Islamic revolution- due to Islam's harmony with human nature- he argues that once individuals really understand Islam, they will adhere to it.[60]

Because *tawḥīd* "is not a negatively philosophical and theoretical declaration" but "is a positively realistic and active declaration",[61] it involves confronting other concepts and ideologies, i.e., the philosophical and practical *jāhilīyyah*. This requires that the Muslims should acquire knowledge of other philosophies and ideologies; also, Islamic activism should confront the material obstacles, foremost among which are the existing political authorities. This confrontation by words and deeds does not apply only to Arab societies but to all societies because the message of Islam is not for Arabs per se, but its subject is man. Therefore, the ultimate message and goal of Islamic revolution is abolishing those regimes and governments that are established on the *jāhilī* basis of men's rule of men and enslavement of others; for, the revolution sets the individuals free in choosing the creed and the lifestyle they want.

As is obvious, this declaration which, for Quṭb, stems, from *tawḥīd,* means

> *the comprehensive revolution in the government of man in all its forms, shapes, systems, and situations, and the complete rebellion against every situation [that is contrary to the principles of Islam] on the whole earth.*[62]

Thus, Quṭb contends, the Islamic state is established on that land ruled by the Islamic system and law whether all or some of the people are Muslims. But the land that is not ruled by Islamic system and law is *dār al-ḥarb* (land of war), no matter what the people believe in (even if it is Islam). What is significant here is that the composition of a society of Muslims does not make it Muslim; only when Islamic law rules the society it can properly be called Muslim. This lends support to Quṭb's previous argument that Islamic government is the government of the law; for the application of Islamic law in a society whether composed of a majority of Muslims or non-Muslims makes it Muslim. The Islamic state is neither defined by specific territories nor by specific races; a Muslim society can be established anywhere. On the other hand, those societies that claim to be Muslim are not, in Quṭb's view, because they do not uphold the law of Islam; in fact they are *jāhilī*. What this means in practical terms is that those societies that existed at Quṭb's time were not Islamic but *jāhilī;* and, thus, needed to be changed. For, any state that fights the Muslims in their religion or *sharīᶜah* also belongs to *dār al-ḥarb* and is part of the overall *jāhilī* structure.[63]

Although *jihād* (struggle) aims at transforming any anti-Islamic status quo and institutions opposing and preventing the free practice of Islam, *jihād* is neither a suicide mission nor a campaign of atrocities. *jihād,* Quṭb announces, has four basic characteristics; the first is "serious realism." That is to say that Islam faces with

> *daᶜawh and explanation those incorrect concepts and beliefs. And faces with power and jihād those regimes and authorities based on those incorrect concepts in order to abolish them.*[64]

Quṭb, as opposed to many other Muslim contemporaries, neither argues nor accepts the argument that Islam launches *jihād* only for defensive purposes and describes this argument as defeatist because Islam does not accept this line of argument. Rashīd Riḍā argues, for instance, that Islam is peaceful unless it is attacked. For Quṭb, Islam is not defensive but "a defence of man himself." And those writers on *jihād* who are defeated spiritually and mentally do not distinguish between the method of this religion in rejecting complusion to embrace Islam and its method in destroying those material and political forces which stand between man and his God. Those who saw *jihād* only as defensive did not understand Islam; it is true that Islam defends the land it exists on, but it also struggles to establish the Islamic system wherever possible. It is necessary to establish that system because it speaks to men wherever they are. But those who understand *jihād* as a defense only are affected by non-Islamic notions (for instance, by the attacks of the orientalists).[65]

To prove that Islam is not defensive only but aims at the elimination of worshipping or subjection to anyone or *al-jāhilīyyah* but God, Quṭb cites the following verses:

And fight in the way of God with those
who fight with you, but aggress not;
God loves not the aggressors.
And slay them wherever you come upon them,
and expel them from where they expelled you;
persecution is more grievous than slaying.
But fight them not by the Holy Mosque
until they should fight you there;
then, if they fight you, slay them-
such is the recompense of unbelievers-
but if they give over, surely God is All- forgiving, All-compassionate.
Fight them, till there is no persecution and the religion is God's;
then if they give over, there shall be no enmity save for evildoers.
The holy month for the holy month;
the holy thing demand retaliation. Whoso commits aggression against you,
do you commit aggression against him
like as he has committed against you; and fear you God,
and know that God is with the godfearing.— II: 187-190

Prescribed for you is fighting, though it be hateful to you.
Yet it may happen that you will hate a thing
which is better for you; and it may happen
that you will love a thing which is worse for you;
God knows, and you know not.
They will question thee concerning the holy month

and fighting in it. Say: 'Fighting in it is a heinous thing,
bid to bar from God's way, and disbelief in Him, and the Holy Mosque,
and to expel its people from it-
that is more heinous in God's sight;
and persecution is more heinous than slaying;'
they will not cease to fight with you,
till they turn you from your religion,...
But the believers, and those who emigrate and
struggle in God's way- those have hope of God's compassion;
and God is All- forgiving, All-compassionate.— II: 212-216
So let them fight in the way of God
who sell the present life for the world to come;
and whosoever fights in the way of God and is slain, or
conquers, We shall bring him a mighty wage.
How is it with you, that you do not fight
in the way of God, and for the men, women, and children
who, being abased, Say, 'our Lord, bring us forth from this city
whose people are evildoers,
and appoint to us a protector from thee,
and appoint to us from thee a helper'?
The believers fight in the way of God,
and the unbelievers fight in the idols' way.
Fight you therefore against the friends of Satan;
surely the guile of Satan is ever feeble. -IV: 77-79

Fight those who believe not in God and the Last Day
and do not forbid what God and His Messenger have forbidden-
such men as practise not the religion of truth,
being those who have been given the Book-
until they pay the tribute out of hand and have been humbled.—
IX: 29
The number of the months, with God, is
twelve in the Book of God,
the day that He created the heavens and the earth;
four of them are sacred.
That is the right religion.
And fight the unbelievers totally even as they fight you totally;

and know that God is with the godfearing.— IX: 36
Leave is given to those who fight because they were wronged- surely God is able to help them.
Who were expelled from their habitations
without right, except that they say 'Our Lord is God...'— XXII: 40

The second characteristic is "active realism," for *jihād* cannot be fought with words only but requires much more preparation: it does not meet reality- for instance, a strong military force- with an abstract theory. *Jihād* is a movement that can operate in stages and takes time and effort as well as organization. The third characteristic is that *jihād*, as a continuous movement, may take many forms and procedures that do not contradict the principles of Islam: it can take the form of writing, assisting others, teaching, self-discipline, and many others. The fourth characteristic is that the regulation of the relations between Muslim societies and non-Muslim ones can only be one of two things: first, that Islam is the basis of international relations; or, secondly, that Islam is permitted peacefully to propagate its call without a barrier from any political regime or material force. Societies should give their peoples the freedom to accept or reject Islam.[66]

As a universal society, the Muslim society is not racial, national or geographical; it is a society open to all mankind regardless of their race, color or language and regardless of religion and belief. More than this, the Muslim society is not a police society; every individual has the right to voice his opinion. For Islam wants freedom of worship for its adherents as well as for worshippers of other religions-[67] though I do not think Quṭb would accept the existence Muslim heretic sects because he would argue that they fall under the law of Islam and are not a distinct religion but have distorted Islam and deserve severe punishment, death or imprisonment.

The societies that are in need of revolutions are the societies that are not based on the Islamic concept of divinity, life, and man. By this definition, Quṭb includes "all existing societies on earth today", as un-Islamic, *jāhilī* societies; this means that

Christian, Jewish, socialist, and capitalist societies are in need of revolutions. Even the Muslim societies do not escape Quṭb's revolution; for although these societies do not believe in the divinity of anyone except God, they have accepted, according to Quṭb, the *ḥākimīyyah* (governance) of others besides God.[68] And notwithstanding Islam's allowing non-Muslims to follow their creeds, it does not allow men to be governed by the laws of men.

Quṭb's argument leads to the conclusion that the highest order of organization is the political, which should be based on Islam; for it is necessary that those political regimes that are based on socialism, capitalism, and Marxism should be abolished, which includes those Muslim societies that follow the West or follow human thought. More to the point, the immediate message is two-fold: first, to discredit the Egyptian government and its ideology and, secondly, to motivate a counter-revolution; and this is why Islam does not try to reconcile itself with Arab nationalism or race and why those governments that advocate Arab nationalism can be overthrown legitimately. For the focal point of the Muslim society is not purity of race or language but *tawḥīd* and the *ḥākimīyyah*. And it is the Muslims' responsibility to ward off evil or *jāhilīyyah* wherever it is found, even in non-Islamic societies. For Islamic ideology should dominate all other aspects of civilization, and if Islam does not aim at reconciliation (patching up) with those un-Islamic societies and concepts and with other creeds and ideologies, the alternative is internal and external war or revolution, especially, if we keep in mind Quṭb's aspiration to transport people from the caravan of darkness and *jāhilīyyah* to Islam and to create a human life in accordance with the Islamic concepts, a life represented in reality by a system that follows the divine method.

But if Quṭb allows people to follow their beliefs and religions, and if he treats communism, liberalism, capitalism as well as Judaism and Christianity as religions, he should not object to their exercise of their political as well as religious beliefs. His notion that Islam seeks to establish an Islamic political order in non-Muslim societies means that Islam's ultimate aim is political domination of the world regardless of whether people believe in *tawḥīd* or not; or, that Islam's real purpose is the propagation of a virtuous life by using political domination as an instrument. In fact, Quṭb's concept cannot be justified exclusively in the name of God; for if Islam's ultimate purpose is political domination of the world in the name of *tawḥīd,* those who do not believe in *tawḥīd* at all or in the same manner as the Muslims do, do have the right to revolt and kill the Muslims in the name of their religions or ideologies. For if the Jews, for instance, can follow their religion under an Islamic regime, would Quṭb accept their claim for Palestine, for example? Put differently, religious beliefs usually include or lead to political beliefs, and religion and politics- or what Quṭb calls systems- are so interwoven that to argue that Christians and Jews can practise completely their religions is an overstatement (and Quṭb should have done better if he did not follow that line of thinking). Moreover, if the aim of the Islamic government is the propagation of Islamic morality and the application of the divine law, there is no point in Islam's political domination of non-Muslim countries in the name of *tawḥīd* since non-Muslims, especially Jews and Christians, are allowed legally to follow their laws and morality. In other words, it would be useless to impose an Islamic government in Britain since the vast majority of that country are non-Muslims, which means that they can follow their own laws and morality. Put simply, the goals of Islamic political theory such as a virtuous Muslim society are frustrated because its aims such as the application of the divine law cannot be attained by its own stipulations such as the freedom of worship.

Quṭb's concept of Islamic ideology is not only very antagonistic to the Egyptian society but also to the Arab countries and the world in general and suffers from exclusiveness due to his perception of things in terms of only either/or. This attitude of seeing only one side has spilled over in to his conception of activism; actually, it is his conception of activism.

Activism, for Quṭb, necessitates the creation of a vanguard *(ṭalīʿah)* that will lead the revival of Islam. This vanguard, to which Quṭb dedicated his book, ***Maʿālim fī al-Ṭarīq,*** needs

signposts and indications in order to understand its role. These signposts should be based on the Qur'ān, its directions, and the concept it gave to the first [Muslim] generation.[69]

The first signpost is that those who are going to be engaged in the Islamic *da^c^wah* (propagation of Islam) should take into consideration the generation of the Prophet and his companions: for the *Qur'ān* was that generation's source of right and wrong. And when necessary they even gave up what was dear to them like friends and relatives as well as their material possessions in order to follow Islam. Islam was a spiritual invasion of peoples and a physical invasion of their governments, and the effects of the first Islamic revolution affected directly or indirectly many revolutionary movements that have occurred- Renaissance, Protestantism, equalitarianism, French Revolution, and experimentalism are examples that Quṭb cites. Therefore, the first step is to teach the Muslims and others the true essence of Islam; the first step in the revolution, i.e., *da^c^wah,* is necessary for the establishment of an Islamic society. Quṭb holds the notion that no Muslim society will be established unless a *da'wah* is set up to enter people anew into this religion or to take them out from the *jāhilīyyah* they reached. *Da^c^wah* is not only necessary in the non-Muslim societies but also in the Muslim ones because, for Quṭb, the absence of activism, which is part of the original nature of Islam, leads society to stagnate.[70]

Another signpost- and another sign of exclusiveness- is that those Muslims who are engaged in the *da^c^wah* should not compromise; for compromise is out of the question because their task is to effect change. Therefore, he states:

The first step in our way is to be aloof from this jāhilī society, its values, and concepts, and not to modify much or little our values and concepts in order to meet with it [the jāhilī society] half-way. No. We and it are at a crossroad and when we go along with it one step, we lose the whole method and the road.[71]

But, it seems, Quṭb contradicts himself by insisting that Islam is not based on attacking other people and that his revolution can be effected by peaceful means. The Islamic *da^c^wah,* which is the first step toward the revolution, he declares, "is a complete declaration of all the facts of this creed in obvious clarity... with wisdom, kindness, amicability, gentleness, and easiness".[72] But, we may say that the possibility of uniting people physically and spiritually in a wise, kind, amicable, gentle and yet, uncompromising way is beyond our comprehension. It is either one of two things, he can be uncompromising and achieve his goals, even if this leads to war; but this can never be gentle and wise and kind; or, he can propagate Islam in a way that people understand and in a gentle, kind, and wise way. If Islamic *da^{c}wah* is a complete declaration of facts, why should the Mulsims resort to war in order to propagate it? And why should the Muslims dominate non-Muslims?

Although Quṭb's insistence that *da^{c}wah* should represent the morality of Islam is understandable, this morality appears from his writings to be a set of limitations and deterrents. Though he denies that Islamic morality is a set of limitations and deterrents but is originally and fundamentally a constructive energy and momentum to continuous development and activism, one can surely see the kind of activism he espouses and the kind of development that would follow from his revolution. But his activism and positiveness are directed mostly at the destruction of governments and ideologies.

Furthermore, Quṭb has problems acknowledging the contributions of other ideologies in the formation of his own. It is true that the message of the *Qur'ān* is primarily to announce the oneness of God and to correct and change the previous concept of God, the universe, and man and is also the proclamation of the brotherhood and equality of men as well as the dissemination of justice, moral and social. But, because Islam contains these principles, Quṭb does not accept resorting to anything that is not Islamic in those important matters; for to describe principles that Islam has advocated before socialism or democracy (like social justice or equality) in non-Islamic terms is, first, a sign of not understanding Islam and other ideologies, and, secondly, of politically subordinating the Muslims to other ideologies like liberalism, socialism, nationalism or a combination of them.

Though morality and ethics are based on freedom from mean inclinations and the liberation of the human spirit,[73] Quṭb's morality is so strict and uncompromising that he even blames

> *those who accept submission to the authority of their people and their government, who are not excused in being overcome [by their rulers]. They [the submissive] are numerous and the tyrants are few. If they [the submissive] wanted liberation, they would have sacrificed [willingly] some of what they had sacrificed disgracefully and unwillingly in the self, honor, and money to authoritarian lords.*[74]

4 - A Comparative Analysis of the Ideologies of Modernism and Fundamentalism

Tawḥīd has become for Quṭb the thread that weaves together all the materials of politics, economics, ethics, theology, and all other aspects of life. Because God, the source of knowledge and of matter, is the creator of both, He is given the ultimate say in political life as well. This understanding of *tawḥīd* is shared by al-Mawdūdī and al-Bannā. Man, they contend, should submit only to God; this submission is not only theological as understood by traditional thinkers, medieval and modern. But more importantly, the fundamentalists endow ultimately this concept of *tawḥīd* with political significance. Their insistence on subjecting the political regime to religion leads them even to consider as infidel and unqualified to rule those individuals who disregard either the establishment or the manitenance of the state on the basis of God's governance or *ḥākimīyyah*. It is ironic that the fundamentalists, like al-Bannā and Quṭb, who reject the teachings of medieval Islamic philosophy, sould seek the same kind of polity, i.e., a polity that is created for and sustained by and that aims at a virtuous society whose ultimate goal is God.

Though the fundamentalists reject many teachings of the modernists, they are by no means traditional. On the contrary, a great portion of their attack is directed at the traditional religious *ᶜulamā'* (scholars); the *ᶜulamā'* are, according to Quṭb, incapable of understanding the true principles of the *Qur'ān*. Following blind imitation and looking for solutions in juristic books which are essentially human and not revealed, their teachings have made the public complacent and have pushed away the educated. On the other side, the fundamentalists level their attacks also on the elites who, though administering the affairs of the Muslims and controlling the government, are ignorant of Islam and are leading their nations to darkness or *jahilīyyah.* Because of the failure of the two, there is a need to create a new group or *ṭalīᶜah* of Muslims who understand truly their religion as well as modernity. Al-Mawdūdī, for instance, acknowledges, as Quṭb and other thinkers do, the weakness of the Muslim civilization and declares the necessity for an Islamic revival because the past is insufficient to strike an Islamic renaissance. It is of primary necessity to find Muslims who can build a new science and philosophy based on pure Islam; those Muslims should take the leadership of science and politics from non-Muslims.[75]

This statement of al-Mawdūdī is of crucial significance for understanding the fundamentalist theory of politics and its difference from the Muslim modernist theory. Because the modernists have not rejected the West altogether but some particular philosophies, they have adopted and accepted many Western political theories like republicanism. For this reason, the modernists have not attempted to put forward a political theory- because it existed already and what is needed is to transport it in into the Islamic milieu. This is not to say that they do not have political teachings, but that their teachings do not amount to a new or a full-fledged political theory: their political thought is mostly of a fragmentary nature put forward for immediate political goals. Moreover, though the modernists have attacked traditionalism, they have not repudiated traditions as such. Perceiving, with validity, that the way for a revival can be by bringing together two traditions, the Islamic and the Western, they have focused their efforts on harmonizing religion with science. And their respect for history is very immense and has culminated in learning and accepting many benefits of both the West and Islam.

Nonetheless, they have never claimed to have, and actually have not, written a complete political theory, for instance, on social justice or *tawhīd* or the principles of politics as legislation and equality and so forth. Their attempts have focused on reviving the intellectual atmosphere in the Muslim lands first, and then on political matters; or in other words, their political teachings are an outgrowth of their intellectual temperament. Put differently, because they have accepted many philosophical ideas produced in the West, they have not hesitated in accepting numerous benefits of Western political systems.

But, except for the period of the Prophet Muḥammad who was inspired and the first two caliphs- to Quṭb- or the first four caliphs- to al-Mawdūdī- who followed the true essence of Islam, the fundamentalists do not, by and large, sanctify history or see it as a guide. Not sanctifying history is one of the challenges to the orthodox establishment of Sunnism as well as to Shiᶜism. Muslim scholars in general, except some philosopers of Islam, have sanctified the past by accepting as imperatives the teachings and interpretations of earlier scholars such as Abū Ḥanīfa, al-Shāfiᶜī, Ibn Ḥanbal, and Ibn Mālik on jurisprudence and al-Ghazālī, al-'Ashᶜarī, and al-Bāqillānī on theology. With the passage of time, their teachings, which were the result of *ijtihād* (independent reasoning), acquired an unchallenged authority as well as a normative status. And because *ijtihād* has been stalled for centuries, even open-minded people such as ᶜAbduh have not challenged their arguments in general.[76]

For instance, ᶜAbduh rejects the notion of human capability to fathom the essence of God and follows traditional theological arguments on God's essence and attributes; thus, ***Risālat al-tawḥīd*** (Treatise of oneness) is nothing more than a simplified edition of medieval treatises on theology. ᶜAbduh's exposition is very traditional except in two points: his refraining from entering disputation that characterized medieval writings (for instance, whether God's attribues are part of His essence or not) and his argument that Islam and reason are not contradictory. The first point is al-Ghazālī's who in ***Tahāfut al-Falāsifah*** (Incoherence of the Philosophers) argues that this kind of discussion is futile since man cannot know whether God's attributes are part of the essence or not. (Al-Ghazālī was chastizing both philosophy and theology). The second point is that of the philosophers such as al-Kindī and al-Fārābī. What ᶜAbduh and other modernists have done is to introduce again to intellectual circles the legitimacy of *ijtihād* by using the past itself. There is nothing wrong in doing so, but the point is made here to show the difference between the fundamentalists and the modernists concerning the past. Also, I am not implying that ᶜAbduh's achievement is minor, but that his efforts were focused on regenerating Islam by recycling past notions of reason and modern science. The reader cannot fail to notice even the traditional structure of his arguments like his description of God's actions.

In sharp contrast to this, the fundamentalists in general perceive as outmoded the past as well as the present in its philosophical, juristic, theological manifestations, whether produced in the East or the West; and historicism which is a main feature of fundamentalism is embodied in its rejection of almost all old and traditional interpretations which are, for the fundamentalists, historically oriented. Though those interpretations and doctrines were suitable for their societies, they are, the fundamentalists contend, by no means of intrinsic value. Their value is historical in showing the Muslims that Islam allows a multitude of interpretations. In other words, they do not look at the truth of arguments in itself but select only those interpretations suitable for modernity. Quṭb and other fundamentalists transform history into a justifying vehicle for renewal, reassessment, and revolution.

Thus, rejecting the past and the present necessitates that the fundamentalists provide an alternative to Islamic and Western political theories. This theory manifests primarily in their understanding of *tawḥīd* and the *ḥākimīyyah* (governance of God). Therefore, Al-Bannā, Quṭb, and al-Mawdūdī proclaim, for instance, that the source of legislation in the new society is God; any truly Muslim society should be directed at obedience to God. Also, they insist that the fundamental characteristic of ethics is obedience to God, i.e., by accepting and applying His teachings.

Thus, whereas the process of history has illuminated the Qur'ān and the *sunnah* for the traditionalists and the modernists, it has become, by preventing a direct understanding of the *Qur'ān* and the *sunnah,* a process of obscurity and dilutions for the fundamentalists. Therefore, history itself has to be disrupted in order to forward a more authentic and direct understanding of the *Qur'ān* and the *sunnah* without recourse necessarily to traditions of philosophy, theology, and jurisprudence. For the fundamentalists, these branches of knowledge, especially the political and the intellectual as opposed to the ritual, have to be reevaluated and verified by a new direct interpretation of Islam. Not only is the history of Islamic nations not accepted as a correct interpretation of Islam, but also Western and socialist doctrines and histories cannot provide to be a model acceptable to the fundamentalists.

This fundamentalist claim is very essential in order to justify the rejection of the past because if the fundamentalists accept the historical or scientific processes as possessing normative claims, neither a new history nor a new science- as al-Mawdūdī believes- will be required but only continuation and development; their insistence on disrupting the existing societies will be a meaningless claim. Hence, in viewing sciences and philosophies as un-Islamic, the creation of purely Islamic sciences and philosophies becomes a must. And because these two aspects of life should be subjected neither to past Islamic civilization nor to foreign civilizations, the fundamentalists find a justification for refusing reconciliation with Western thought; they even perceive that there is an essential contradiction between the conception of man in Islam and other systems. It is not reason per se or science per se, al-Mawdūdī argues, that bestows honor on man, but what really does bestow honor is man's rising from obligatory instinctual worship of God to the level of human, willed worship. If man worships other than God or is detracted from worshipping God- al-Mawdūdī believes that the West is doing so- he is less honored than animals because animals are still at least on the instinctual level.[77]

Many notions that the fundamentalists hold can be traced to Muḥammad Asad, a convert to Islam. He argues, for instance, that the Muslims should not look to the West as a regenerating force. If they do, Islam is "a spent force". Asad argues like Quṭb, al-Banna and al-Mawdūdī, that Western education of Muslim youth is bound to undermine their will to believe in the message of the Prophet. Hence, one can find that with Western-educated Muslims religion is losing ground. The cause of this loss is that Western thought is antireligious and imposes itself on the religious potential of the young Muslims. In fact, an argument can be made that Muḥammad Asad is the father of modern fundamentalism; for, first, he wrote before al-Mawdūdī and Quṭb or al-Bannā; and, secondly, the fundamentalist writers are very aware of his writings and quote him frequently-especially Quṭb and al-Mawdūdī.

The argument so far has been that the fundamentalists want to create a new society based entirely on Islam. And because they are reluctant to accept (consciously) Western principles or to follow Western outlooks or even Islamic political thought, they insist on "Islamic authenticity" in any theory, social and political; even in determining, for instance, the form of government; they shy from using, and are at least reluctant to use, terms like "republican", "democratic" or "socialist". On the other hand, the modernists, though rejecting some medieval political theories of Islam, find no contradiction in imitating the West or in adhering to Western and Islamic notions of politics. Al-Afghānī, ᶜAbduh, and Iqbāl accept the republican form of government as an ideal.[78] Al-Afghānī accepted, for instance, the rule of Ottoman caliph ᶜAbdul Ḥamīd for the modernization of the Muslim *'ummah* through a spiritual and political regeneration of the Muslims and through adopting Western institutions.

However, I do think that Quṭb's and al-Mawdūdī's attacks on the West, Christianity, and Judaism are partly due to what they percieve as profound normative differences in, for instance, the concept of God or modern Western morality. On the other hand, their attacks are partly due to political and historical circumstances. Another reason for attacking the West is Quṭb's perception of Western distortions of Islam. He wants the Muslims to read a history of Islam that is not written by foreigners. The reason is that athough he considers that there are some positive changes in the attitude of Western scholarship to Islam, the West is still full of prejudice against the Muslims because of the opposition between the ambitions, interests, goals of the West and the Muslims. And he sees that the Westerners' claim of being neutral in their studies of Islam is a myth. What imperialism and colonialism have tried to do, Quṭb argues, is to make the Muslims not proud, and to assign to Europe the best role in the making of humanity, therefore, encouraging the Muslims to give up their culture and to admire the European culture. And many of the Muslims become an easy bedfellow to colonialism. Because European history does not give other cultures their place in history, Quṭb maintains that it is a service to humanity if they are studied not only from a Western but also from other perspectives, including Islam. This study should be not only of events exclusive to one culture but also of relationships between nations. In other words, this history should be not only of events exclusive to one words, this history should be comparative history which accords to each nation its place and role in the making of humanity and seeks to uncover the nature of the relationships between different nations.

Also, what has been said so far- in addition to different historical circumstances- can help us see why the modernists like Iqbal, ᶜAbduh, and al-Afghānī aimed at reformation more than revolution. Also, this can help us understand why the fundamentalists view revolution as a viable alternative to reformation. Rejecting the past and even the present and viewing existing societies as corrupt and unjust at their roots, the fundamentalists see that there is nothing to reform, but transformation of societies is the avowed motto and principle of the fundamentalists, especially al-Bannā, Quṭb, and, to a lesser extent al-Mawdūdī (discussed later).

The first step in this process of transformation is to disregard the past except for the periods of the Prophet and the first two caliphs because the former contains legislative procedures; the second, a correct practical application of some Islamic principles such as in not forcing themselves on the community and in being elected by the community after consultation. Though they should have considered it as a good example of applying Islam to the life of community, *the Muslim should, by no means, try to imitate that period* and should aim at creating a society that no one has attempted before, a materially and morally advanced society. *The first society in Islam was not materially but morally advanced;* hence, the new society is not a replica of the first.

Hence, a statement like ".... to the Muslim mind, nothing in the present or the future could possibly ever be as good as that exquisite society erected by Muhammad and transfixed forever by his death," or the statement "the object of true Islamic reform cannot be to create a new society, rather, it must have as its ultimate end the re-establishment of the Prophet's ideal community,"[79] does not accurately capture the consequences of fundamentalist attitudes towards an ideal Muslim society. Although Quṭb considers the first community as the best example of an Islamic nation because its principles were *tawḥīd* and justice, and although he considers the first two caliphs as representing the best example of the exercise and transition of power by the consent of the community, those principles of *tawḥīd*, justice, *shūrah, ijmāc* are attainable again and even they can be understood differently. Because the *Qur'ān* was the basis of the Muslim community, the death of the Prophet does not deter the accomplishment of an ideally Muslim society. The arguments of Quṭb and the rest of the fundamentalists stipulate implicitly and explicitly that the principles of Islam are attainable and are, through continuous reinterpretation, valid for all ages. If this is not true, the fundamentalist endeavor then, i.e., the attainment of a perfect Muslim society, is a futile one. Thus, the mere attempt to establish a new- and Quṭb insists on "new"- Muslim society forwards, at least in theory, the notion of the attainability of a perfect Muslim society- and it is perfect because it is governed essentially by the *Qur'ān-* and the perfection or idealization of the Prophet Muḥammad stems from his application of the *Qur'ān* and from following its prescriptions. Furthermore, because the concepts of *tawḥīd*, morality, and justice as well as electing the ruler are by no means unattainable, the ideal new Muslim society is something to be achieved and is distinguished from the first Muslim society by its material advancement.

It has become a common practice to define fundamentalism as- and to quote Richard Stephen Humphreys-

> *the affirmation, in a radically changed environment, of traditional modes of understanding and behavior. In contrast to conservatism or traditionalism, which assumes that things can and should go as much as they have for generations past, fundamentalism recognizes and tries to speak to a changed milieu, and altered atmospher of expectations. Fundamentalism is by no means a blind opponent of social change, but it insists that change must be governed by traditional values and modes of understanding.*[80]

In the quotation above, Humphreys captures only half the truth. First, what are the traditional modes of understanding and behavior? Are they the modes of the public, theologians, the philosophers, the sufis, the jurists or a combination of those? Or are the Holy *Qur'ān* and *sunnah* meant by modes? Humphreys is not clear in defining "traditional modes of understanding," but refers to the Holy *Qur'ān* and "the lawyers and theologians of medieval Islam." But if by traditional modes of understanding, is meant the Holy *Qur'ān* and the *sunnah,* it is wrong because the Qur'ān and the *sunnah* are sources of and the material of understanding, not modes. The questions that interest the fundamentalists are the questions of understanding, reading, and interpreting the *Qur'ān* and the *sunnah.* In their answers, the fundamentalists reject the traditional public understanding because they perceive that the public is ignorant about Islam. In other words, the public did not understand; ignorance is its mode, and, therefore, the public need to be educated about Islam. Furthermore, the fundamentalists dismiss philosophy as unwarranted; here another mode of understanding is rejected. As to the theologians' mode of understanding, it is also rejected by the fundamentalists because theology submerged itself in unfathomable questions such as the characteristics of God. The sufis are discredited as well because they encouraged laziness and helped the deterioration of Muslims societies; in other words, they have nothing positive or constructive to afford the Muslims. Hence, their mode of understanding is rejeced as well.

As to the jurists, the fundamentalists perceive them as fulfilling the needs of their societies, and their (the jurists') teachings belong to a specific past generation. Even though scholars like al-Ghazālī or Ibn Taymīyyah are revered, their teachings belonged to a different historical epoch- and one fails to find, for instance, any reference to al-Ghazālī for support in Quṭb's attack on Muslim philosophers, though al-Ghazālī could have saved Quṭb some energy. In fact, the political teachings of individuals like al-Ghazālī and Ibn Taymīyyah are not in harmony with the political teachings of the fundamentalists, espcially on matters of the ruler's qualification, the form of government, and the like. As to contemporary scholars, they received a tremendous amount of attacks from the fundamentalists for their subservience to temporal power and for their imitation.

In short, the fundamentalists, especially Quṭb and al-Bannā, have offered an untraditional, new, comprehensive interpretation of Islam. Although they are mistaken in leaving the interpretation of the Holy *Qur'ān* to the understanding of the individual without a guide- because so many people cannot even read it, let alone understand or interpret it- this only goes to show that this notion of the individual's freedom to interpret the *Qur'ān* itself undermines all traditional modes of understanding and behavior. Not only this, but also the fundamentalists stress the notion that traditional Qur'anic exegeses are not binding on the Muslims- and Quṭb himself attempted to reinterpret the *Qur'ān* the way he saw fit.

If by behavior is meant political behavior, fundamentalist behavior is not traditional- a notion that Humphreys disregards. Traditional political behavior has been, on the public side, submissive and, on the government side, authoritarian; both of which are rejected by the fundamentalists. But if by behavior is meant values such as the prohibition of pre-marital sexual activity, theft or murder or as preserving family structures, reverence for older people or enjoining the good, it is correct; but the basis of acceptance is not the scholars' stipulations but arises from the *Qur'ān* itself. But on important issues such as theology and jurisprudence, fundamentalism as propagated by especially Quṭb, at-Mawdūdī and Bannā is non-traditional.

Two political concepts, among many, should make clear the untraditional and revolutionary aspects of fundamentalism; one is *ijmāᶜ*, the second is revolution. *Ijmāᶜ* (consensus) which has been accepted as a legal and theological concept is transformed by fundamentalism into a political doctrine. Muslim scholars have traditionally used this doctrine as a tool to interpret revelation and the *sunnah;* once the consensus (of the scholars) was reached in a specific matter, the outcome was binding on the Muslims. In terms of theology, law, politics, and other fields of knowledge, the *ijmāᶜ* of a specific generation acquired a normative and legislative status. The most well-known *ijmāᶜ* was that of the tenth century where scholars of the time agreed, for instance, that *ijtihād,* especially in jurisprudence was not warranted anymore. Note that up to that century what is meant by *ijmāᶜ* anyway is the agreement of scholars and not necessarily of all people.[81]

By stripping off the doctrine of *ijmāᶜ* from its theological and juristic components, the fundamentalists, and especially Quṭb, have, instead transformed it into a main demand in matters of politics. First of all, *ijmāᶜ* should not be limited to scholars, but should be conducted by all people. All Muslims, scholars or not, have the same rights in terms of formulating new concepts or in terms of political behavior; in order to do this, Quṭb and others have channelled this doctrine into a political vehicle. Thus, Quṭb, for instance, argues that the consensus of the people is necessary for the election as well as the legitimacy of Muslim rulers, and that those rulers who ascend to power without the approval of their people, though they may apply the *sharīᶜah,* are illegitimate. Whereas medieval thinkers such as al-Māwardī accepted the seizure of power on the condition that the usurper would apply the *sharīᶜah,* the fundamentalists totally reject this view because of their belief that God entrusted people as a whole with authority and legitimacy; and whether scholars approve or disapprove of usurpation, the fundamentalists do not accept any justification for the usurpation of power.

This attitude towards politics spills over towards Muslim scholars and thinkers who have been elitist in their approach to knowledge and politics. Scholars, whether theologians, jurists or philosophers have accepted and have been accepted traditionally as the authorities on matters of theology and jurisprudence, notwithstanding the nonexistence of clergy in orthodox Islam. Contrary to this, the fundamentalists reject all kinds of intellectual and political elitism; though they acknowledge differences in human faculties, these differences should not be institutionalized. For instance, those who traditionally and theoretically had chosen the caliphs or *ahl al-ḥal wa al-ᶜaqd* have no more rights than the rest of the Muslims; all Muslims should enjoy the same rights in terms of electing or disposing of rulers.

In addition to this, Quṭb renders *ijmāᶜ* on theological matters unnecessary and not restricted to a specific group of people; all people should enjoy reading and understanding the *Qur'ān* and the *sunnah* according to their abilities. In other words, there is no one or more legitimate interpretations of Islam insofar as they do not contradict the *Qur'ān* and the *sunnah*; theology and exegesis as well as jurisprudence become wide open to interpretation and reinterpretation, The only concepts to which Quṭb and other fundamentalists ask unwavering adherence are the *tawḥīd* and *ḥākimīyyah* of God. Hence, the *ijmāᶜ* of the Muslims becomes the embodiment and application of *tawḥīd* and *ḥākimīyyah*; *tawḥīd* manifests in the unity of Muslims under the *Qur'ān,* and *ḥākimīyyah* manifests in adhering to the *sharīᶜah*. Both concepts, *tawḥīd* and *ḥakimīyyah*, are the principles of regeneration; or else, the regeneration is lacking its essential characteristics that distinguish it from secular or un-Islamic movements because Muslim regeneration aims not only at eradicating injustices as many other movements do but also at the creation of a Muslim society under the banner of the Holy *Qur'ān*.[82]

But the fundamentalists are not aware that if a concept like *tawḥīd* is left to every individual, many of those individuals are going to understand it in anthropomorphic, pantheistic terms which undermines the very essence of *tawḥīd* in Islam. In actuality, this might also mean many Iqbāls or ᶜAbduhs- whose understandings are rejected by Quṭb- who advocate outright reinterpretation of Islam through science.

The other point to illustrate the fundamentalists' rejection of an accepted political behavior as well as mode of understanding is revolution. Muslims in general have accepted traditionally just or unjust rulers who adhere, even nominally, to *sharīᶜah*- in modern times, some modernist Muslim thinkers co-operated with unjust government, like ᶜAbduh with the Egyptian government. Many jurists and thinkers such as Aḥmed b. Ḥanbal prohibited revolution; the Muslims were asked to obey the victorious ruler. Ibn Taymīyyah, al-Ghazālī, Ibn Jamāᶜah and others required obedience even to unjust or heretical rulers once victory was achieved. The reason for this is that the evils of revolution were thought to outweigh its benefits. And the modernist thinkers such as ᶜAbduh and Iqbāl follow more or less the same path.[83]

Ḥasan al-Bannā and other fundamentalists looked at revolution as an ethical concept and a political obligation, and Quṭb's writings on revolution represent a new understanding. Revolution is not only a means to fight enemies of Islam but acquires, more importantly, theological, metaphysical, and political implications; for Islam is the religion of revolution in the fields of ethics, metaphysics, politics, and economics. The revelation of Islam was a revolution against the status quo or *al-jāhilīyyah* in its all unjust political, metaphysical, and religious manifestations. Furthermore, al-Mawdūdī as well as other fundamentalists argue that all messengers of God were advocates of revolution, renewal, and transformation of political, social, ethical, and economic structures. Moreover, for Quṭb, al-Bannā, and al-Mawdūdī, revolutions are universal, favor no specific group, and do not aim at revenge, but aim at justice and happiness.[84]

What should be noted here is that revolution for most fundamentalists has become a part of or is Islam itself. For them, the rise of fundamentalism is not only invited by a particular environment "produced of a crisis situation characterized by economic difficulties, moral and ideological confusion and political instability".[85] On the contrary, the non-existence of revolution is a sign of crisis, of laziness and economic injustices and moral and political instability. Islamic political and moral norms are revolutionary; the absence of revolution is a sign of moral weakness and political stagnation. And this is why Quṭb, for instance, insists on the necessity of activism before and after the creation of a Muslim society; for revolution is a moral responsibility because of its instrumentality in creating and maintaing a Muslim society and in education, culture, economics, government, and politics.

The most important aspect of *tawḥīd* in relation to political behavior- and this is by no means a traditional mode of understanding- is its being the substance and the motto of Islamic revolution. *Tawḥīd* is a concept that revolutionizes the mind which sooner or later will be embodied in a popular movement, and the goal of this revolution is the transformation of the outlook as well as the heart of individuals. In many ways, it is also the transformation of what is secular into the religious; for instance, a visa or a passort should not be required from Muslims entering other Muslim countries: the Muslim's passport is his religion. In other words, Muslims quo Muslims have rights beyond the limits of particular citizenship because the *tawḥīd* of God and unity of people are the bond that should tie together all facets of life.

Put differently, what the Muslim revolution aspires to is the creation, the continuation, and attainment of a moral, strong, and happy society erected on *tawḥīd* and *waḥdah* (unity). Thus, those societies that are not based on and do not continue to serve *tawḥīd* and *waḥdah* are in state of moral and political bankruptcy or *jāhilīyyah*, notwithstanding any material gains and progress. This bankruptcy is not only an indication of bad regimes but also of the unhappiness and misery of mankind. Consequently, a rich, as opposed to a bankrupt, society entails a people whose mind is not preoccupied with lust, selfishness, infidelity, and disunity. And because Muslim societies are on the road to total bankruptcy and *jāhilīyyah*, the only solution to their problems is a comprehensive movement, i.e., a revolution, similar to that of the Prophet Muḥammad that uprooted bankruptcy and *jāhilīyyah*.[86]

Furthermore, the fundamentalists blamed the failure of

Muslims on neglecting *tawḥīd* and true Islam, which led to the deterioration of Muslim *'ummah.* Both modernists and fundamentalists cite religious and scientific reasons for the calamities that beset the Muslim lands but their difference is not only of emphasis but also of conception. Thus, al-Afghānī, argues that, for instance, the failure of the Ottoman empire is due to its lack of material force and science and that the success of Christian governments was due to the progress of science and material force. But Quṭb and al-Mawdūdī attribute the causes to Muslims' neglect of true Islam which led to authoritarianism and stagnation. On the other hand, for Quṭb, it was not science and material force per se but what caused them, i.e., the neglect of true Islam. Quṭb looks inward to Islam and rejects Western thought and science because success, though in need of material force, is essentially a religious matter. Ultimately, for the fundamentalists, the cause of defeat is the outcome of deviating from the spirit of Islam.

This revolution should not be imposed by a coup or an elite but should, in the opinion of most fundamentalists including Quṭb, be "natural." "Natural" means that the state should not try to undermine the activities of the advocates of Islam who should be allowed to disseminate freely Islamic teachings. But if the freedom of speech of the Muslim callers is denied or hampered, there is sufficient grounds to taking arms against the government. Freedom of speech is very important to the fundamentalists because it is the instrument they need to disseminate their ideas and to transform people's mental attitudes and to create a new psychology.

All these activities necessitate the existence of a group or a *ṭalīʿah* whose raison d'etre is strugge, *jihād.* Al-Bannā, al-Mawdūdī, and Quṭb see that this party should carry the seeds of revolution and its principles, *tawḥīd* and justice and, ultimately, should assume power. Assumption to power should not be the result of employing force but of popular conviction.[87] Put differently, this *ṭalīʿah* should advocate Islam and its teachings, including the political. When people are shown the advantages of Islamic teachings and are convinced of their viability, the Muslims, the fundamentalists contend, will opt naturally for an

Islamic government. Hence, societies should be able to decide what kind of society they want and, at the same time, Islam should be allowed to preach its messages. Armed resistence is allowed when Islam is suppressed.

Here I find it important to point out that al-Mawdūdī is pro-reform, but, at times, he is contradictory: sometimes he supports revolutions; other times, he is against it. In one particular place, the distinction he makes between reform and revolution is that the former begins with deliberation and thought. Reform tries to remove the causes of corruption not by using destructive force except when it is absolutely necessary. On the other hand, revolution is based on anger, indignation, and hatred. In trying to eliminate corruption, it brings other extremes. He is reluctant to advocate destructive revolution because it destroys the social fabric of society. And usually, destructive revolutions are brought about for desperate reasons- and incidently, al-Mawdūdī shows preference toward traditional arguments like those of al-Ghazālī. But the reforms he envisions are no less radical than the revolution advocated by Quṭb except on economics. Quṭb, on the other side, conceives of no other solution for decaying societies except by revolution. Though he does not advocate murder, the Muslims should not compromise. His concept of revolution (like reform for al-Mawdūdī) starts with educating individuals about the true meaning of Islam.

Notwithstanding the fundamentalists agreement on many issues there are still some differences. Al-Mawdūdī believes that the majority do not enjoy a calm, reasoning mind; hence, the few should plan the path for the whole. The elites enjoy wealth, reason, pride, and governmental positions; in fact, the real power of a nation is in its elite which makes the nation good and whose corruption makes the nation corrupt; therefore, the corruption of Muslims is due to the deterioration of their elite.[88] For him, reform and change should come from above. But for Quṭb and al-Bannā the direction of change should come from below and move upwards; to al-Mawdūdī the direction is from above downwards. The upward movement leads to the destruction of wealth and priviliges and transforms the whole fabric of society; conversely, the downward movement tries to maintain existing structures but infiltrates the branches of government since it does not aim at complete break with power structures and tries to use them to redress substantively social evils.

Apparently, al-Mawdūdī is less radical or more conservative; his conservatism stems from fear of revolutionary changes which might not be controlled. One of those changes that he does not want to occur is the redistribution of wealth. Within fundamentalism one can distinguish two attitudes or theories toward economics. Though all fundamentalists agree that God is the real owner of possessions, and that it is part of man's trust to use it in a good way, however, they differ on the best way to fulfill this trust: Quṭb wants to limit it, and al-Mawdūdī leaves the door open. Al-Mawdūdī, in opposition to Quṭb, allows the commercial utilization of general resources like water and mineral by private enterprises and individuals, but still argues that if the resources are not used, they should be given to others for their utilization. Governments should not interfere in, and should respect and secure individual ownership. The governments should not, for instance, take from the rich and give to the poor. In a similar manner to liberalism, he maintains that the function of the government is to abolish obstacles preventing individuals from exerting themselves. But the role of government for Quṭb is much more radical than that; the government can control the whole economy if there is a necessity and should interfere to remove inequity and excessive wealth.

Moreover, for al-Mawdūdī, though social and class distinctions are prohibited, individuals can accumulate as much wealth as wanted because it is the right of the individual to be distinguished from others; for instance, "a man who owns a car can drive it and those who do not own [cars] should walk. And those who are crippled cannot but hop along".[89] Put differently, individuals have the right to have unequal starting points. But Quṭb views the responsibility of the government and society as securing equal starting points or else there is no real equality and justice.

What should be noted here is that the fundamentalists are by no means in agreement with each other on economic matters; their opinions range from unbridled capitalism to stifling socialism and are all advocated in the name of Islam and justice. What they are in agreement on, however, is that Islam will and should play the major role in politics.

Footnotes:

1 Quṭb, *Hādhā al-Dīn,* see, p 123, no. 7. p. 33; also, on the same topic, see p. 32 and *passim.*

2 Quṭb, *Ma[c]rakat al-Islām wa-al-Ra'simālīyyah*, p. 60, also see p. 49.

3 Quṭb, *Hādhā al-Dīn,* p. 19, also, on this topic see pp. 16-18, and Quṭb, *Ma[c]ālim fī al-Ṭarīq*, pp.49, 114 & *passim.* Quṭb, *Fī Ẓilāl al-Qur'ān,* Vol. 1, Part 3, p. 34 (hereafter cited as *Fī Ẓilāl); and see Quṭb, Fiqh al-Da[c]wah* (The understanding of the Call), (Bayrūt: Mu'ssasat al-Risālah 1970), pp. 60-61. See also, *Al-[c]Adālah al-Ijtimā[c]īyyah fī al-Islām*, p. 105, and *Tafsīr Sūrat al-Shūrah* (The Interpretation of the Chapter on Consultation) (Bayrūt: Dār al-Shurūq, n.d.), p. 51 (hereafter cited as *Shūrah*).

4 Quṭb, *Hādhā al-Dīn,* p. 190. On *al-ḥākimīyyah,* see also Quṭb, *Mūqawwamāt,* pp. 109, 133-135, 137 145-46, 173, 176-86.

5 Quṭb, *Al-[c]Adālah,* p. 113, and see p. 107.

6 Thomas Hobbes, *Leviathan,* Part I, 57-58. But, for Hobbes, "Mahomet, to set up his new Religion, pretended to have conferences with the Holy spirit, in forme of a Dove." (Part I, *Chapters:* 12, 57-58). References are to the Penguin ed. 1968.

7 Jean-Jacques Rousseau, *The Social Contract,* an eighteenth century translation by Charles Frankel (N.Y: Hafner Publishing Company, 1947), IV. 8, p. 118.

8 Locke, *Second Treatise of Government* (Indianapolis: Hackett Publishing Co., 1980), para. 168.

9 *Ibid.,* paras. 243 and 13.

10 *Ibid.,* para. 32.

11 *Ibid.,* paras. 6 & 61.

12 Hobbes, *Leviathan,* Ch. XI 47.

13 Quṭb, *Al-[c]Adālah*, p. 111. On the relation between law, government, and society, see, for instance, N.J. Coulson, *History of Islamic Jurisprudence,* 1st. ed. 1967 (Edinburgh: Edinburgh University Press, pb. 1974), pp. 120-48; on the differences between *sharī[c]ah* and Roman law, see Ann K.S. Lambton, *State and Government in Medieval Islam: Introduction to the Study of Islamic Political Theory: The Jurists* (Oxford: Oxford University Press, 1981), *Chapters I* and *II*, pp. 1-42. Also, see H. A. R. Gibb, *Mohammadanism* (N.Y: Oxford University Press, reprint, 1976), pp. 34-45.

14 On the necessity of Muslims' choice, see Quṭb. *Ma[c]ālim*, pp. 71-74. On the duties of the rulers in Islam, see Muḥammad 'Amārah, *Al-Islām wa-Falsafat al-Ḥukm* (Islam and the Philosophy of Government), (Bayrūt: al-

Mū'assasah al-ᶜArabīyyah li-Dirāsāt wa-al-Nashr, 1980), pp. 613-646. ᶜAmārah outlines and analyzes the different demands and views by the Shīᶜites and the Sunnites as well as the functions and duties of the ruler. On the Caliphate, see also Lambton, *State and Government in Medieval Islam, Chapter* IX "The extinction of the Caliphate" where the opinions of Ibn Taymīyyah, Ibn Jamāᶜa, al-Māwardī, and al-Ghazālī are contrasted. On the early Muslim state, see Hodgson, *The Venture of Islam,* Vol. 1, "The Classical Age," (Chicago: Chicago University Press, 1974), pp. 187-230; and on the spread of absolutism, see pp. 280-314.

15 Quṭb. *Al-ᶜAdālah,* p. 107. Also, see pp. 108 and 73.

16 *Ibid.* pp. 206-7. On accepting force and the requirement of being from Quraysh, see, for instance, Ibn Taymiyyah, *Minhāj al-Sunnah al-Nabawīyyah* (The Method of the Prophetic Traditions), Vol. 1, (Bayrūt: Maktabat al-Khayyāt, n.d.), p. 281; al-Ghazālī, *Al-Iqtiṣad fī al-Iᶜtiqād* (What is Essential in Creed), (Al-Qāhirah: Maṭbaᶜat al-Ḥussein al-Tijārīyyah, n.d.), pp. 105-106; al-Māwardī's *Al-Aḥkām al-Sulṭanīyyah* (Sultanic Rules), (Al-Qāhirah: 3rd. ed. 1973), pp. 33-34. On the qualifications of the rulers and a summarization of major opinions on them, see al-Māwardī, *al-Aḥkam al-Sulṭānīyyah,* pp. 5-21; Reuben Levy, *The Social Structure of Islam,* 1st. ed. 1957 (Cambridge: Columbia University Press, reprint 1965), pp. 168-69 & 271-299; ᶜAmārah, *Al-Islām wa-Falsafat al-Ḥukm,* pp. 315-492. Also, see, on the Caliphate, H.A.R. Gibb, *Studies on the Civilization of Islam,* 1st. ed. 1962 (Princeton: Princeton University Press, pp. 1982), pp. 22, 140-49 & 151-64. And Gustave E. Von Grunebaum *Medieval Islam,* 1st. ed. 1946 (Chicago: The University of Chicago Press, 1971), pp. 157-60.

17 Quṭb, *Fiqh,* p. 61. See also, Quṭb, *Maᶜālim,* p. 50, Quṭb, *Ra'simālīyyah,* pp. 67, 80 & 75.

18 Quṭb, *Fiqh,* p. 84. See Quṭb, *Ra'simālīyyah,* p. 60. Also, see idem, *Naḥwa Mujtamaᶜ Islāmī,* pp. 46-52.

19 Quṭb, *Al-ᶜAdālah,* p. 167. See also, pp 102-5.

20 In 827 the caliph Ma'mūn forced the theologians and jurists to consent by writing on paper that the Holy *Qur'ān* was created- the Muslims believe that the Holy *Qur'ān* is the eternal word of God. The majority of the theologians and jurists accepted his demand. Aḥmad Ibn Ḥanbal (d.855) was uncompromising and was imprisoned as well. For more details on this event, see Gustave E. Von Grunebaum, *Classical Islam,* tr. Katherine Watson (Chicago: Aldine Publishing Company, 1970), pp. 94-95.

21 *Ibid.,* pp. 167-69; see, also, p. 157, and Quṭb, *Fī Zilāl,* Vol. 1, Part 3, p, 329. Actually, on this and other requirements Quṭb is closer to the Kharijis in rejecting the limitation of the caliphate to the tribe of Quraysh. One of the differences between the Sunnites and the Shiᶜites is that the latter insist that the Imam should be not only from Quraysh but specifically

from *'ahl al-bayt* (the descendents of both ᶜAlī, the Prophet's cousin, and Fāṭima, the Prophet's daughter). The importance of Quṭb's rejection of this and other requirements is twofold: (a) rejection of the reasoning behind and the development of this concept, and (b) giving the contemporary Muslims a leeway to find different qualifications. On Muᶜawīyah, see ᶜAmārah, *Al-Islām wa-Falsafat al-Ḥukm,* pp. 75-/125.

22 Quṭb, *Al-ᶜAdalah,* p. 111, and see, Quṭb, *Maᶜālim,* p. 132.

23 Quṭb, *Maᶜālim,* pp. 58, 63-69 & 72.

24 On differences between the Shiᶜite and Sunnite attitudes towards government, see Lambton, *State and Government,* pp. 246-263; F. E. Peters, *Allah's Commonwealth* (N.Y.: Simon & Schuster, 1973), pp. 544-634; and, Hamid Enayat, *Modern Islamic Political Thought,* pp. 8-15. And see footnote 21.

25 Quṭb, *Al-ᶜAdālah,* p. 107, and see, Quṭb, *Ra'simālīyyah,* p. 70.

26 Quṭb, *Hādhā al-Dīn,* pp. 39-42, and see, Quṭb, *Ra'simālīyyah,* p. 66, and Quṭb, *Tafsīr 'Ayāt al-Ribā* (The Interpretation of the Verses on Usury) (Bayrūt: Dār al-Shurūq, 1970), p. 84 (hereafter cited as *Ribā*). On *Shūrah,* its history and definition, see ᶜAmārah, *Al-Islām wa-Falsafat al-Ḥukm,* pp. 57-72. Also, see Quṭb, *Ra'simālīyyah,* p. 72, Quṭb, *Ribā,* p. 84, and Quṭb, *Al-ᶜAdālah,* pp. 37 & 108.

27 Quṭb, *Ra'simālīyyah,* p. 53, and Quṭb, *Al-ᶜAdālah, p. 98.*

28 *Quṭb, Hādhā al-Dīn,* p. 85.

29 *Ibid.,* p. 87. Also, see, Quṭb, *Ra'simālīyyah,* p. 58; Quṭb, *Maᶜālim,* pp. 59 & 89, and Quṭb, *Al-Islām wa-Mushkilāt al-Ḥaḍārah,* pp. 7-9. Also, for more information on this topic, see Quṭb, *Naḥwa Mujtamaᶜ,* p. 13 and *passim.*

30 Quṭb, *Ra'simālīyyah,* p. 116. See also, Quṭb, *Fiqh,* p. 92, Quṭb, *Fī Ẓilāl,* Vol. 4, Part 13, pp 2008-10, and Quṭb, *Maᶜālim,* p. 12. See also *Mūqawwamāt,* pp. 15-23, 26, 29, 34, 160 and 165.

31 Quṭb, *Rā'simālīyyah,* p. 25. On socialism and Marxism see, *Mushkilāt,* p. 6 and *passim;* and see idem, *Naḥwa Mujtamāᶜ,* pp. 33-38, 86-87 & 88-98. On capitalism, see *ibid.,* p. 83 and *passim.*

32 Quṭb, *Al-ᶜAdālah,* p. 33; also, pp 39, 73 77 & 82. And see, Quṭb, *Fī Ẓilāl,* Vol. 2, Part 5, p. 689.

33 Quṭb, *Al-ᶜAdālah* p. 82; see also, pp. 41-2, 45-46, & 82-83, and Quṭb, *Al-Ra'simāliyyah,* p. 52.

34 Quṭb, *Al-ᶜAdālah,* p. 47; and, pp. 115-16. Also, see idem, *Ra'simālīyyah,* pp. 34-36 & 55.

35 Quṭb, *al-ᶜAdalah,* p. 55.

36 Quṭb, *Ra'simālīyyah,* p. 84; see also p. 47.

37 *Ibid.*, p. 49.

38 Quṭb, *Al-ᶜAdālah,* pp. 72 & 164.

39 *Ibid.*, pp. 56-58.

40 *Ibid.*, pp. 66-67.

41 *Ibid.*, pp. 67-68.

42 Quṭb, *al-ᶜAdālah,* p. 86. And see Quṭb, *Fī al-Tārīkh,* pp. 33-34.

43 Quṭb, *Fī al-Tārīkh,* pp. 34-35; and see pp. 32-33 and 76. Also, see *Al-ᶜAdālah,* pp. 73-80 & 119.

44 Quṭb, *Ra'simālīyyah,* p. 59. Also, see idem, *Fī Ẓilāl,* Vol. 2, Part 5, p. 689, Quṭb, *Al- ᶜAdālah,* pp. 35 & 113, and Quṭb, *Fi al-Tārīkh,* pp. 36.

45 Quṭb, *Al- ᶜAdalah,* p. 59.

46 On the economics of Egypt and its control by an elite, see, Roger Owen, "The Ideology of Economic nationalism: 1919-1939," pp. 1-9 in Marwan R. Buheiry, *Intellectual Life in the Arab East, 1809-1939,* (Beirut: Center For Arab and Middle East Studies/ American University of Beirut, 1981).

47 Quṭb, *Fī Ẓilāl,* Vol. 1, Part 2, p. 234; also, see Part 1, p. 235 and Part 4, p. 587.

48 Quṭb, *Al-ᶜAdālah,* p. 60; and see, *Ibid.*, pp. 61-65.

49 *Ibid.*, pp. 69-70 & 124, and Quṭb, *Ra'simālīyyah,* p. 40. Also, see, *Al-ᶜAdālah,* pp. 46-47.

50 Quṭb, *Al-ᶜAdālah,* p. 123.

51 *Ibid.*, p. 184, and see p. 131. On the theoretical prescriptions of the *Qur'ān* on economics and on the historical development of economy, see Maxim Rodinson, *Islam and Capitalism,* 1st. ed. 1966 (Austin: University of Texas Press, 1981). The author approaches the topic from a Marxist point of view.

52 *Ibid.*, p. 142; and see also, Quṭb, *Fī al-Tārīkh,* p. 32. *Zakāt* is an obligatory tax on the Muslims and is a religious duty.

53 Quṭb, *Ra'simālīyyah,* p. 44. See also, *Ibid.*, pp. 46-47, and Quṭb, *Al-ᶜAdālah,* p. 157-58.

54 Quṭb, *Al-ᶜAdālah,* p. 145; see also pp. 132-137 & 144-51. For more information on the effects and ills of usury, see pp. 137-39.

55 Quṭb, *Al-ᶜAdālah,* p. 151. On the importance of *zakāt* see, idem, *Fī Ẓilāl,* Vol. 1, Part 3, p. 328.

56 Quṭb, *Maᶜālim,* p. 26; also, see p. 101, and Quṭb, *Ra'simālīyyah,* p. 70. Also, see idem, *Al-ᶜAdālah,* p. 250.

57 Quṭb, *Fī al-Tārīkh,* pp. 23-24.

58 *Ibid.*, pp. 24-25.

59 Quṭb, *Ra'simālīyyah,* p. 28.

60 Quṭb, *Hādhā al-Dīn,* p. 48.

61 Quṭb, *Ma^cālim,* p. 68.

62 *Ibid.,* pp. 69-71. Also, see Quṭb, *Ma^cālim,* pp. 67 and *passim.* Also, Quṭb quotes in *Social Justice* (p. 67) the following verses to support his argument: III: 64; XII: 40 & XLIII: 84.

63 Quṭb, *Hādhā al-Dīn,* pp. 87-88, and Quṭb, *Ma^cālim,* p. 159. In *Ma^cālim* (pp. 149-51) Quṭb cites the following Qur'anic verses: V: 50; IV: 76; VI: 153; VIII: 72-75; XLV: 50 & LXIII: 22.

64 Quṭb, *Ma^cālim,* p. 64. *Jihād* has been usually translated into English as holy war. In Arabic it means struggle which can be spiritual and material, with oneself or with others. The connotation of *jihād* is much wider than war, holy or otherwise.

65 *Ibid.,* pp. 65, 66, 72, & pp. 81-91. For instance, see Rashīd Riḍā's opinion in M.A. Zaki Badawi *The Reformers of Egypt* (London: Croom Helm, 1967), p. 114. This book is worthwhile reading and focuses on basic themes in the writings of al Afghānī, ^cAbduh, and Rashīd Riḍā.

66 Quṭb, *Ma^cālim,* pp. 64-65; and see, *Hādhā al-Dīn,* pp. 11 & 91. See the verses in footnotes 63 & 65.

67 Quṭb, *Al-^cAdālah,* pp. 107 & 198. Also, see Quṭb, *Fī Ẓilāl,* Vol. 1, Part 2, pp. 186-87, Part 2, pp. 187-92, and Part 3, pp. 294-95. And see Quṭb, *Naḥwa Mujtama^c,* pp. 92-99, 102-20, 123 & 134. Also, Quṭb, *Ma^cālim,* p. 67.

68 Quṭb, *Ma^cālim, pp. 162-63. Also, see idem, Naḥwa Mujtam^c,* p. 62.

69 Quṭb, *Ma^cālim,* pp. 12 and 11.

70 *Ibid.,* pp. 14-15, and, Quṭb, *Al-^cAdālah,* p. 197, Quṭb, *Hādhā al-Dīn,* pp. 65-67, and Quṭb, *Fiqh,* pp. 32 & 88-89.

71 Quṭb, *Ma^calim,* p. 22, and see, Quṭb, *Fiqh,* pp. 15-31.

72 Quṭb, *Fī Ẓilāl,* Vol. 4, Part 14, p. 2155.

73 *Ibid.,* Vol. 4, Part 12, p. 1901, and, Quṭb, *Hādhā al-Dīn,* pp. 29-30.

74 Quṭb, *Hādhā al-Dīn,* p. 11.

75 Al-Mawdūdī, *Naḥnu wa al-Ḥaḍārah al-Gharbīyyah* (Bayrūt: Mu'assasat al-Risālah, 1983), pp. 47-51 & 23-25.

76 See on Muḥammad ^cAbduh, *Risālat al-Tawḥīd* (Bayrūt: Al-Mu'assasah al-^cArabīyyah li-Dirāsāt wa al-Nashr, 2nd. ed., 1981), pp. 17-51.
For a brief essay on and references to al-Ghazālī's understanding of the science of logic as not being contrary to religion, see Michael Marmura, "Ghazālī's Atitude to the Secular Sciences and Logic," in *Essays,* Hourani, pp. 100-109. Also, for more details see al-Ghazālī, *Tahāfut al-Falāsifah* (Al-Qāhirah: Dār al-Ma^cārif, 1957), "The Introduction" and "Problem No. 1",

pp. 74, 77-78, 83-87 & 89-124, and *al-Munqidh min al-Ḍalāl* (Al-Qāhirah: Maktabat al-Jundī, 1973); and, on the division of philosophy, pp. 47-57. On ^{c}Abduh's reluctance to involve himself in controversies, see his treatment of the Muslim philosophers where he explains their differences from the main orthodoxy without commending or censuring them, *Risālah,* pp. 28-32.

77 Al-Mawdūdī, *Mafāhīm Islāmīyyah* (Kuwait: Dār al-Qalam, 1977), pp. 24-25. See also Muhammad Asad, *Islam at a Crossroad,* 1st, ed., n.d. (Lahore: Arafat Publications, 1963), pp. 83-84.

78 For instance, see Iqbal, *The Reconstruction of Religious Thought in Islam,* p. 157.

79 Thomas Naff, "Towards A Muslim Theory of History," in *Islam and Power,* ed. A. Dessouki (Britain: Hellenic Mediterranean Center for Arabic and Islamic Studies, 1981), p. 28.

80 Richard Humphreys, "Islam and Political Values in Saudi Arabia, Egypt and Syria," in *Islam and Power,* ed. Dessouki, p. 108.

81 On traditional understanding of the *Qur'ān* and the *sunnah,* see Peters, *Allah's Commonwealth,* pp. 41-134; Gibb, *Mohammadanism,* pp. 24-35 & 36-48; Gibb, *Studies,* pp. 186-207; Levy, *The Social Structure of Islam,* pp. 150-91; B. M. Sharif, ed., *A History of Muslim Philosophy* (Germany: Heimatverlag, 1966), for instance, p. 697; Bernard Lewis, "Politics and War," in *A Legacy of Islam* (Oxford: Oxford University Press, 1974), p. 160; and J.J. Saunders, *A History of Medieval Islam* (London: Routledge and Kegan Paul, 1965), for instance, pp. 133-35.

82 On the reasons for modern Islamic revival and its beginning, see Gibb, *Mohammadanism,* pp. 111-31. On modern concepts of the Islamic state, see Enayat, *Modern Islamic Political Thought,* pp. 69-110. On the lack of leadership and existence of absolutism, see Cragg, *Contemporary Counsels in Islam,* pp. 181-93.

83 Al-Afghānī chastises ^{c}Abdūh for his suggestion to leave Egypt for a place where al-Afghānī is not under political pressure and where he can establish a school for leaders. Also, al-Afghānī wondered why ^{c}Abduh and his friends did not establish a party to fight the British in Egypt. Al-Afghānī and Egyptian fundamentalists were revolutionaries, and did not reconcile themselves with the British. On these issues see M. ^{c}Amārah, *Muslimūn Thuwwār* (Revolutionary Muslims), (Bayrūt: al-Mū'assasah al-^{c}Arabīyyah li-Dirāsāt wa-al-Nashr, 1979), p. 154 and the whole chapter on al-Afghānī. Also, ^{c}Amārah, *Al-Islām wa-al-Thawrah* (Islam and Revolution), (Bayrūt: al-Mū'assassh al-^{c}Arabīyyah li-Dirāsāt wa-al-Nashr, 1980), pp. 234-38. Also, ^{c}Amārah, ed. *Al-A^{c}māl al-Kāmilah* (Complete Works), Part II, Political Writings, (Bayrūt: al-Mū'assasah al-^{c}Arabīyyah li-Dirāsāt wa-al-Nashr), p. 333.

In some way or another, al-Afghānī's advice for organization was heard by the fundamentalists who established a party and fought the British.

84 Fon instance, see al-Mawdūdī, *Al-Jihād fī-Sabīlilāh,* 1st. ed. n.d. (Bayrūt: Mū'assasat al-Risālah, 1983), pp. 25-28.

85 A. Dessouki, "Isalmic Organization," in *Islam and Power,* p. 113.

86 On al-Afghānī, see, for instance, "al-Khaṭirāt," in *Al-'A[c]māl al-Kāmilah,* ed. [c]Amārah, pp. 9-13. On the fundamentalists' view, see Asad, *Islam at a Crossroad,* p. 3. The quotation is from al-Mawdūdī, *Naḥnu,* p. 79.

87 For example, al-Mawdūdī, *Minhāj al-Inqilāb al-Islāmī (Bayrūt: Mu'assasat al-Risālah, 3rd. ed., 1981),* p. 56; and al-Mawdūdī, *Naḥnu,* pp. 193-194.

88 *Ibid.,* pp. 207-9 & 230-32.

89 Al-Mawdūdī, *Nizām al-Hayāt fī al-Islām,* 1st. ed., n.d. (Bayrūt: Mū'assasat al-Risālah, 1983), p. 54; and see also, pp. 50-53.

CONCLUSION

Quṭb's thought is best understood in terms of the contemporary history of the Islamic world. Partly, fundamentalism, of which Quṭb is one of the main advocates, is the product of contemporary political crises; however; it cannot be viewed as only a reaction against the perception of a hostile environment. For it forwards a new political theory-notwithstanding the relevance and importance of contemporary problems in shaping some of its notions, for instance, of the West. Still the importance of fundamentalism stems from its preference to advocate Islam, instead of, for instance, socialism. Although the militancy of fundamentalism can be attributed to the crises of contemporary social and political life, the substance of its teachings need to be viewed as normative statements about God, reason, science, history, politics, and economics; the understanding of which requires a closer look at the principles of Islam more than at transitory political phenomena.

Quṭb himself acknowledges the relation between political environment and its influence on the writer; for he does not believe in the benefit and adequacy of theoretical writings if isolated from the problems of society and reality. His belief that thought should aim at improving existing societies does not lead him to exclude the writing of a political theory. Quṭb's theory is tightly linked to life, political and moral; its survival and success are also dependent on the continuation of the same political atmosphere; for instance, his doctrine of revolution aims at eradicating stagnation of the Muslim world and unjust governments. Similarly, his doctrines of social justice and economics are directed toward eradicating injustice and poverty prevalent in his and surrounding societies; and, his doctrine of divine and man-made laws is expounded in order to encourage the creation and preservation of morality.

Quṭb's writings are composed primarily for the benefit of contemporary Muslims, and not as eternal treatises on politics, though he believes that the principles of Islam and the Holy *Qur'ān* are eternal. Because he believes in the historicity of human thought, as distinguished from divine knowledge, and the necessity of constant revision of thought and additions of ideas, he never claims to have written a treatise valid for all ages; his claim is the validity of Islam for all ages, which necessitates that every generation should develop and reinterpret the principles of the Holy *Qur'an* in order to prevent the stagnation of the Muslims and to further their progress.

But fundamentalism lacks the tools to be the intellectual motivating force for an Islamic revival because any revival is not only in need of political activism but also of a new philosophy, espcially a political one, in order to stimulate and rejuvenate Islamic thought. An Islamic revival cannot take place if philosophy, theology, and other disciplines are repudiated as un-Islamic; for if these tools are neglected, the reinterpretation of Islam will be based on shaky grounds that will be blown away with the lightest wind. In other words, fundamentalism is impoverished in terms of theology, philosophy, history, and, what it accepts, science- for none of the fundamentalists is a scientist. In fact, what they have to offer does not amount to a coherent and well-argued intellectual system, though it is still a comprehensive system.

Notwithstanding their acceptance of the Holy *Qur'ān* and the *sunnah* as the bases of all normative principles, the Holy *Qur'ān* and the *sunnah* are overshadowed by politics. In fact, besides their political significance, one cannot fathom the fundamentalist concept of *tawḥīd,* for instance. Adherence to *tawḥīd* should characteristically manifest in the political regime because if it does not the political regime as well as the people living under it are suspect in their principles or lives a *jāhilī* life. Consequently, to the fundamentalists, political philosophy shoulders the role of metaphysics; for man cannot conduct intelligently a discourse on God, reason, moral law, but he can know the political principles: equality, social justice, private ownership, and so forth. Thus, the fundamentalists do not force people to worship God- at least this is what they advocate- but they do aspire to spread an Islamic government wherever and whenever possible. In some ways, if fundamentalism is stripped of its political principles or political philosophy, it ceases to make sense or exist; for if God, reason, law, morality and so forth cannot be known by abstract thinking, and those that are known have primarily political significance, the absence of political philosophy makes God's existence and truth in general irrelevant and unprovable; for God's relevance can only be seen in a political context.

In short, fundamentalism has very little to offer in terms of creating an intellectual edifice that can propel the Muslims to greatness or make them feel proud- though the Holy *Qur'ān* and the *sunnah* are a great legacy for the Muslims.

Of course, Quṭb did not write a decisive treatise on the harmony or disharmony of philosophy and religion. His writings have an aura of immediacy, urgency, and impatience- many of his arguments are ad hominem. In some ways, he felt he had to do it all- write on politics, philosophy, economics, law and be active against the government. Because of its stagnation, Quṭb was extremely dismayed with *al-Azhar*, the prestigious Sunnite center for learning, which he considered to be full of useless and irrelevant books. The study of the Holy *Qur'an* was overshadowed by teaching grammar and rhetoric, theology, logic, and, law; and the Holy *Qur'ān* was never taught without commentaries. But Quṭb viewed the Holy *Qur'ān* as a book of call *(daʿwah)* and the constitution of an order, and a method of thinking and a *nizām* of life, and not as a book of novels, amusement or history. Furthermore, he was dismayed with the intellectuals who were brought up and educated under European colonial powers, and with the rest of the people who were ignorant.[1] Thus, for Quṭb, neither Europe in its intellectual and political expansion nor the *ᶜulamā'* in their intellectual and political stagnation were to be looked to as models to be followed in developing an independent Muslim society. Both the colonial powers and their local spokesmen, on the one hand, and the *ᶜulamā'*, on the other, hand, for Quṭb, contributed to the stagnation of the Muslims.

In contemporary Islamic thought there are two major Islamic intellectual tendencies towards the West: (a) those who believe that the acquisition of modern knowledge must be limited to technological and practical spheres; and (b) those who believe that the Muslims should not only acquire technology but also its intellectual underpinnings.[2] Quṭb was one of the champions of the first tendency; for he thought that the West which was capable of exporting technology was incapable of exporting morality that would suit the Muslims. Although Western technology and morality were the products of modern philosophy, Quṭb felt that the Muslims can disassociate the one from the other. In order to accept Western technology, the Muslims do not have to accept its morality or, for Quṭb, the lack of it. Notwithstanding his perception that modern science and Islam were compatible, his contention was that Westen morality and Islam were incompatible, regardless of admirable principles in Western morality like freedom, human dignity, and so forth.

In order to eradicate the root causes of the troubles in the Muslim lands and the creation of a Muslim leadership, Quṭb embarked on a two-fold campaign: to construct a new Islamic ideology and to attack many fields of knowledge and most of the past and the reader of Quṭb will find many terms like true Islam, true Christianity, and true human rights as opposed to false Islam, false Christianity and false human rights. Quṭb's rebellion was very pronounced in terms of the past; he was more radical in his teaching than Al-Afghānī or ᶜAbduh, due to differences in temperament and because the time he lived in was harsher whether internally or externally. Thus, thinkers like al-Afghānī and ᶜAbduh hoped that institutions in the Muslim world would develop on Western lines, but Quṭb wanted development to be from the inside because he could not co-exist with the outside world, i.e., the *jāhilīyyah.*

Quṭb's appeal can be traced to many factors: First, he tried to justify social justice and freedom in Islamic terms; instead of adhering to democracy and socialism, he explained the important issues for the Muslims (like the choice of the Muslims for their government and rulers or social justice) without reference to what he and others considered foreign ideologies that did not include God as the underpinning of their principles. In other words, he offered religious justification for democractic as well as socialist principles; the principles of Muslims' choice and social justice became religious as well as political duties- i.e., the principles of government in Islam. By so doing Quṭb preempted the advocates of both democracy and socialism and was able to show the Muslims that Islam and modernity were compatible; their compatibility resulted from Islam itself. If the most revered principle in democracy was the choice of people in their governments, Islam offered this principle before any other ideology- but this principle, according to Quṭb, has not been fully developed in the Muslim lands. And if the most revered principle in socialism was social justice, Islam, as interpreted by Quṭb, offered also this principle and considered it as a legal, political, and ethical issue. Therefore, what Quṭb did- and his fame is due to - was to create a new Islamic political ideology that encompassed the best in the Western tradition which had been accepted by the majority of people without negating or subordinating Islam. Thus, a Muslim could be a Muslim by insisting on social justice and the choice of the people; he did not have to be a democrat or a socialist. By so doing, Quṭb was able to reinforce the notion that Islam was valid for all ages and that its principles could integrate diverse conditions and changing realities. Hence, the Muslims did not have to relegate the Holy *Qur'ān* only to prayers, funerals, or the personal domain, but it was their lasting constitution. All that the Muslims had to do was to study critically the Holy *Qur'ān* not as a book of the past but as a guide that contained stipulations that were valid for all ages- something that the majority of the Muslims believe in.

Throughout his justification of how the Muslims should

conduct their government and life, Quṭb extensively used the Holy *Qur'ān*. Whether it is revolution, social justice or the Muslims' choice- all of the basic notions he advocated were based on Qur'anic verses. And though many of these verses have been interpreted and used differently (on *shūrah,* for instance), Quṭb argued against any authority besides the revelation itself; hence, he gave the Muslims an argument for not seeing that they were bound by previous interpretations or authorities; the Muslims could shape the government they want. In other words, Quṭb provided a new hope for reviving Islam by insisting that Islam was not its history; for history itself could be dismissed as being only a manifestation and was not a normative statement about what was correct or incorrect. Thus, the Muslims could create a new and modern history that might accommodate any immediate or contemporary issue.

What also made Quṭb famous was his conversion to fundamentalism as well as his execution. After his journey into modernism, Quṭb rejected it as based on shallow premises- a topic that other fundamentalists seized upon and expounded in their literature. Also, his fame is partly due to his formulation of a theory of political violence that the contemporary Islamic movement has been attached to. Whether it is *al-Jihād al-Islāmī, al-Takfīr wa al-Hijrah, al-Jihād, Tanzīm al-Fanīyyah al-ᶜAskarīyyah, Jund Allāh* - all these are theoretical followers of Sayyid Quṭb. Also, there is an intellectual school that follows and elaborates his theories. This school includes Mustafā al-Khudayrī, Abd al-Majīd al-Shādhly, and Muḥammad Jawād Yāsīn. This school has penetrated in one way or another the ideologies of contemporary Islamic movements. Also, his execution put on him the final touches of sacrifice and sincerity- because with those who die for a cause, their beliefs cannot be questioned, supposedly. And being a martyr in Islam is one of the highest ranks of belief and worship; and Quṭb, in the eyes of the fundamentalists and others, paid the price of his belief.

Footnotes:

1 Sayyid Quṭb, *Ma^calim*, pp. 64-65. On the stagnation of *al-Azhar* see Fazlur Rahman, *Islam and Modernity: The transformation of an Intellectual Tradition* (Chicago: The University of Chicago Press, 1982), pp. 36-37 & 98-100.

2 For more information on this topic see, Rahman, *Islam and Modernity,* pp. 46-58.

BIBLIOGRAPHY

Part I. Primary Sources

A. Sayyid Quṭb

1. *Al-^{c}Adālah al-Ijtima^{c}īyyah fī al-Islām*
2. *Afrāḥ al-Rūḥ.*
3. *Amrīkā allatī Ra'aytu*
4. *Al-Aṭyāf al-Arba^{c}ah*
5. *Ashwāk*
6. *Dirāsāt Islāmīyyah*
7. *Fī al-Tārīkh: Fikrah wa-Minhāj*
8. *Fī Ẓilāl al-Qur'ān*
9. *Fiqh al-Da^{c}wah*
10. *Hādhā al-Dīn*
11. *Ḥlm al-Fajr*
12. *Islām aw lā Islām*
13. *Al-Islām wa-Mushkilāt al-Ḥaḍārah*
14. *Al-Islām wa-al-Salām al-^{c}Alamī*
15. *Al-Jihād fī Sabīl Allāh*
16. *Khaṣa'īs al Taṣawwur al Islāmī wa-Muqawwamātuh*
17. *Kutub wa-Shakhṣīyyāt*
18. *Li-Mādhā A^{c}damūnī?*
19. *Al-Madīnah al-Mas'ḥūrah*
20. *Ma^{c}rakat al-Islām wa al-Ra'simālīyyah*
21. *Ma^{c}rakatunā ma^{c}a al-Yahūd*
22. *Mashāhid al-Qiyāmah fī al-Qur'ān*
23. *Muhimmat al-Shā^{c}ir fī al-Ḥayāt wa-Shi^{c}r al-Jīl al-Mu^{c}āṣir*
24. *Mūqawwamāt al-Taṣawwur al-Islāmī*

25. *Al-Mustaqbal li-Hādhā al-Dīn*
26. *Ma^{c}ālim fi al-Ṭarīq*
27. *Al-Naqd al-Adabī: Uṣūluhu wa-Manāhijuhu*
28. *Naqd Kitab Mustaqbal al-Thaqāfah fī Miṣr*
29. *Qāfilāt al-Raqīq*
30. *Al-Qaṣaṣ al-Dīnī*
31. *Tafsīr 'Āyat al-Ribā*
32. *Tafsīr Sūrat al-Shūrah*
33. *Al-Taṣwīr al-Fannī fī al-Qur'ān*
34. *Ṭifl fī al-Qaryah*
35. *Al-Shāṭi' al-Majhūl*
36. *Sīnā' bayna Aṭmā^{c} al-Isti^{c}mārīyyin wa-al-Ṣhyunīyyin.*

B. General

Jamāl al-Dīn Al-Afghānī

1. *Al-Waḥdah al-Islāmīyyah*
2. *Al-Rad ^{c}alā al-Dahrīyyīn*
3. *Al-^{c}Urwah al-Wūthqāh.*

Muḥammad ^{c}Abduh

1. *Al-^{c}Urwah al-Wūthqāh*
2. *Inḥiṭāṭ al-Muslimīn*
3. *Al-Islām wa-al-Rad ^{c}alā Muntaqidīh*
4. *Risālat al-Tawḥīd*
5. *Al-Islām Dīn al-^{c}Ilm wa-al-Madanīyyah.*

Muḥammad Rashīd Riḍā

1. *Al-Khilāfah aw-al-Imāmah al-^{c}Uẓmāh*
2. *Tārīkh al-Ustādh al-Imām.*

Muḥammad Iqbāl

1. *The Reconstruction of Religious Thought in Islam*
2. *Islam as a Moral and Political Ideal.*

Abū al-'A^{c}lā al-Mawdūdī

1. *The Political Theory of Islam*
2. *The Ethical Viewpoint of Islam*
3. *The Process of Islamic Revolution*
4. *Islamic concepts*
5. *We and Western Civilization*
6. *The Way of life in Islam*
7. *Al-Ḥukūmah al-Islāmīyyah*

8. *Al-Khilāfah wa al-Mulk*
9. *Al-Muṣṭalaḥāt al-'Arba^c^ah.*

Ayatollah Khomeini

1. *Al-Ḥukūmah al-Islāmīyyah*
2. *Al-Juhūd al-Nafsīyyah.*

Ḥasan al-Bannā

1. *Majmū^c^at Rasā'il al-Imām al-Shahīd.*

^c^Ali Sharī^c^atī

1. *On the Sociology of Islam*
2. *Marxism and Other Western Fallacies.*

Part II. Secondary Sources.

^c^Abbās, Muḥammad Yūsuf ^c^Abd Allāh. *Miftāh fī Ẓilāl al-Qur'ān.* ^c^Ammān: Maktabat al-Aqsā, 1972.

^c^Abd al-Ḥamīd, Maḥmūd. *Al-Ikhwān al-Muslimīn.* Al-Qāhirah: Dār al-Da^c^wah, 1978.

^c^Abd al-Rāziq, Alī. *Al-Islām wa-'Uṣūl al-Ḥukm.* Bayrūt: al-Mu'assasah al-^c^Arabīyyah wa al-Dirāsāt wa al-Nashr, 1972.

Abdel-Malek, Anwar. *Egypt, Military Society: The Army Regime, the Left, and Social Change under Nasser.* Translated by Charles Lam. New York: Random House, Inc., 1968.

Al-^c^Aẓm, Yūsuf. *Rā'id al-Fikr al-Islāmī al-Mu^c^āṣir.* Bayrūt: Dār al-Qalam, 1980.

Al-Balīhī, Ibrāhīm Ibn ^c^Abd al-Raḥmān. *Sayyid Quṭb wa-Turāthuhu al-Adabī wa al-Fikrī.* Riad/Saudi Arabia, 1972.

Al-Bushrī, Ṭāriq. *Al-Ḥarakah al-Siyāsīyyah fī Miṣr* (1945-1952). Al-Qāhirah: Dār al-Shurūq, 3rd. ed., 1983.

Al-Fārābī. *Arā' Ahl al-Madīnah al-Fāḍilah.* Al-Qāhirah: Maktabat Muḥammad ^c^Alī Ṣubḥ, n.d.

——. *Rasā'il al-Fārābī.* India: Matba^c^at Majlis Dā'irat al-Ma^c^ārif al-^c^Uthmānīyyah, 1926.

Ahmed, Jamal M. *The Intellectual Origins of Egyptian Nationalism.* London: Oxford University Press, 1960.

Aḥmad, Rīf^c^at Sayyid. *Al-Ḥarakah al-Islāmīyyah fī Miṣr wa-Irān.* Al-Qāhirah: Sīnā li al-Nashr, 1989.

——. *Al-Dīn wa al-Dawlah wa al-Thawrah.* Al-Qāhirah: Dār al-Hilāl, 1985.

Al-Huḍaībī, Hasan. *Du^c^āt Lā Quḍāt.* Al-Qāhirah: Al-Itiḥād al-Islāmī al-^c^Alāmī li al-Munaẓẓamāt al-Ṭullābīyyah, 1977.

Al-Ghazali, Muhammad. *Our Beginning in Wisdom* Washington, D.C.: American Council of Learned Societies, 1953.

Al-Ghazālī, Abū Ḥāmid. *Tahāfut al-Falāsifah.* Translated by Ahmad Kemal. Lahore: Pakistan Philosophical Congress, 1963.

——. *Al-Munqidh min al-Ḍalāl.* Al-Qāhirah: Maktabat al-Jundī, 1973.

——. *Al-Iqtiṣād fī al-I*ᶜ*tiqād.* Al-Qāhirah: Matbaᶜat al-Hussein al-Tijārīyyah, n.d.

Al-Husri, Khaldun S. *Three Reformers: A Study in Modern Arab Political Thought.* Beirut: Khayyaṭ's College Book Co., 1966.

Al-Khabāṣ, ᶜAbd Allah A. *Sayyid Quṭb al-Adīb al-Nāqid.* ᶜAmmān: Maktabat al-Manār, 1983.

Al-Māwardī. *Al-Aḥkām al-Ṣulṭānīyyah.* Third Edition. Cairo, 1973.

ᶜAmārah, Muḥammad. *Al-Islām wa-Falsafat al-Ḥukm.* Bayrūt: al-Mū'assasah al-ᶜArabīyyah li-Dirāsāt wa-al-Nashr, 1980.

——. *Muslimūn Thūwwar.* Bayrūt: al-Mū'assasah al-ᶜArabīyyah li-Dirāsāt wa-al-Nashr, 1979.

——. *Al-Islām wa-al-Thawrah.* Bayrūt: al-Mū'assasah al-ᶜArabīyyah li-Dirāsāt wa-al-Nashr, 1980.

Amīn, Samīr. *'Azmat al-Mujtam*ᶜ *al-*ᶜ*Arabī.* Al-Qāhirah: Dār al-Mustaqbal, 1985.

Atiyeh, George N. *The Contemporary Middle East 1948-1974. A Selective and Annotated Bibliography.* Boston: G.H. Hall. 1975.

Arberry, Arthur J. *The Koran Interpreted.* New York: The Macmillan Co., 3rd. ed. 1969.

Armajani, Yahya. *Middle East: Past and Present.* New Jersey: Prentice-Hall Inc., 1970.

Asad, Muhammad. *Islam at a Crossoroad.* Lahore: Arafat Publications, 1963.

As-Said, Labib. *The Recited Koran.* Translated by Bernard Weiss, M.A. Rauf, and Morroe Berger. New Jersey: The Darwin Press, 1975.

Averroes. *Tahāfut al-Tahāfut.* Al-Qāhirah: Dār al-Maᶜārif, 1981.

Badawi, M.Z. *The Reformers of Egypt.* London: Croom Helm, 1978.

Baer, Gabriel. *Studies in the Social History of Modern Egypt.* Chicago: University of Chicago Press, 1969.

Barakāt, Muḥammad Tawfīq. *Sayyid Quṭb: Khulāṣat Ḥayātuh, Minhājuhu fī al-Ḥarakah, al-Naqd al-Mūwajjah Ilayh.* Bayrūt: Dār al-Daᶜwah, 197?.

Berger, Morroe. *Islam in Egypt Today: Social and Political Aspects of Popular Religion.* Cambridge: Cambridge University Press, 1970.

Berque, Jacques, "Islam and Revolution," in *Islam, Philosophy and Science.* International Seminar on Islam. Paris: UNESCO, 1980.

Binder, Leonard. *The Ideological Revolution in the Middle East.* New York: John Wiley and Sons, Inc., 1964.

——. *Islamic Liberation: A Critique of Development Ideologies.* Chicago: University of Chicago Press, 1988.

Butterworth, Charles E. "Prudence Verses Legitimacy." *Islamic Resurgence in the Arab World.* Edited by A.H. Dessouki. New York: Praeger Publishers, 1982.

——. "Philosophy, Stories, and the Study of Elites." *Elites in the Middle East.* Edited by William Zartman. New York: Praeger Publishers, 1980.

——. "New Light on the Political Philosophy of Averroes." *Essays on Islamic Philosophy and Science.* Edited by George Hourani. New York: State University of New York, 1975.

Buheiry, Marwan, ed. *Intellectual Life in the Arab East, 1908-1939.* Beirut: Center For Arab and Middle Eastern Studies/ American University of Beirut, 1981.

Carre, Olivier. "Le combat-pour-Dieu et l'Etat islamique chez Sayyid Qotb, l'inspirateur du radicalisme actuel." *Revue francaise de science politique.* No. 4, August, 1983, Vol.33, pp. 680-705.

Choueiri, Youssef M. *Islamic Fundamentalism.* M.A: Twaynel/G.K. Hall, 1990.

Cragg, Kenneth. *Counsels in Contemporary Islam.* Edinburgh: Edinburgh University Press, 1956.

Cudsi, A.A. *Islam and Power.* London: Croom Helm, 1981.

Curtis, Michael, ed. *Religion and Politics in the Middle East.* Boulder/ Colorado: Westview Press, 1980.

De Boer, T.J. *The History of Islam.* English Translation. London, 1933.

Dekmejian, R. Hrair. *Egypt Under Nasir: A Study in Political Dynamics.* New York: State University of New York Press, 1971.

——. *Islam in Revolution: Fundamentalism in the Arab World.* New York: Syracuse University Press, 1985.

Dessouki, A.H., ed. *Islamic Resurgence in the Arab World.* New York: Praeger Publishers, 1982.

——. "Arab Intellectuals and Al-Nakba: The Search for Fundamentalism," *Middle Eastern Studies* (1973): 445-46.

Enayat, Hamid. *Modern Islamic Political Thought.* Austin: University of Texas Press, 1982.

Esposito, John L. *Islam and Development: Religion and Sociopolitical Change.* New York: Syracuse University Press, 1980.

Fa'īz. Aḥmad. *Ṭarīq al-Da^cwah fī Ẓilāl al-Qur'ān*. 2 Vols. Bayrūt, n.d.
Faḍl Allāh, Mahdī. *Ma'a Sayyid Quṭb fī Fikrihi al-Sīyāsī wa-al-Dīnī*. Second Edition. Beirut, 1979.
——. *Al-Shūrah: Ṭabī^cat al-Ḥākimīyyah* fī al-Islām. Bayrūt: Dār al-'Andalus, 1984.
Faḍl Allāh, Muḥammad Ḥ. *Al-Ḥarakah al-Islāmīyyah. Bayrūt: Maktabat al-Jīl,* 1979.
——. *al-Islām wa-Mantiq al-Qūwah,* 3rd. ed. 1986.
Fakhry, Majid. *A History of Islamic Philosophy*. New York: Columbia University Press, 1970.
Gibb, H.A.R. *Modern Trends in Islam*. Chicago: Chicago University Press, 1947.
——. *Studies on the Civilization of Islam.*: Princeton: Princeton University Press, 1982.
——. *Mohammedanism*. Oxford: Oxford University Press, 1976.
Guindi, Fadwa, El-. "Religious Revival and Islamic Survival in Egypt", *International Insight*. May-June 1980, pp. 6-10.
Haddad, Yvonne Y. "The Qur'anic Justification for an Islamic Revolution: The Views of Sayyid Qutb." *The Middle East Journal*. Winter 1983, Vol. 37, No. 1, pp.14-29.
——. "The Islamic Alternative." *The Link*. Vol. 15, No.4, Sept./ Oct. 1982, pp. 1-14.
——. "Sayid Qutb: the Ideologue of Islamic Revival." *Voices of a Resurgent Islaṃ*. Edited by John Esposito. New York, Oxford: Oxford University Press, 1983.
Haim. S.G. *Arab Nationalism*. London: University of California Press, 1962.
Halpern, Manfred. *The Politics of Change in the Middle East and North Africa*. Fourth Edition. Princeton: Princeton University Press, 1970.
Ḥamūdah, ^cĀdil. *Sayyid Quṭb: min al-Qaryah ilā al-Mishnaqah*. Al-Qāhirah: Sīnā li al-Nashr, 1987.
Halliday, Fred, and Alavi, Hamza. eds. *State and Ideology in the Middle East and Pakistan*. New York: Monthly Review Press, 1988.
Ḥamūdah, Husayn Muḥammad. Asrār *Ḥarakat al-Ḍūbāṭ al-Aḥrār wa al-Ikwān al-Muslimīn*. Al-Qāhirah: Al-Zahrā' li al-I^clām al-^cArabī, 1985.
Harris, Christina P. *Nationalism and Revolution in Egypt*. West Port/ C.T: Hyperion Press, 1981.
Hasan, S. Badrul. *Syed Quṭb Shaheed*. Lahore: International Pakistani Publishers, 1980.

Heyworth-Dunne, James. *Religious and Political Trends in Modern Egypt.* Washington, 1950.

Hilāl, [c]Alī al-Dīn. *Al-Sīyāsah wa al-Ḥukm fī Miṣr: 1923-52.* Al-Qāhirah: Maktabat Nahḍat al-Sharq, 1977.

Hiro, Dilip, *The Rise of Islamic Fundamentalism.* New York: Routledge, 1989.

Hitti, Philip. *History of the Arabs.* New York: St. Martin's Press, 1970.

Hodgson, Marshall G.S. *The Venture of Islam.* Chicago: Chicago University Press, 1961.

Hudson, Michael. *Arab Politics.* New Haven: Yale University Press, 1977.

Hunter, Shireen. ed. *The Politics of Islamic Revivalism: Diversity and Unity.* Bloomington: Indiana University Press, 1988.

Husaini, Ishak M. al-. *The Moslem Brethren.* Beirut: Khayyat's College Book Co., 1956.

Hussain, Asaf. *Political Perspectives on the Muslim World.* New York: St. Martin's Press, 1984.

Hussain, Asaf. *Islamic Movements in Egypt, Pakistan, and Iran.* Great Britain: Mansell Publishing Limited, 1983.

Hussein, Mahmoud. *Class Conflict in Egypt 1945-1970.* New York: Monthly Review Press, 1973.

Imām, [c]Abd Allāh. *[c]Abd al-Nāṣir wa al-Ikhwan al-Muslimīn.* Al-Qāhirah: Dār al-Mawqif al-[c]Arabī, 1981.

Karpat, Kemal. *Political and Social Thought in Contemporary Middle East.* New York: Praeger Publishers, 1982.

Keddie, N. *Scholars, Saints, and Sufis.* Berkeley: University of California Press, 1972.

——. *An Islamic Response to Imperialism.* Berkeley: University of California Press, 1973.

Kepel, Gilles, *Muslim Extremism in Egypt: the Prophet and the Pharaoh.* Berkeley: University of California Press, 1985.

Kerr, Malcolm. *Islamic Reform.* Berkeley: California University Press, 1966.

Khadduri, Majid. *War and Peace in the Law of Islam.* Baltimore, 1955.

Khālidī, Ṣalāḥ [c]Abd al-Fattāḥ. *Sayyid Quṭb, al-Shahīd al-Ḥayy.* [c]Ammān: Maktabat al-Aqṣā, 1981.

——. *Naẓarīyyat al-Taṣwīr al-Fannī 'inda Sayyid Quṭb.* [c]Ammān: Dār al-Firqān, 1983.

Lapidus, Ira A. *Contemporary Islamic Movements in Historical Perspective.* Berkeley: Institute of International Studies/ University of California Press, 1983.

Lambton, Ann K. *State and Government in Medieval Islam: Introduction to the Study of Islamic Political Theory: The Jurists.* Oxford: Oxford University Press, 1981.

Lawrance, Bruce B. *Defenders of God: The Fundamentalist Revolt against the Modern Age.* San Francisco: Harper and Row, 1989.

Leiden, Carl, ed. *Conflict of Traditionalism and Modernism in the Muslim Middle East.* Austin: University of Texas Press, 1967.

Lerner, Ralph and Mahdi, Muhsin, eds. *Medieval Political Philosophy.* Ithaca/ New York: Cornell University Press, 1963.

Levy, Reuben. *The Social Structure of Islam.* Cambridge: Columbia University Press, 1965.

Lewis, Bernard. *Islam.* New York: Walker and Company, 1976.

Mahdi, Muhsin, trans. *Al-Farabi Philosophy of Plato and Aristotle.* New York: Cornell University Press, 1969.

Mitchell, Richard P. *The Society of the Muslim Brothers.* London: Oxford University Press, 1969.

Moussalli, Ahmad S. *Al-Fikr al-Islāmī al-Mu^c^āṣir, Dirāsāt wa-Shakhṣīyyat: Sayyid Quṭb.* Bayrūt: Dār Khudr, 1990.

——. *Qira'āt Naẓarīyyah Ta'sisīyyah fī al-Khiṭab al-Islāmī al-Uṣūlī.* Bayrūt: Dār al-Nāshir, 1992.

——. *Al-Uṣūlīyyah wa al-Niẓam al-Dawlī.* Beirut: Center For Strategic Studies, Research and Documents, 1992.

——. *"Al-Uṣūlīyyah al-Islamīyyah* wa al-Nizām al-Dawlī." *Al-Ḥiwār.* Summer 1990.

——. "Naẓarīyyat al-Ma^c^rifah ^c^inda al-Uṣūlīyyah al-Islāmīyyah." *Al-Ijtihād.* Spring 1991.

——. "Sayyid Quṭb's View of Knowledge." *The American Journal of Islamic Social Sciences.* Vol. 7, No. 3, 1990.

——. "Sayyid Quṭb: The Ideologist of Islamic Fundamentalism." *Al-Abḥāth.* Spring 1990.

Mortimer, Edward. *Faith and Power.* London: Faber and Faber, 1982.

Munson, Henry. *Islam and Revolution in the Middle East.* New Haven: Yale University Press, 1988.

Nadawī, Abū al-Ḥasan, al-. *Mudhakkirāt Sā'iḥ fī al-Sharq al-^c^Arabī.* Al-Qāhirah: Maktabat Wahbah, 1954.

Nāṣir, Jamāl 'Abd al-. *Falsafat al-Thawrah.* Al-Qāhirah, 1952.

Peretz, Don. *The Middle East Today.* New York: Holt, Rinehart and Winston, 1978.

Peters, F.E. *Allah's Commonwealth.* New York: Simon and Schuster, 1973.

Peroncel-Hugoz, Jean-Pierre. *The Raft of Mohammed, Social and Human Consequences of the Return to Traditional Religion in the*

Arab World. New York: Paragon House, 1988.
Pipes, Daniel. *In the Path of God: Islam and Political Power.* New York: Basic Books, 1983.
Qāsim, Maḥmūd. *Dirāsāt fī al-Falsafah al-Islāmīyyah.* Al-Qāhirah: Dār al-Maᶜārif, 4th. ed. 1972.
Quṭb, Muḥammad A. *Sayyid Quṭb al-Shahīd al-Aᶜzal.* Al-Qāhirah: al-Mukhtār al-Islāmī, 1974.
Rahman, Fazlur. *Islam and Modernity: The Transformation of an Intellectual Tradition.* Chicago and London: The University of Chicago Press, 1982.
Reischauer, R.J., and Thompson, J.H. *Modernization in the Arab World.* Princeton: D. Van Nostrana Co., 1966.
Rodinson, Maxime. *Islam and Capitalism.* London: Penguin Books, 1977.
Roff, William R. ed. *Islam and the Political Economy of Meaning: Comparative Studies of Muslim Discourse.* Berkeley: University of California Press, 1987.
Rosenthal, Erwin I.J. *Political Thought in Medieval Islam.* Cambridge: Cambridge University Press, 1958.
——. *Islam in the Modern National State.* Cambridge: Cambridge University Press, 1965.
Rubin, Barry M. *Islamic Fundamentalism in Egyptian Politics.* New York: St. Martin's Press, 1990.
Sadat, Anwar al-.*In Search of Identity.* New York: Harper, 1978.
Safran, Nadav. *Egyptin Search of Political Community: An Analysis of the Intellectual and Political Evolution of Egypt 1804-1952.* Cambridge: Harvard University Press, 1961.
Said, Edward. *Orientalism.* New York: Vantage Books, 1979.
Saunders, J.J. *A History of Medieval Islam.* London: Routledge and Kegan Paul, 1965.
Shadī, Ṣalāḥ. *Safaḥat min al-Tārīkh: Haṣād al-ᶜUmr.* Al-Qāhirah: Al-Zahrā' li al-Iᶜlām al-ᶜArabī, 3rd. ed. 1987.
Shafīq, Munīr. *Al-Islām wa-Taḥadīyyat al-Inḥiṭāṭ al-Muᶜāṣir.* (Lundun: Dār Tāha li al-Nashr, N.D.
——. «Two Trends and Five Historical Phases of Contemporary Islamic Thought." *Al-Muntaka,* Vol. v, 14, No. 1, 1989.
Sharabi, Hisham. *Nationalism and Revolution in the Arab World.* Princeton: Princeton University Press, 1966.
——. *Arab Intellectuals and the West: The Formative Years, 1875-1914.* Baltimore: The John Hopkins University Press, 1970.

Sharif, B.M. *A History of Muslim Philosophy.* Germany: Heimatverlag, 1966.

Shepard, William E. "Islam as a 'System' in the later Writings of Sayyid Qutb." *Middle Eastern Affairs.* Vol. 25, No. 1, January 1989.

Sivan, Emmanuel, and Friedman, Menachem. *Religious Radicalism and Politics in the Middle East.* Albany/ N.Y.: State University of New York Press, 1990.

Sivan, Emmanuel. *Radical Islam, Medieval Theology, and Modern Politics.* New Haven and London: Yale University Press, 1985.

——. *Radical Islam and Modern Politics.* New Haven and London: Yale University Press, 1985.

Smith, Wilfred C. *Islam and the Modern World.* London: Oxford: University Press, 1957.

Sonn, Tamar. *Between Qur'an and Crown: The Challenge of Political Legitimacy in the Arab World.* Boulder/ Colo.: Westview Press, 1990.

Taheri, Amir. *Holy Terror: The Inside Story of Islamic Terrorism.* Johannesburg: Hutchinson Ltd., 1987.

Taylor, Alan. *The Islamic Question in the Middle East Politics.* Boulder/ Colo.: Westview Press, 1988.

Tibi, Bassam. *The Crisis of Modern Islam: A Preindustrial Culture in the Scientific-technological Age.* Salt Lake City: University of Utah Press, 1988.

ᶜUthmān, Muḥammad Fatḥī, *Al-Fikr al-Islāmī wa al-Taṭawwūr.* Al-Qāhirah: Dār al-Qalam, 1961.

Vatikiotis, Panayiotis J., ed. *Nasser and His Generation.* New York: Praeger Publishers, 1968.

——. *The Modern History of Egypt.* London: Weidenfield and Nicolson, 1969.

Von Grunebaum, G.E. *Modern Islam.* Berkeley and Los Angeles: University of California Press, 1962.

——. *Medieval Islam.* Chicago: University of Chicago Press, 1971.

——. *Classical Islam.* Chicago: Aldine Publishing Company, 1980.

——. *Modern Islam: The Search for Cultural Identity.* Westport/Conn.: Greenwood Press, 1983.

Watt, W. Montgomery. *Islamic Survey.* Edinburgh: Edinburgh University Press, 1968.

——. *Islamic Philosophy and Theology.* Edinburgh: Edinburgh University Press, 1962.

——. *Islamic Fundamentalism and Modernity.* New York: Routledge, 1988.

Wright, Robin B. *Sacred Rage: The Crusade of Modern Islam.* New

York: Linden Press/ Simon and Schuster, 1985.
Wolfson, Harry A. *The Philosophy of Kalam.* Cambridge: Harvard University Press, 1976.
Yousef, Michael. *Revolt against Modernity: Muslim Zealots and the West.* Leiden: E.J. Brill, 1985.
Zakarīyyah, Fu'ād. *Al-Ḥaqīqah wa al-Wahm fī Al-Ḥarakah al-Islāmīyyah al-Mu*ᶜ*āṣirah.* Al-Qāhirah: Dār al-Fikr, 1986.

INDEX